Jessie Bernard

Jessie Bernard

The Making of a Feminist

Robert C. Bannister

Rutgers University Press   New Brunswick and London

Women's Bldg

Library of Congress Cataloging-in-Publication Data

Bannister, Robert C.
  Jessie Bernard : the making of a feminist / Robert C. Bannister.
    p. cm.
  Includes bibliographical references.
  ISBN 0-8135-1614-5 (cloth)—ISBN 0-8135-1615-3 (pbk.)
  1. Bernard, Jessie Shirley, 1903– . 2. Sociologists—United
States—Biography. 3. Feminists—United States—Biography.
  I. Title.
  HM22.U6B4717   1991
  301'.092—dc20
  [B]   *90-34390*
                                                              CIP

British Cataloging-in-Publication information available

12/26/00

Contents

Acknowledgments

This biography of Jessie Bernard developed unexpectedly from research on a more comprehensive and still uncompleted project on
women in the social sciences in the interwar years, as well as from my
earlier *Sociology and Scientism*. Both projects were funded by grants
from the National Endowment for the Humanities, the most recent
under the program of Fellowships for College Teachers and Independent Scholars for 1988–1989 (grant FB-25878). I am also indebted to
Swarthmore College, whose generous research support, liberal sabbatical policy, and fine interlibrary loan and word-processing services
make it possible to combine scholarly interests with the demands of
undergraduate teaching.

Among the many individuals who have assisted me along the way, I
am uniquely indebted to Jessie Bernard. Although this study is not an
official biography, nor even one she particularly likes, Professor Bernard generously provided me with unpublished autobiographical
sketches and other materials concerning her career, patiently answered my questions during two separate interviews in her apartment
in Washington, D.C., and granted me permission to use materials in
the Luther and Jessie Bernard Papers without restriction. For additional information and assistance I am also indebted to Raphaela Best
and Dorothy Lee Jackson. With all historians of American sociology, I
am also indirectly indebted to Bernard's late husband, Luther Lee
Bernard, who had the abiding good sense to save stuff most of us
throw away.

Among the many librarians who have facilitated my researches into
the history of sociology, I want especially to thank Peter Gottlieb and
his staff at the Pennsylvania State University Library for making my
many visits to the Bernard Papers such a pleasure. For permission to

quote from materials in their possession, I wish to thank the Pennsylvania State University, the University of Chicago, the Michigan Historical Collections, and the University of Washington. Thanks are due also to Arlie Hochschild of Berkeley, Alice Rossi of the University of Massachusetts, and Kathryn Kish Sklar of SUNY Binghamton for permission to quote from their letters in the Jessie Bernard Papers, as well as to Professor Rossi for comments concerning the early history of the Sociologists for Women in Society. All photos appear courtesy of the Historical Collections and Labor Archives, Pattee Library, The Pennsylvania State University.

Finally, I am indebted to scholars who endured earlier versions of this study: to Finnish and American colleagues who heard it all first in a paper presented at the Second Tampere (Finland) American Studies Conference, May 1987; and to Rosalind Rosenberg of Barnard College and Dee Garrison, who read and commented on successive versions of the entire manuscript. All remaining errors of fact or interpretation are, of course, my own doing.

Chronology

1880 Early in the decade, Bossie Kantar (later Bettsy Kanter), maternal grandmother, immigrates to the United States with daughter Bessie (Bernard's mother).

ca. 1890 Bessie Kanter marries David Revici (later Ravitch).

1898 Birth of Clara (later Lambert), sister.

1901 Birth of Samuel (brother).

1903 (June 8) Born Minneapolis, third child of David and Bessie Ravitch (later Ravage). Ravitch family moves to house on Lake and Eleventh Streets, Minneapolis.

1908 Birth of Maurice (brother).

1919 (June) Graduates public high school.

1920 (January) Enters University of Minnesota.

1921 First meets Luther Bernard (late in year or early 1922).

1923 B.A., University of Minnesota (magna cum laude).

1924 M.A., University of Minnesota. "An Investigation into the Changes of Attitudes in Jews of the First and Second Generation under Influence of Social Environment" (Harris Prize).

   (December) First paper to American Sociological Society.

1924–25 Luther teaches at Cornell; Jessie in Minneapolis.

1925 (September 23) Marries Luther Lee Bernard in secret ceremony in upstate New York.

1926 (February–August) Sails to Argentina with L.L.B.

1927 (January–July) At University of Chicago with L.L.B. studies with George Herbert Mead, Robert Park, and Ellsworth Faris.

   (September) New Orleans, L.L.B. teaching at Tulane (through June 1928).

1928   (September) Chapel Hill, North Carolina. L.L.B. teaching at University of North Carolina (through June 1929).

1929   Moves to St. Louis, where L.L.B teaching at Washington University.

1930   (September–October) Researching history of social science in libraries in St. Louis and throughout South.

1931   First attempt at job-hunting.

1932   (December) Paper before ASS "An Instrument for the Measurement of Success in Marriage."

1933   (December) Paper before ASS: "Experimental Comparison."

1935   (Spring) Attends International Sociological Institute meetings in Brussels with L.L.B.

        (May) Defends doctoral dissertation at Washington University. "An Instrument for the Measurement of Neighborhood with Experimental Application."

        (September–December) In Paris to transcribe diaries of positivist Henry Edger.

        (December) returns to New York via England.

1936   (April) Files for divorce and leaves for Washington, D.C. Divorce petition withdrawn ca. July.

        (May) Employed Railroad Retirement Board (Bureau of Labor Statistics). Lives in temporary quarters at 44 C Street Northeast, and 22 East Capitol Street.

        (November) Transferred to Works Progress Administration.

1937   (July) Moves to apartment at 42 Independence Avenue Southwest, where she remains until leaving Washington for St. Charles, Missouri, three years later.

        (Fall) Transfers to Bureau of Labor Statistics, in cooperation with Bureau of Home Economics, for survey of national consumer expenditures (until 1940).

1940   (September) Begins teaching at Lindenwood College, St. Charles, Missouri (to 1947). Lives alternately in St. Charles and St. Louis to 1947.

1941   (July 23) Birth of first child, Dorothy Lee.

1942   *American Family Behavior.*

1945	(July 2) Birth of second child, Claude.
1947	(September) Begins teaching at Pennsylvania State University.
1949	*American Community Behavior* (rev. ed. 1962).
	Public exchange with George Lundberg over "values."
1950	(June 2) Birth of third child, David.
1951	(January) Death of Luther Bernard.
1951–63	Active in Society for the Study of Social Problems (SSSP) within American Sociological Association.
1953	President of Eastern Sociological Society.
1953–54	Vice-president of the American Sociological Association. On sabbatical in Graz, Austria. Daughter Dorothy Lee at International School in Geneva.
1954–59	Dorothy Lee at George School.
1956	*Remarriage.*
1957	*Social Problems at Midcentury.*
	(Summer) trip to Panama and Ecuador.
1958	*Dating, Mating, and Marriage* (with Meahl and Smith).
1959	Dorothy Lee enters Sarah Lawrence.
1959–60	Visiting professor at Princeton.
1961	Moves to Washington, D.C. Commutes to Penn State (to 1964).
1961–62	On sabbatical. Dorothy Lee at London School of Economics.
1963	(June) Dorothy Lee graduates from Sarah Lawrence.
	(Summer) Dorothy Lee and Brick in Chicago after her graduation.
	(August) Joins Iron Mountain Project.
	(September) Son Claude to Johns Hopkins.
	(December) Daughter's marriage at Friends Florida Avenue meeting in Washington.
1964	Contributes to Project Camelot.
	(June) Retires from Penn State, Research Scholar Honoris Causa.
1966	*Marriage and Family among Negroes*
1968	*The Sex Game.*
	(Spring) First attends meeting of a "woman's liberation" group in Washington, D.C.

1971	*Women and the Public Interest.*
	(February 12–14) Attends reorganization meeting of Sociologists for Women in Society at Yale University.
1972	*The Future of Marriage.*
1973	*The Sociology of Community.*
1974	(January) Bernard suffers heart attack.
	Visiting Fellow, National Institute of Education (1974–1975).
	The Future of Motherhood.
1975	Scholar in Residence, United States Commission on Civil Rights (1975–1976).
1976	ASA establishes Jessie Bernard Award.
1980	Visiting Professor, Mills College.
1981	*The Female World.*
	Visiting Professor, University of California, Los Angeles.
1982	Visiting Professor, University of Delaware.
1987	*The Female World from a Global Perspective.*

Introduction

This feminist perspective may not be as epochal as Freud's but almost.
Once you "catch it," it makes all the difference in how you see the world.
—Jessie Bernard to Ernest Havermann, June 2, 1977

In 1970, at the age of sixty-seven, Jessie Bernard joined the feminist revolution.[1] The occasion was a meeting of the Women's Caucus at the annual meeting of the American Sociological Association (ASA) in Washington. The caucus traced its origins to a survey conducted in the spring of 1969 by Alice Rossi, then at Goucher, on the status of women in sociology. At the San Francisco meetings that summer, the Women's Caucus organized to discuss her findings. The facts were disturbing if predictable. Whereas almost half of the male sociologists holding doctorates were full professors, only 16 percent of the women with doctorates held that rank. Not one of the forty-four professors of sociology at five elite universities was female. At a meeting at Yale in early 1971, the Women's Caucus reconstituted itself as the Sociologists for Women in Society (SWS), with Bernard listed as one of half a dozen persons to contact concerning the work of the group.[2]

For Bernard this commitment had been in the works for some time. Early in 1968, with NOW, WEAL, WITCH, and other militant organizations moving to center stage, she first learned of an emerging "women's liberation" movement through the underground press. Interested, but still viewing the movement in a detached, academic fashion, she wangled an invitation to a consciousness-raising session only to discover that her professorial manner "threatened" one of the younger participants. Seated on the floor amidst the assembled, she could not imagine that she was "giving off bad vibrations." But the incident set her thinking. By 1970 she was ready to join her colleagues in the Women's Caucus. This decision, as it turned out, launched what she later termed her "fourth revolution."[3]

During the next two decades, Bernard's writings on feminism were prodigious, including six books and a dozen or more contributions to scholarly journals. In them she addressed an ever-wider audience: first in the staid and analytical *Women and the Public Interest* (1971); then in *The Future of Marriage* (1972) and *The Future of Motherhood* (1974), both reprinted in popular paperback editions; and most recently in *The Female World* (1981) and *The Female World from a Global Perspective* (1987). For *The Female World* and her other scholarly achievements, she was awarded the W. J. Goode Prize of the American Sociological Association in 1985, and four years later, the association's Career of Distinguished Scholarship Award.[4] Meanwhile, she attended countless feminist conferences, supported young women seeking positions in sociology, and battled sex discrimination at every level. In the mid-1970s, she served one year as Visiting Fellow at the National Institute of Education and a second as Scholar in Residence in the research office of the United States Commission on Civil Rights.

In her feminist writings, Bernard synthesized and embellished the work of others rather than stake out radically new territory. Her starting point was the assumption that men and women have occupied and will continue to inhabit separate and distinct worlds. In *The Sex Game* (1968), written before her feminist conversion, this premise provided the occasion to apply game theory to the war of the sexes. In *The Future of Marriage* it underlay the contention that every marriage is in reality two marriages—one his, the other hers—and the conclusion that marriage, as currently constituted, posed a distinct hazard to female health. In *The Female World* she traced the consequences of this separation in western history and culture since the Middle Ages.

From this premise, Bernard pursued two major lines of inquiry. The first, in the jargon of the trade, was the "sociology-of-knowledge theme"; that is, the role of gender in shaping, not only sociology and the academic disciplines, but also the fundamental values and commitments of all human societies.[5] More simply: do men and women think

differently and, if so, why and what difference has this made throughout history? In the early seventies she examined this issue with respect
to science and social science, drawing a distinction between what she
termed "agentic" and "communal" styles in research, the former (masculine) aiming at power and control, the latter (feminine) seeking
understanding.[6] In *The Female World* she extended the analysis to language, literature, and folk culture.

Bernard's second major concern was more strictly sociological. She
sought to define and explore the word of women, not simply as it im-
pinges upon the male world, but as an integral and valid sphere in itself.
"The female world," she wrote, "is a sociological entity with a characteristic demographic structure (age, marital status, education, income,
occupation), a status and class structure, [and] . . . a characteristic culture." As such, it has a "boundary maintenance system" (mechanisms
for defining who's in and who's out) but also "faultlines" of ethnicity,
class, and race. In earlier sociology, this polarity between male and
female sphere was anticipated in various dichotomies: *Gemeinschaft-
Gesellschaft* (Ferdinand Tönnies), primary-secondary (Charles Horton
Cooley), Apollonian-Dionysian (Ruth Benedict), although none drew
these distinctions with gender in mind.[7]

THROUGHOUT HER CAREER Bernard's maverick eclecticism made it
difficult to place her on the political spectrum, a difficulty compounded by her insistence that rationality somehow placed her above
the battle. "As a matter of fact, I am not a knee-jerk radical or even
liberal," she once bristled when her daughter made this charge. "My
position on issues where I seem to be radical is one I arrive at on the
basis of logical or moral persuasion rather than automatic conviction."[8] During the thirties and early forties, she rarely commented
on domestic politics even though she was working in various New
Deal agencies at the time, perhaps because her husband, Luther,
loathed FDR, but, more importantly, because she shared the still-
widespread belief that true social science should be value neutral.
Although in the fifties she displayed some of the characteristics of a
liberal cold warrior, she vigorously opposed McCarthyism while joining

ostensibly radical sociologists in founding the Society for the Study
of Social Problems (SSSP).

Likewise, Bernard's feminism does not quite fit the conventional
categories. Describing liberals and radicals within the movement in
the early 1970s—the principal split as she then saw it—she refused to
identify with either camp, but instead played the mediator to whom all
ferment was a good thing.[9] In her subsequent writings she quoted or
cited works covering virtually the entire spectrum of feminist opinion
as it had then developed: liberal, radical, socialist, psychoanalytic, and
even existentialist.[10] Yet, when the footnotes were tallied, her own
assumptions and proposals remained quintessentially liberal.

Through most of her earlier life Bernard was a feminist only in the
sense that she was a woman who took advantage of opportunities to
gain professional success and a measure of individual autonomy. After her late 1960s conversion, she continued to think initially in terms
of individual opportunity and personal adjustment (whether through
elimination of overt discrimination or consciousness-raising) leavened
by a vision of more humane social policies through the adoption of
"feminine" values—a position one observer has termed "welfare liberal feminism."[11] Although stressing the integrity of a separate female
world, Bernard shied from the radical feminist indictment of male
oppression or their proposals for social reconstruction through new
biological technologies, the creation of a "lesbian nation," or other
separatist strategies. In keeping with her longstanding antipathy toward communism, she showed little interest in socialist or Marxist
versions of feminism.

As a result, even the works Bernard cited sometimes taught less
complete lessons than their authors intended. Shulamith Firestone's
Dialectics of Sex (1970), for example, illustrated "utopian" ferment.
Simone de Beauvoir's *Second Sex* (1952) was one attempt to define a
separate women's sphere (an excessively pessimistic and separatist
analysis in Bernard's view). And Nancy Chodorow's *Reproduction of
Mothering* (1978) merely underlined the importance of the mother-
daughter relationship.[12]

Bernard's own proposals were accordingly moderate: equal opportunity under the law, the elimination of sex-typed work roles, and,
closer to home, the greater sharing of housework and increased child

care. Although she viewed the Equal Rights Amendment as a "symbol" of these changes, she was not outspoken in its support.[13] While occasionally appearing to endorse affirmative action, her statements were notably equivocal. Cautiously optimistic, she saw no end to the problems between men and women. "Despite the dreams of the Utopists and idealists, there is no all-purpose, perfect way to relate to one another," she concluded in *The Female World*. "Sometimes a whole culture may 'tilt' in the direction of the male ethos, sometimes in the direction of the female, sometimes in a direction different from both."[14]

Since separatist analyses historically have been double-edged where women are concerned (witness the "social feminism"[15] of the Progressive Era), Bernard's brand of feminism, by her own admission, disturbed some liberal feminists who feared that any concession to difference undermines a commitment to genuine equality. At the same time, her failure to endorse more extreme measures (whether radical or socialist) has meant that she is more often cited as a role model or a source of inspiration than for her contributions to feminist analysis.[16]

W hy, then, a study of Jessie Bernard rather than of any number of other feminists, many bolder and more original? One answer lies in her age and professional prominence at the time she joined a movement whose supporters not only were much younger, but were rebelling against an academic establishment of which, by any normal standard, she was a card-carrying member. Born in Minneapolis in 1903, she entered the University of Minnesota at age sixteen and a half. There she acquired a B.A. (magna cum laude), wrote a prize-winning M.A., and eventually met her future husband, her forty-four-year-old professor of sociology, Luther Lee Bernard. Although slowed in obtaining her doctorate by the real and imagined demands of his career, she presented her first paper to the American Sociological Society (later "Association") at age twenty-one and published several articles in sociology journals before earning her Ph.D. at Washington University in 1935. In 1942, she produced the first of the six books she was to write during her teaching career.

Moving to Penn State in 1947, she contributed regularly to the leading scholarly journals, while amassing enough honors, committee memberships, and professional positions to cover a half-dozen pages of vita.

By virtue of her age, Bernard also represents the so-called postfeminist generation of American women. Born at the turn of the century, too young to share in the prewar ferment for women's rights, middle-class women of this generation instead took advantage of new opportunities to build careers as academics or other professionals, apparently indifferent, and sometimes hostile, to the organizations, efforts, and values of earlier suffragists. A roll call of some of the big names among her contemporaries tells some of the story: Margaret Mead (b. 1901) in anthropology; Margaret Bourke-White (1904) in photography; Susanne K. Langer (1895) in philosophy; Lillian Hellman (1905) in the theater. To these might be added other women in the social sciences: the antropologists Ruth Bunzell (1903), Gladys Reichard (1893), Cora Dubois (1903), and Hortense Powdermaker (1896), for example; or the sociologists Ruth Shonle Cavan (1896), Helen MacGill Hughes (1903), Helen M. Lynd (1896), Mirra Komarovsky (1906), Irene Taeuber (1906), and Dorothy Swain Thomas (1899). If Bernard's scholarship has been less distinguished than that of these contemporaries—Komarovsky, certainly, and the other sociologists arguably—she has been more outspoken and has written more extensively in support of feminism than most of her cohort. With the exceptions of Margaret Mead (whose relations with feminists were complex, to say the least) and Helen Hughes, these women were barred by death, infirmity, or conviction from lending support to the women's revolution of the late 1960s.[17]

Bernard, as it happens, also treated in her scholarship three major themes that shaped her own career and those of women professionals of her generation, thus serving as both subject and witness in her own case. One is the decline in the percentage of women in the male-dominated professions starting in the late 1920s. In *Academic Women* (1964) she detailed this decline within college and university faculties, a finding scholars have since confirmed in other fields. A second theme is the role of gender in shaping the agenda of sociology; for example, in studies of social class or mobility. A third, as represented by her distinction between "agentic" and "communal" science, is the charge that the natural and social sciences have been shaped by masculine rather than feminine values, a distinctive theme in feminist scholarship during the past two decades.

A final reason for examining Bernard's career is that, in defining her feminism, she abandoned or modified many of her earlier convictions, even while tending to downplay this fact. During most of her career she took positions that were, if not antifeminist by present standards, at least afeminist or unfeminist. In *American Family Behavior* (1942), passing references to "feministic agitation" and "militant feminists" were detached at best.[18] In *Academic Women* she drew feminist fire for her conclusion that factors other than discrimination accounted for the relative absence of women in academia.[19] When one young woman labeled *The Sex Game* "sexist," Bernard agreed.[20]

Accordingly, several themes in Bernard's feminist writings flew in the face of theories and approaches with which she has been associated. During the 1930s, as a proponent of her husband's behaviorist sociology, she practiced agentic science with a passion: measuring, quantifying, and tabulating everything from success in marriage to neighborhood relations. During the early 1970s she attacked this approach for its masculine bias. In the 1950s, she called for a sociology of conflict, apparently giving struggle a permanence in human affairs. Two decades later, she wondered if a cooperative social order might be not only possible but more profitable. Throughout most of her career, she rejected cultural relativism and was skeptical of the anthropologists' dictum *omnis cultura ex cultura* (all culture from culture).[21] In *The Female World* she pictured a distinctly "female culture" (and social science) powerful enough to shape society to its own purposes, even though this argument coexisted uneasily with an earlier commitment to the Enlightenment ideal of universal reason.[22]

That Bernard for most of her adult life was an avowed champion of science and a woman professional par excellence raises other questions. Was she earlier seduced by an inherently male view of the world? Or did she adopt the outlook and approach of her male colleagues for much the same reasons as they did? Did her description of the "female world" mark an epochal discovery? Or, on her road from positivism to feminism did she simply adopt the latest sociological fashion? Did the feminist sociologist finally see the truth that eluded the value-free positivist? Or is Bernard one of those individuals who, having done an about-face on an issue, fails to recognize that she could be wrong both times?

━━━━━━━━━━

A ddressing these questions, this study necessarily treats several more general issues in the history of twentieth-century feminism. Among the most important are the fate of prewar feminism in the two decades following the passage of the suffrage amendment; the impact of professionalization on women and the role of gender in shaping the style and agenda of academic social scientists; and the sources of the "feminine mystique" of the 1940s and 1950s and of the attack upon it in the wake of the revival of feminism in the 1960s.

Although historians have long debated the extent and timing of the apparent demise of prewar feminism in the interwar years, the situation was less one of persistence or decline than of transformation.[23] During the 1910s, as the historian Nancy Cott has noted, the term "feminism" first came into general use just as the phrase "the woman movement" began to sound archaic if not downright ungrammatical. Although narrower in its appeal, feminism was "broader in intent" than suffragism or the movement for women's rights in that it proclaimed "revolution in all the relations of the sexes." Moreover, this new consciousness embodied paradoxes that were relatively invisible in the earlier struggles: sexual equality with sex differences; individual freedoms to be gained and enjoyed through sexual solidarity; diversity among women and recognition of a basic unity. Although the need to integrate the two eras remained a challenge, the very existence of these paradoxes heralded the beginning of a new era rather than the end of an old.[24]

Unfortunately for prewar activism, however, the two halves of the equation were easier to combine in theory than in practice. As a professionalized, consumer-oriented society took shape in the 1920s, women of Jessie Bernard's generation experienced a new freedom that offered individual opportunity but at the same time threatened older forms of female solidarity. During her college years, Bernard was liberated by prewar standards, just as later she gained success and individual autonomy through her profession. But she was not a feminist by the standards of prewar activism, by current understanding of the term, or by the lights of the post-1960s revival.

The reasons were several, or so this study will argue. One was the intersection of gender and ethnicity in her own life. Ethnicity is often discussed in terms of its effects in alienating middle-class WASP activists from potential allies among new immigrants.[25] Yet ethnicity is important here because for much of Bernard's early life her Jewish background was at least as important to her as her sex. Missing from her background were elements common to the life histories of many other American feminists and women achievers: a Quaker or dissenting Protestant past; a family history of doing good; a sturdy, self-reliant mother and a supportive, high-minded father. Rather, the situation was quite the reverse: hardworking Jewish immigrant parents who strove for worldly success in the conventional ways and a youth torn between devotion to parents and a rejection of much that they represented.

A second factor was the new social freedom itself. As an undergraduate at the University of Minnesota in the early twenties, Bernard enjoyed the decade's heady mix of prosperity and permissiveness. If not a feminist by earlier or later standards, she defied most conventional expectations concerning proper womanly behavior in her romance and marriage with her professor husband, her unconventional demeanor (especially where homemaking was at issue), and her ambition for the independence and recogition a career would bring. Her ongoing struggle for individual self-expression and personal liberation worked against a sense of a world divided by sex, and hence of common cause based on gender, even if this individual liberation was a necessary detour on the road to her later feminism.

A third was the strength of gender stereotypes and Bernard's inability to transcend them. Most prewar feminists, instead of attacking prevailing definitions of femininity, accepted and ultimately reinforced these stereotypes, leaving potential postwar successors few resources with which to oppose the flapper (whose lifestyle older feminists generally disapproved) or, eventually, the "feminine mystique" of the forties and fifties. Bernard again is a case in point. Despite her liberated behavior, she could never quite escape prevailing notions of what a women should be: whether the flapper ideal of the 1920s (even if the bespectacled and relentlessly studious Jessie made a less than convincing specimen) or a new cult of domesticity that led her to lobby her recalcitrant and aging husband in the late 1930s to allow her to have children—a four-year campaign that finally paid off when the first of three arrived in 1941. Vestiges of these assumptions resurfaced in the feminism of Bernard's later years, specifically in her insistence on the permanence of difference.

All this is not to deny that many women were victimized by discrimination, which was often strongest in the area where they had earlier made gains—notably in the professions—a backlash that assumed epidemic proportions during the 1930s.[26] Bernard herself experienced concrete obstacles to a career in the form of the nepotism rules and general discrimination against women that worsened during the depression. But for several decades, intellectual and personal struggles provided a more subtle barrier to self-realization and independence than overt discrimination.

THE IMPACT of professionalism on women—a second theme of recent feminist scholarship—also remains in debate. On the surface, at least, the figures suggest that women of Bernard's generation were increasingly the exceptions in the traditionally male professions. During the 1920s, different professions witnessed setbacks for women in varying proportions. In academia, for example, women made up 30 percent of college faculties by the 1910s (many, of course, in women's colleges). But by the late 1920s, virtually every index of female participation was down: the proportion of women students, of Ph.D.s, and of faculty members. If some of these changes paved the way for female monopoly in selected occupations (nursing, social work, or secondary school teaching), the short-run consequences for women professionals were not cheering. By the early 1930s, journalists were sounding an obituary for the "vanishing race of pioneer women" of the prewar years.[27]

The relation of women to the professions, however, was never simply a matter of numbers. On the one hand, professionalization is generally agreed to have worked against organized feminism (even though one can argue that individual success in a career should be seen as one sort of fulfillment of the earlier crusade for women's rights). Viewed in terms of feminist consciousness and organized activity, the professional "angle of vision," as Cott has put it, was "counterproductive to feminist practice."[28]

On the other hand, women no less than men of this generation were enormously attracted by the ideals of professionalism. One reason was that entry typically required neither a large outlay of capital (as in business) nor public clout through the vote (as in politics)—a consideration that explains its appeal to the children of immigrants, male and female, as to any other aspirants to middle-class status. Others were doubtless money, prestige, and the promise of doing useful work, although the first applied to Bernard only in that a desire to obtain a stable income in order to have children motivated her initial entry into academia.

A final and more important attraction was psychological and personal: the professional emphasis on reason, scientific standards, and objectivity promised escape from the burden of gender and from an immigrant past. To the fledgling professional, whether in sociology or other fields, a rigorously objective science, in Cott's words, "constituted an alternative to subjectively determined sex standards."[29] So, also, it provided standards to replace the curious, if not downright embarrassing, ways of one's ancestors. To be scientific was not simply to espouse the male virtues of objectivity and control but to embrace a clean, well-lighted standard to replace the candles of tradition: in short, to be modern and American.

Unfortunately, this latter aspect of professional ideology held problems, as Bernard's case also will illustrate. Rationality and objectivity, especially as defined in the interwar years, directly opposed conventional conceptions of women as emotional and subjective. What, then, was the price of "acting like a man"? Since professional standards were also methods of regulating entry and advancement this question involved more than self-image. As scientific objectivity translated into group research, financed by large, bureaucratically organized foundations, could women social scientists function as effectively as in the age of individual scholarship, even those who chose to compete? Although Bernard through the 1950s played this game with skill and success, much of her later feminism was a reaction against this world and its values.

At the personal level, there was also a price to be paid. A central thesis of this biography is that the twentieth-century culture of professionalism (to borrow Burton Bledstein's phrase) fed on a radical disjuncture in the lives of practitioners between public and private, subjectivity and objectivity, emotion and intellect, tradition and science. Bernard experienced this disjuncture in extremis. Liberation from convention in her case did not necessarily bring freedom in any meaningful sense, since her marriage to Luther, and through him to the ideal of scientific rationality, brought restraints almost as confining as those of nineteenth-century morality. Accepting the professional ideal and its ideology of disinterested objectivity was not simply a matter of being one of the boys in order to succeed, but implicitly of accepting crippling stereotypes concerning the irrationality and unreliability of "feminine" values, and ultimately of one's inner self. For male sociologists such as Luther Bernard, "science" meant mastery and control; that is, being even more a man. For a woman such as Jessie Bernard, it meant accepting that she could be a success professionally only if she stopped, in some sense, being herself. Thus the central paradox of her career: the professionalism that promised (and finally delivered) personal success and autonomy was bound to assumptions that retarded feminist consciousness, as she later understood it. Despite her feminist "epiphany" (as she termed it) in the late 1960s, she continued to wrestle with this paradox throughout her career.

FINALLY, although less directly, Bernard's career sheds light on several factors that contributed to at least one strain of feminism by the late 1960s. Concerning the effects of World War II, there is a growing consensus that, whatever women's real gains in the workplace, the disruption and insecurities of the early 1940s, coupled with the efforts of advertisers and the media to mobilize women first for war and then for peacetime prosperity, helped create the "feminine mystique" that would come under fire two decades later. Although historians continue to debate whether these developments laid the basis for a new cult of domesticity or for a future feminism, Bernard's embrace of motherhood in the late 1930s and 1940s and her growing attention to "woman's role" in her sociological work were important preconditions to her eventual support of feminism.[30] The rise of fascism, the Holocaust, and the cold war, although not immediately undermining her earlier faith in science, paved the way for her later attack on its masculine bias.

At the same time, Bernard's conversion owed little or nothing to the pockets of organized feminism that persisted during the lean years of the 1950s, diminished in size if not in spirit.[31] Rather it was a direct product of the 1960s. Unlike many younger women, Bernard did not personally experience the misogynous underside of the counterculture.[32] But she was not immune to the public turmoil of the decade as she explored the uncharted and often painful path of single parenthood. This experience provided the precipitating crisis, if not the underlying causes, of her open embrace of the new movement.

Although Bernard is the focus of this study, it is not a biography in the life-and-times tradition, but rather a case study of the forces in twentieth-century American life that have shaped one woman's thinking about gender and the relation of the sexes, and of the effect of these assumptions on her scholarly work. The subtitle "The Making of a Feminist" might as easily be "From Positivism to Feminism" or even "Sexism and Sociology."

As an account of one life, this study does not pretend to provide a complete history of any of the various themes around which the chapters are organized, whether Jewish life in Minneapolis (chapter 1), student culture in the twenties (chapter 2), anti-Semitism in the interwar years (chapter 3), the "feminist mystique" of the late 1930s and 1940s (chapter 4), the impact of World War II and the Holocaust (chapter 5), cold war liberalism (chapter 6), women in academia (chapter 7), single parenthood (chapter 8), or feminist theory (chapter 9). Much more could be (and has been) written about each. As concerns sociology, more also could be said about several key episodes in which Bernard participated; the struggle to "democratize" the American Sociological Society during the 1930s; the battles of Parsonians and conflict theorists in the 1950s; the use of academic "experts" in the controversial Project Camelot; and the activities of the SWS after 1970. In each instance, I have attempted to provide enough to explain Bernard's (often peripheral) role and no more.

What this individual record does allow is an almost unique opportunity to explore the relationship between the public and the private, the professional and the personal. Whatever may be the case for the rest of us (and on this point, readers will doubtless differ), Bernard's social theory, professional activities, and personal life are virtually impossible to untangle. The extraordinary written record that Luther and Jessie Bernard together have deposited at the Pennsylvania State University confirms what might otherwise be speculation. Intimate discussions and the most private of thoughts are reported, not imagined. Quotations are given exactly as they appear in the record. None are made up for the good reason that they do not have to be.

The richness of the written record and the focus on Bernard's personal life raise two other issues that deserve comment. One concerns the use of relatively few personal interviews. For this, the reasons are several. Most of the individuals with whom Bernard associated before 1968 have died, an exception being her lover in the years following her husband's death (herein called "Ezra"). Ezra made it clear when Bernard was writing *Self-Portrait of a Family* (1978) that he did not wish to cooperate in any public discussion of their relationship. No sociology department records exist at Penn State, nor could I locate anyone there or at Princeton who could provide further information concerning her career there.[33] Moreover, Bernard's nonfamily associations, with very few exceptions, were and continue to be intellectual and professional, rather than personal and private. When not working in the library or at her typewriter, she attended conferences and meetings, not church socials or neighborhood coffees. Despite her celebration of the "female world" of Gemeinschaft, her own world before and after her feminist conversion was the functionally ordered, professionally organized one of Gessellschaft. To judge from the contents and tone of her extensive correspondence, the public record of debts and differences tells most of the story.

For Bernard's activities since the late 1960s, there are, to be sure, a number of sociologists and others who might have been interviewed, and their absence may be viewed as a weakness. Yet, it is debatable whether a fuller history of American sociology during the past two decades, or even of the Sociologists for Women in Society, would contribute to fuller understanding of Bernard's published work. What is certain is that both are topics of enormous complexity, and beyond the scope of this study.

A related matter concerns privacy and resulting gaps in the record. Ideally, the conflict between principles and personalities during the past two decades should be treated in the same detail and with the same frankness as for the earlier years. In practice, people have feelings. Thus, some minor details concerning Bernard's personal and family life are omitted where their inclusion would add little to the story but possibly cause discomfort or embarrassment. In several cases, names are changed (when Bernard did so in her published work) or withheld. For similar reason, reports in letters to Bernard concerning discrimination and/or departmental infighting during the 1970s are not detailed, despite the fact that they clearly contributed to her support of feminism. Finally, on Bernard's instruction, letters judged sensitive were removed from the most recent addition to the Jessie Bernard Papers (August 1989) at the discretion of the staff at the Pennsylvania State Libraries. Although I was thus not able to see them, I am told they consist of a file about six inches in depth.

This study is also not an intellectual history of the analytic or internal variety, quite simply because Bernard has not been a deep thinker. Although ideas have been her business, she has always found their surfaces more interesting than their depths, and their uses more compelling than their logical structure. On this point, lest it appear unfair, we have her own testimony. "[It] has occurred to me that [an] adverse effect of a protected and sheltered life may be a kind of emotional shallowness," she wrote in a recent autobiographical sketch. "When I dip into the great classics I become aware of a certain superficiality in my own emotional equipment. I read them with a feeling that I am missing something."[34] Her eclecticism as a sociologist invites a study of "influences."[35] It also may be applauded (as it was at a recent award ceremony at the ASA) for its "maverick" quality.[36] But neither approach alters the fact that Bernard's work for the most part has lacked the system or distinctive vision of a Robert Park or a William F. Ogburn, two of her mentors, or of a David Riesman, a C. Wright Mills, or half a dozen other modern sociologists whose careers overlapped hers. By her own account, most of the terms she contributed to sociological discourse—"biculturality," for example—failed to catch on. Others made good copy—"stag effect" for male networking, or "shock theory of marriage"—but had little applicability beyond the specifics they describe. If stylistically she escaped the worst excesses of her jargon-prone colleagues, her informal, almost breezy style does not merit extended literary analysis. Yet, precisely because she has functioned somewhere in a middle ground between academic sociologist and popularizer, Bernard provides an unusually sensitive barometer of the social and intellectual cross-currents of this century.

This book, finally, is also about the roots of contemporary feminism. Here the focus is less on the specifics of Bernard's analysis than on underlying themes and patterns. Her "conversion" in the late 1960s was neither the public expression of views she had somehow really believed all along, nor an eleventh-hour epiphany with no roots in past experience.[37] Rather, it was a natural extension of themes in her earlier sociological work and a response to the many forces that had shaped her life and career. Just as her early sociology expressed a deep ambivalence toward her past and herself as a Jew and a woman (or so I argue), so her road to feminism during the 1940s and 1950s involved coming to terms with her Jewish background (beginning with her affiliation with the Society of Friends in the late 1930s) and a reassessment of her femininity, initially, it paradoxically, through her enthusiastic embrace of motherhood in the same years. Coupled with the experience of fascism and the cold war, these reassessments underlay an increasing skepticism toward science and the sort of sociology she had been doing. Finally, the experience of single parenthood against a background of the upheavals of the 1960s led to new appreciation of the affective, communal dimensions of experience, now labeled "feminine."

Bernard's feminism, to put it another way, was a product of specific conditions from 1910 through the 1960s, not simply a dusting-off of complaints that surfaced in the antebellum women's rights movement or in pre–World War I suffragism. Whereas the thrust of the earlier phases of the women's movement was primarily legal and political, and perhaps secondarily economic and social, this latest phase added critiques of marriage, the family, and immobilizing cultural stereotypes, not to mention social analysis of far greater sophistication and complexity than previously developed. Whereas earlier feminists looked to professional advancement as one avenue to female liberation, their latest descendents have expressed ambivalence if not outright hostility toward professionalism as traditionally conceived. Echoing these themes, Bernard's feminism was in large part a reaction against an earlier and exaggerated vision of the power of reason and science, and more personally of the half-realized price paid for professional success. It was also a product of manifold tensions in American life as the nation entered its "modern" phase, tensions dramatized in her often-tumultuous private and professional life. For this very reason, Bernard's road to feminism provides a particularly revealing picture of the ways social change has shaped American social thought since the turn of the century.

1
Third Child (1903–1919)

> There is no happier fate for a man than to live his life in a culture never challenged, a culture he is never called upon to justify; to eat and speak and dress and pray without ever realizing that there are other ways of doing these simple things.
>
> —Jessie Bernard, "Biculturality"

A carefree culture was a luxury that Jewish immigrants of the generation of Jessie Bernard's parents would never know. On both sides, her ancestors were from Transylvania, the poetically named portion of Eastern Europe that historically has been Austrian, Hungarian, Rumanian, or Russian, as the political tides dictated. When the issue arose, family members considered themselves Rumanian. Their move to the United States began in the early 1880s when Jessie's maternal grandmother, Bossie Kantar, recently widowed for a second time, left her three grown sons and migrated with Jessie's mother, Rebecca, then not quite twelve, to New York. A decade later, this daughter returned home briefly to marry a man whom her three brothers had chosen for her, a candlemaker who hoped to recoup his faltering fortunes in the United States. In the early 1890s, the young couple settled in Minneapolis.[1]

For the newcomers, the United States, first of all, meant new names. At Ellis Island, David Revici, Jessie's father, became David Ravitch. By the time of the census of 1900, Bossie Kantar was Bettsy Kanter, and her daughter Rebecca (Rifke) was Bessie. Two decades later Ravitch was Ravage, just as Jessie Sarah (her given names) in time became Jessie Shirley. For the family as a whole, as she later noted, the census also had its own special language: "foreign born" for the parents; "native white, both parents foreign," for the children.

Socially, Minneapolis was ethnically if not racially diverse. Although in 1890 native-born settlers outnumbered the foreign born by two to one, Scandinavians constituted some 55 percent of the latter. In 1880 the city's population was approximately 50,000, of whom 2,500 were Jews. By 1900 the total population had reached 202,000, with Jews at 8,000, slightly less than 4 percent. After 1900, a flood of Eastern Europeans swelled the Jewish population as poor and largely uneducated immigrants fled the ghettoes of Russia, Poland, and Lithuania. Blacks, a distinct minority, numbered only some 2,500 by 1910, less than 1 percent of the population.[2]

The pattern of Jewish settlement by 1900 reflected the successive stages of immigration, as nationality groups clustered for emotional and economic support. Arriving first in the 1870s, Jews from Germany, Austria, Bohemia, and Hungary established thriving commercial enterprises and staked out their neighborhood on the soon-fashionable West Side of the city. Eastern European arrivals from the 1890s onward clustered on the North Side, where over 80 percent of the city's Jews lived by 1910. A middle stratum consisted of Eastern Europeans, mostly Rumanians, who arrived after the first Germans but before mass migration at the turn of the century. Better off educationally and economically, typically shop owners or in sales, they established an enclave on the South Side. To this group belonged Jessie's parents.[3]

Despite its ethnic diversity, Minneapolis remained an outpost of New England Yankee culture. The great milling names—Pillsbury, Loring, Washburn—were the success stories of the New Englanders who had trekked north from Ohio and Illinois a generation earlier. With the coming of the railroad in the 1870s, transportation also became an important industry. Within another decade, the Northern Europeans who had laid the rails made up much of the city's middle and working classes. Unlike other cities, where newcomers gradually filtered into the ruling elite, the old Yankees and their heirs consolidated their social and economic power in Minneapolis. More than half a century later, two sociologists reported, young Jews in Minneapolis enjoyed fewer economic opportunities than in eastern cities.[4]

The city many remembered, in any case, was predominantly Yankee. *New York Times* reporter Harrison Salisbury, born in Minneapolis five years after Bernard, called it a "Victorian City in the Midwest." Of the state as a whole, a Federal Writers' Project survey concluded that the "Yankees" left an "indelible stamp," despite the "incalculable debt" to other European countries.[5] Bernard agreed. "Sometimes I say, in fact, that I went to a New England Academy," she recalled of her schooling. The curriculum was classical in the grand style, including four years of Latin, and even Greek for those who wanted it. The teachers too, most of them women, were "stamped with a New England brand." The great American writers were of course New Englanders; the chief statesman was Alexander Hamilton, the architect of the Federalist party. Only years later did Bernard realize that southerners Jefferson and Washington were far greater men.[6]

The Ravitch home was on Lake Street at Eleventh Avenue, an area still suburban when they moved in soon after Jessie was born. "Most of the houses were of the geometrically square type, with generous front and back porches," she later wrote in "Sarah Gordon," one of several novels she wrote in the late twenties. Lawns and shrubbery made up for whatever the house may have lacked architecturally. Once fashionable, the lower part of Lake Street was quickly becoming heavily trafficked and commercial. But their block "still retained some of its old flavor."[7]

Jessie's most vivid memories of her house, however, were of what it was not. For one thing, it was not in the ghetto, but far from even the closest Jewish quarter, that of their fellow Rumanians on the South Side. The Ravitch family, in fact, were the only Jews in the neighborhood. "River Avenue [Lake Street] was extremely far away," she wrote, again in "Sarah Gordon." Far away from friends; far from Jewish shops; far from the synagogue. "Sarah [Jessie] never had any intimate Jewish friends except her cousins," she continued, exaggerating her own situation only slightly. The house, for another thing, was not really theirs. Although they had bought and paid for it, someone else's ancestors had built it and planted the tall oaks in the yard. The Ravitches, like the fictional Gordons, were "mere intruders."[8]

Like most American children, Jessie was aware of social and ethnic differences without quite knowing what to make of them. Her neighborhood friends had names like Oleson and Hansen; a Greek Orthodox church stood a block to the west; and a former slave named Peebles fascinated the neighborhood children (only two other blacks lived in the area, both married to white women). But she remained innocent of the hostility of "old" toward "new" immigrants, just as she was blind to the tensions between grain traders and farmers or employers and workers that would burst forth in later Minnesota history.[9]

Mostly, in fact, Jessie had fond memories of these years: outings with parents, confidences with her sister, and visits to cousins. If Jews were a minority in this new land, the fact caused few problems. She had been "only vaguely conscious of myself as a Jew," she recalled two decades later. She changed her middle name from Sarah to Shirley, not out of shame, but simply because it was more like the names of her friends. Pressed on the issue of anti-Semitism, she claimed that she had experienced little if any during her youth. The issue, she told alumni of her alma mater in 1970, "had been worked through" by the 1940s. To a biographer she spoke almost casually of the "whole bit about my Jewish background"—the "bit" suggesting how inconsequential she now thought it.[10]

The reality, as one might suspect, was more complicated. Happy memories of family life, although doubtless genuine, masked tensions that racked her early life. If resolved after a fashion by the 1940s, the problem of identity—Jew versus American—plagued her earlier years more than she cared to remember. Tensions within Judaism—between German and non-German, Reform and Orthodox—also left their mark. Although she could not have realized it then, the years of youth set her sociological agenda for a good many years to come.

———

T he Ravitch family, to all appearances, was the classic American success. Starting as a "butter-and-eggs man" delivering dairy products, Jessie's father, David, moved into haberdashery, then into buying up bankrupt stores throughout the upper Midwest, and finally into real estate. "He is no longer a peddler," she wrote in a lightly disguised account of his rise. "He is a broker."[11] The children arrived in girl-boy order: Clara in 1898, Sam in 1901, Jessie in 1903, and Maurice five years later. A network of uncles, aunts, and cousins helped one another along. Just as David's brother had started him in dairy delivery, so David brought another brother into the men's clothing store, overlooking his worthlessness as a salesman and refusal to work on Saturdays.[12]

Below the surface, however, things were less tranquil, in part as they are in almost all families, in part because of the special strains of being "foreign" in a still-Yankee world. Jessie's relations with her father were a case in point. As she later told it, she was his special favorite, and he hers. "I basked in the warmth of my adoring and adored father," she reminisced, recalling the evening ritual of helping him draw homemade wine from a basement barrel, or sitting snugly in his lap on Sunday horse-and-buggy rides. At the same time, her sharpest memories were of paternal fallibility, even weakness: of a failure when she was four to bring her a doll without being asked, when she was sure he could read her mind; of being left at home while older siblings enjoyed a long-awaited summer trip to North Dakota; or of her brother's similar disappointment when, believing that he was to spend the summer alone with his father, he found himself left with an uncle. On another occasion, David forbade his daughters to spend the night with girl friends (a firm family rule) and ordered them to their rooms, only to remember that the varnish he had applied on the stairs was still wet. With a desperation peculiar to beleaguered males, he then lined the stairs with newspapers, bits of which remained embedded in the varnish, as Jessie remembered, "a long time."

Jessie's memories of her mother were also mixed, although, as with her father, possibly clouded by a wrenching break of later years. Since arriving in the United States, Bessie Kanter's life had been a round of hard work and self-sacrifice. As a teenager, she toiled in the garment district of New York for a weekly wage of three dollars, which she dutifully turned over to her mother. During these years, or so young Jessie was told, she once marched in a women's rights parade and another time joined a workers' demonstration. But, by the time Jessie arrived, the burdens and responsibilities of marriage were taking their toll: first a miscarriage and a resulting grief never mentioned; then four children in a decade. Although an avid reader, Bessie's tastes ran to the newspaper equivalent of today's soaps: her particular favorite was a series called "Married Life." Her favorite songs were the current hits: "After the Ball Is Over" and "Why Did You Wink Your Eye?" After decades of denial, she was more interested in women's clothes than in women's rights. When, on one occasion, a solicitor from the League of Women Voters invited her to a meeting, she complied more in gratitude for the personal attention shown than out of concern for the vote.[13]

In later years, though not for want of trying, Jessie found little in her mother in the way of a feminist model. Quite the opposite. Her mother's devotion to her father and dependence upon him demonstrated "Some Disadvantages of Being a Happily Married Woman"— the title of a curious essay Jessie wrote when her own marriage was anything but happy. Her mother's "complete satisfaction in my father isolated her from other women," she observed (anticipating a theme of *The Female World*). "Her personality seemed to be bled white when he was gone." The conclusion: "A happy marriage deprives a woman of initiative, drive, leadership!"[14]

The power in the family and the source of Jessie's fondest memories was her grandmother Kanter. It was she who gave permissions, provided moral guidance, and dispensed discipline when necessary, all the time helping with the cooking and the housework. It was she also, as Bernard wrote twenty years later, "who set the Jewish stamp on our home": saying prayers before and after every meal; providing blessings for virtually every occasion. But in the process she also overshadowed her daughter. "She was a much more important person than our mother," Bernard added, in a characteristically frank assessment.[15] Not surprisingly, Bettsy Kanter provided the role model in Bernard's later conversion to feminism. "Almost as important as God himself," she wrote of her grandmother in the early 1970s. "Obviously His wife."[16]

The network of uncles, aunts, and cousins was also not the source of comfort many Americans like to imagine. Older settlers in the Jewish community resented the arrival of newcomers since family claims often drained valuable resources.[17] In the novel "Sarah Gordon," Bernard dramatized this issue as it applied to her own family. "The Solomon Gordons hated him," she wrote of rich Uncle Isador from whom the family must borrow money for a new house, "because they knew that his theories were wrong, and still he had succeeded, whereas their own theories were right, and they had not." To this was added that children born in the new country lorded it over those born abroad. "[Sarah] had always boasted proudly that she was native born

American," she wrote of her fictional self. "Not all her cousins were, and those who were felt superior and slightly condescending to those who were not."[18]

For the two older Ravitch children, a perennial casus belli was the issue of when, where, and with whom they might socialize. "My sister fought my father tooth and nail," Jessie recalled of Clara's rebellion over this issue. When her brother Sam proposed to date a young woman of whom his mother disapproved, her anger and frustration were so visible that Jessie remembered them years later. Made literally ill by the demands of his Yankee schoolteachers, hounded by his parents to enter a prestigious profession, Sam also carried a burden of bitterness against his father into adult life. The younger brother, for reasons unexplained, had an ungovernable tendency to escape from the house whenever possible.

Clara, as the oldest, was the first to explore the outer world. In the process, she provided Jessie a model of sorts, despite their up-and-down relationship in later years. It was Clara who majored in English (strengthening Jessie's resolve to do the same). It was also Clara who first studied the sciences and social sciences, zoology and anthropology being favorites. From one of these courses she brought home a text in social psychology by William McDougall (whose theory of instincts Jessie's future husband was then in the process of demolishing); from another, the theory of evolution; and from a third, the professor himself, Albert E. Jenks, chairman of the Anthropology Department at the University of Minnesota. When the professor graced their home, the Ravitches were deeply honored. But when Clara elaborated some of the latest theories (evolution, in particular), the family poked "good-natured fun." "Prof said so" became the family joke, armor of a sort against the modern world.[19]

On matters of taste and life-style, Clara also served as emissary of modern science and expertise. Lettuce and celery must replace the rich, heavy *vorspeise* of roasted eggplant, chopped onion, and olive oil; milk must be substituted for coffee. In America, each person must have individual napkins, individual knives, and, above all, privacy. Windows must be opened to the Minnesota winter to provide fresh air, even though, as Jessie later recalled, "it meant pneumonia, colds, and sinus infections for us all."[20]

The amused skepticism of these recollections in fact veiled feelings more truthfully revealed in Jessie's later fiction. In one particular story, Jessie as Ruthie recounted how her sister "Helen" brought the latest American habits into the home. "Everything American had prestige and therefore Helen [Clara] had prestige," she wrote. In this version the family jokes seemed less amusing. "When the Kaplans [Ravitches] protested or grumbled or showed dissatisfaction with anything Helen did," the story continued, "Ruthie despised them."[21]

To the bespectacled, sometimes rumpled, always studious Jessie, her American, more glamorous sister represented a life-style that was tempting, if not quite attainable.[22] In still another sister-story, Clara as Audrey was the well-dressed New Yorker, buoyed by her successful work with a child-study group (by the late 1920s, Clara was working in a similar position with Lucy Sprague Mitchell at Columbia).[23] Jessie as Lucy Page was a dowdy doctoral assistant in psychology, working for a Professor Smith whom she feared and idolized. At dinner at Audrey's Lucy is a source of amusement to two young men, who lament the faults of "scientific women" who "become too truthful and direct for their main business in life, which is to charm men." Currying their favor, she tells stories on her professor, only to be overwhelmed by guilt when she meets him the next day. Perhaps she should give up her assistantship, she suggests, to which Smith replies that he has a substitute already in mind. Feeling betrayed, Lucy runs from the office to an unanticipated sensation. "She had expected relief from inner torment to result from her conference," the story concludes. "But she had never anticipated this lovely joyous peace." Now part of her sister's world, in spirit at least, she spies a former lab associate, deep in thought and oblivious to her appearance. Lucy gloats at the sight of her friend's wrinkled stockings: "She allowed herself for the first time to laugh at them."[24]

A lthough Jessie's grandmother put the Jewish stamp on the household, her parents had some definite ideas of their own concerning religion. "My mother hated gentiles, in her cheerful, matter-of-fact way, all her life," Bernard later wrote. "Nothing could surpass the contempt and scorn in her voice when she spoke of our playmates as *veesta goyim* or *shiksas* or *schootzim.*" When Clara reported that anthropologists no longer believed in "pure" races, they were horrified since it implied that her father's blue eyes and her mother's blond nieces were something less than Jewish.[25]

From these religious convictions flowed a number of dos and don'ts. Do work hard, but avoid manual labor. On one occasion, so the story went, the family was scandalized to hear that the husband of one of Jessie's cousins was seen wearing overalls and was placated only when assured that he contracted for painters, but did not himself do the work. Study hard, but beware of heretical ideas—a lesson Clara had already learned concerning evolution. Do marry and have children, but not outside the faith. A favorite story of Jessie's father concerned a messenger who, when confronted with the task of telling an old Jewish man that his daughter had died, first approached him with the statement that she had eloped with a Gentile. "I would rather have seen her dead at my feet," the old man wailed. "She is dead, sire," the messenger replied.[26]

Jessie also lived with the ever-present tension between Jewish and Gentile culture. One Christmas it was stockings hung innocently over the fireplace by Jessie and her sister, and their father ripping them down after administering a good tongue-lashing.[27] On another occasion, it was the taunt of a playmate that Jews had killed Jesus. In high school, it was a subtle attempt by a favorite teacher to convert her, an incident she decided not to report to her parents.[28] Although she maintained friends among all groups, it was an uphill struggle. During her school years, she was forbidden to date Gentile boys or to bring them into her home.[29] "My Jewish friends and my non-Jewish friends did not feel . . . at home in one another's presence," she recalled in a lengthy, but unpublished analysis years later.[30]

The issue of the death of Jesus so absorbed her that she opened the novel "Sarah Gordon" with a fictionalized account of one childhood confrontation. "Mama, *why* did we kill Jesus?" Sarah asks. "Who said we killed him?" her mother replies with a flash of anger in her eyes. "Why Frances Locke told me so. We killed him and he was God's little boy." "Who is Frances Locke?" the mother shrieks in excited Yiddish. *"Veesta shiksa* . . . It's a lie!" Ordered not to play with the offending

Frances, Sarah nonetheless returns several days later with the news that a Sunday school teacher was the authority. "But we didn't kill God's little boy . . . did we Mama?" Sarah pleads. "No, of course not," her mother explains, forced finally to tell the whole story. "The Romans killed him and blamed it on the Jews."[31]

Anti-Semitism in Minneapolis was not, of course, confined to children. When Eastern European Jews moved to the North Side in the 1890s, they lived in ghettoes as much for self-protection as from economic necessity. Local lore had it that it was physically dangerous for a Jew to live above Fifth Street North.[32] Social and service organizations, from the Rotary to the Automobile Club, denied membership to Jews. The result, two sociologists later concluded, was "the systematic exclusion of Jews from participation in the community's social and civic life.[33]

Despite these realities and her own experiences, Jessie held to the conviction that she was American first and only incidentally a Jew. "I felt myself to be an American and I did not want to acknowledge any relationship with Europe," she wrote when finally coming to grips with the issue in the forties. She identified America with herself, and when grownups spoke well of the country she took it as a personal tribute. When a newly arrived cousin claimed that Russian scenery was the equal of American, she took it as a personal affront. America was unproblematic. Everyone—playmates, teachers, the newspapers—told her she was American. The result, she realized in hindsight, was a kind of complacency. Eventually, she (and her generation) would have to confront the uncomfortable fact "that we were not as American as we supposed."[34]

Soon after high school, the first hint of this fact intruded. Graduation night was a triumphant vindication of Jessie's faith in America. In the Roll of Honor she had been elected Best Looking and Most Courteous among the girls. "I was certainly among the most maudlin," she later wrote, recalling graduation-night hugs and kisses and promises to keep in touch forever. But then parents intervened to take each girl back to her separate world. The following autumn, this same lesson was reinforced at the funeral of one of the girls in her group. Suddenly Jessie felt alienated by the customs and rituals that in death claimed her friend back to the ancient and (to her) alien faith of her parents. "I learned that whenever adults—parents, that is—or boys were involved, something happened and we were not the same." Although her friends—Catholic and Protestant, as well as Jew—continued to see one another, it was not the same. "Like iron filings we seemed to become polarized and . . . lined up according to our ancient ways."[35]

IRONICALLY, although hardly a surprise, the tensions Jessie knew best were within the Jewish community itself. The poverty of the East European newcomers shocked and embarrassed the well-established Germans. Addressing the poverty of North Siders through charity soon became a form of status-seeking among them. German-Jewish organizations, even the Minneapolis chapter of B'nai B'rith, excluded the newcomers. Backlash against the mass influx after 1900 in turn cost older Jewish residents some hard-won gains. The Athletic Club, for example, excluded from membership the sons of Jews who were already members. The Ravitches and others in the middle presumably got it both ways: condescension from German Jews and rejection through association with the newcomers. The results would appear, often between the lines, in Bernard's later discussions of their situation.[36]

The city's synagogues, reflecting these divisions, ran the gamut from extremes of Orthodoxy to the Reform Temple (as it was called) of the West Side Germans. As members of the South side synagogue, the Ravitches joined those who were attempting to carve a path between West Side Reform Judaism and varieties of North Side Orthodoxy—a middle position finally called Conservative Judaism. Although their services were in Hebrew, as Jessie described them in a later account of the Jews of "Milltown," there was singing (but no instrumental music) and women were allowed to sit downstairs, both innovations unacceptable to the Orthodox. When even these compromises failed to stem the exodus to the Reform Temple, younger members organized a new synagogue, Beth El. By the forties, the two Conservative synagogues together claimed almost eight hundred families as members.[37]

For those leaving the faith, the two most popular destinations were Christian Science and Unitarianism. For the first, the "tender-minded," as she called them, Jessie had nothing but scorn. "Few members of the community credited these Jews with sincerity," she remembered. "The motive attributed to them was that of cowardice.... They were ashamed of their heritage."[38] A review of the writer Paul Cowan's autobiography decades later kindled these same thoughts. On his mother's side, Cowan (né Cohen) came from a family that, having embraced Christian Science in 1910, celebrated Christmas extravagantly and ate ham and sweet potatoes for Easter. It took their grandson, now a fifth-generation American, to undo the damage by finally embracing his Jewish past.[39] Unitarianism, in contrast, was less a competing religion than a way of learning Christian history and theology while remaining a Jew. "They remained loyal to their faith, at least in words." Bernard wrote of the "Milltown" Jews who attended Unitarian services in ever-increasing numbers, "while they drank at the stimulating fountain of New England's transmutation of Christianity."[40]

At home, a friend of her father's named Diamond brought alive the rationalist strain of Reform Judaism without the snobbery of the West Side Temple. A disciple of Voltaire and an avowed agnostic, he proclaimed untiringly how happy and free he was. He also, as it happened, had a house in the best part of town, complete with a study lined floor to ceiling with books. David Ravitch told his daughter that Diamond protested too much. No one could be that happy! But the visitor made a definite impression on young Jessie, who later told his story on several occasions. Neither eccentric nor atheist (as David Ravitch believed), Diamond represented those Jews in late eighteenth-century Vienna and elsewhere who had felt the liberating winds of the Enlightenment. To her own daughter, Bernard later told this whole story of Jewish emancipation from stultifying traditions and rituals.[41] "It was eerie," she wrote in an autobiographical account of her encounter with Diamond, "to have even this evanescent contact with the Enlightenment."[42]

Jessie was not long content with South Side Conservative Judaism, nor did she think of joining the Reform Jews of the West Side. But the combination of rationality, affluence, emancipation, and assimilation that Diamond and the Germans represented was not lost on her when, within a few years, she encountered, in Auguste Comte, neopositivism, and in Luther Bernard the latest recrudescence of the Enlightenment spirit.

What sort of Jew, then, was young Jessie Bernard after all distinctions are made? The appearance of a biography of Hannah Arendt six decades later returned her again to this question.[43] Arendt's piercing analysis of Jews through history left her in awe. In the presence of Arendt's work, she felt like the child on a *Saturday Evening Post* cover gazing "fascinated but uncomprehending" at a honeymooning couple in the next railway seat (a fitting image given Bernard's roots in Norman Rockwell's middle America). Particularly interesting was Arendt's distinction between Jewish "parvenus" and "pariahs"—the first trying without success to make it in the Gentile world; the second weaving "the strands of their Jewish genius" *as Jews* into the fabric of European culture. Arendt, of course, was a pariah—indeed, "a pariah for all seasons." But what was Bernard herself?[44]

Striking similarities in their backgrounds, as she saw them, gave the question special meaning. Although the two never met, they were roughly contemporaries (Arendt was born in 1906). The Königsberg of Hannah's childhood and the Minneapolis of Jessie's, although light-years apart culturally, showed similar patterns of Jewish settlement. As girls, both received weekly religious instruction, but nonetheless became fascinated by the person of Jesus and troubled by the taunt that their ancestors had murdered him. Both came under the sway of charismatic university professors—in Arendt's case, the philosopher Martin Heidegger. But differences proved finally more important. Whereas Arendt had lived in one of the city's ghettoes, Jessie had not. Just as Minnesota was not East Prussia culturally, so Bernard never knew the passionate intellectual debates that were a daily part of Arendt's home life. "She had powerful convictions [and] believed strongly in making judgments," Bernard observed. "My own background had instilled in me just the opposite." German rather than Rumanian, Arendt "was elitist, even snobbish, vis-à-vis East European Jews." And the positivist L. L. Bernard was not, after all, the existentialist Heidegger.

Was Bernard thus a parvenu? Somehow this term also did not fit. Although she had sometimes found herself "passing" in Gentile company, "smiling foolishly" at anti-Jewish jokes she did not understand, even sticking up for WASPs when everyone else was on the attack, she had never shared the parvenu's fear of being unmasked. Perhaps

English needed some equivalent of the Spanish distinction between *estar* and *ser,* the first referring to a variable state (wherein one consciously chooses to become something, in this case Jewish), the second to an inherent quality (being a Jew)—a state of belonging, as Arendt put it, "as a matter of course, beyond dispute or argument."[45] Sammy Davis, Jr., and Elizabeth Taylor became Jewish but were not Jews. Jessie Bernard was a Jew, but not Jewish. As she moved into the world beyond high school, however, this distinction was not always easy to maintain.

LOOKING BACK, Bernard ascribed her optimistic, trusting, and sometimes naive outlook on life to her special position as third child. Clara had led the way without benefit of an older sister; Sam bore the brunt of the career expectations of parents and teachers; Maurice shouldered the pain that Jessie's marriage later caused their parents. "I was the protected one," she wrote, "the enchanted one, the untested one."[46]

Her future husband, Luther L. Bernard, characteristically took a different view as he analyzed her youth years later. Her "dogmatic, self-centered family" had wounded each of their children, Jessie included. Clara almost escaped, since she was born before they "had sufficient security and determination to immolate her." But the others paid double. "I suppose many an old hatred filled Jew said to your parents that they let Clara run wild and that they must get in their work early with Sam," Luther continued. The result in all cases was what he termed a "phantasy complex" born of the inability to accept, or to break totally from, the Jewish reality. "Sam . . . had the phantasy complex the same as you, apparently. But he fell between the two worlds—Jewish and normal—and never entered into either, so he is a stranger to all worlds except the lost and roving world, which lives in a world of fantasy and escape from reality, like yours" (the latter most likely a reference to Sam's serious drinking problem, among others, in his later years). Her parents blamed this brother for his troubles "when they should dress in sackcloth and ashes, like their ancestors, and beat their breasts and say: 'Oi, oi, oi, what fools and sinners we were. We have utterly ruined one son and may yet ruin a son and a daughter.' "[47]

Sheltered or immolated? Naive or fantasy-prone? Although the truth was somewhere in between, the result was the same so far as the lessons Jessie learned, or rather did not learn, during her youth. In turn-of-the-century Minneapolis, the problems were there, but she did not yet see them. The trauma of Americanization, generational strife, ethnic and social conflict, and anti-Semitism so subtle it sometimes seemed invisible. More than she realized, these issues set her intellectual agenda for years to come. Culture versus environment. Factors determining whether children associate with family or friends, in or out of the neighborhood. Jews in a Gentile world, and what she later termed "biculturality." Dating and mating. The role of conflict in society.[48] The nature and future of the family. For the moment, however, at age sixteen and a half, she was off to the University of Minnesota for her freshman year.

2
Héloïse (1920–1926)

Very Dearest Abelard. . . . Do you love me infinitely more than anyone ever loved his lady?
—Jessie Ravitch to Luther Bernard, August 24, 1922

W hen Jessie arrived on the campus of the University of Minnesota in January 1920, the postwar party was just beginning. "To Bob—or Not to Bob?" This "tantalizing question," proclaimed the *Minnesota Daily*, was "causing the greatest discussion American women have ever engaged in."[1] Casting her vote for modernity, Jessie bobbed, and for a time uneasily adopted the protective coloration of the flapper. And short hair, she soon discovered, was only the beginning. The year before she arrived there had been a "corsetless coed" movement. "Women were wearing garter belts to keep their stockings up or just rolling them below the knee," she remembered. Flappers had already replaced the camisole and corset-covers with the brassiere as a symbol of liberation. A flood of new books raised fashion to the level of art. "My tastes were 20th century," Bernard continued, noting that her favorite authors were Edna St. Vincent Millay, Floyd Dell, and, not surprisingly, fellow Minnesotan F. Scott Fitzgerald.[2]

Scholarship was also part of the mix. Although not yet the multiversity of later times, the University of Minnesota numbered some 8,600 students in 1920, more than double the enrollment a decade earlier.[3] The faculty had expanded accordingly, as the university took steps to modernize its departments. Headed for an English major, Jessie took classes with some of its most distinguished members, among them Richard Burton, a Johns Hopkins Ph.D. who titillated the students with Jane Austen's comment that no woman over twenty-three could excite affection in the male breast; Elmer E. Stoll, a world-famous Shakespearean scholar, who shocked the class with the announcement that Shylock was a comic character; and one Stanley Rypins, son of a prominent rabbi and a recent Rhodes scholar, who scandalized Jewish Minneapolis by marrying outside the faith. In other departments, Jessie also studied with some of the biggest names: Alvin Hansen and N.S.B. Gras in economics; Karl Lashley in psychology; and Pitirim Sorokin, the distinguished Russian émigré, in sociology. She sometimes joked that she had attended Harvard, since the last four eventually taught there.[4]

Among its faculty, Minnesota also boasted a number of distinguished women: in history, Alice Felt Tyler, later author of the highly regarded *Freedom's Ferment* (1944); in English, the novelist Mary Ellen Chase, Marjorie Nicholson, Anna A. Phelan ("statuesque and the very archetype of Pallas Athene"), and the venerable Maria Sanford ("the first woman college professor)";[5] and in chemistry, Lillian Cohen. Many years later, Bernard saw clearly the barriers these women had faced. Since Tyler was married to another Minnesota professor, nepotism rules kept her a permanently temporary section leader. Nicholson and Chase, sensing a ceiling to their ambitions, soon left for Columbia and Smith respectively. They were "great luminaries," Bernard later remembered: they "dazzled" her.[6]

This memory, however, almost certainly told more about her later convictions than her views at the time. At the University of Minnesota of the early 1920s—to judge from the *Minnesota Daily*—the "woman question" had lost much of its prewar urgency. Male students typically recognized the issue only to express vestigial uneasiness in open opposition to the flapper craze or in attempts at light-hearted humor. A particularly vitriolic editorial in the fall of Jessie's freshman year condemned the wearing of what it called "kindergarten skirts." "No one has to think twice," the editor lectured, "to know that the short skirts worn by the ultra-fashionable group are bringing not only severe criticism upon their wearers, but also sneers and unpleasant remarks from men—men whom these women consider their friends as well as those whose opinions mean nothing." In the same issue a columnist lampooned the new permissiveness: "It takes cheek to kiss a girl" the exchange went. "Yes, and sometimes the girl is willing to furnish the check." "What do you mean 'only sometimes'?" A month later, a correspondent contributed a sardonic commentary on "Feminine Masculinity." Now that women were equals, he opined, they need expect no special courtesies. Indeed, if "masculine femininity" was to be the rage among women, why not "a husky man playing the part of a coy and demure girl." Since this thought was too awful, perhaps "assertive women" should think twice.[7]

A few women students sporadically attempted to extend women's liberation to campus affairs. "Men Wash Dishes as Fair Sex Seeks [Office] 'Position' " read a headline in October 1920, reporting that women students no longer sought housework to aid them through school, but office jobs. "The psychology of men and that of women are different things," announced the director of the University Employment Agency, with an air of revelation. Women had had enough of dusting and dishwashing and felt their independence threatened when taking on domestic work, while men were quite willing "to try anything once, even polishing the parlor table." Other evidence was more direct, although rare. During Jessie's fifth term, the campus women's organizations rose up to protest the exclusion of females from the Gridiron Banquet, an annual student roast of "tyrant profs." "Girls are mistreated by professors as well as the men," one woman noted, claiming equal right to be in on the fun. (Another plotted with her boyfriend to go disguised in his place, only to be foiled when a sorority sister squealed.) In the fall of Jessie's senior year, the campus YWCA and the Women's Student Government Association designated November 21 "Maria Sanford Day," thus honoring past triumphs.[8]

When the issue came up, Jessie also opposed bastions of male privilege. As a member of Kappa Rho, the women's debating society, she was reported in her sophomore year as taking the affirmative in a debate "Resolved, that Men's Literary Societies should be abolished from the Campus."[9] But, to judge from letters and other written work, the issue rarely came up, at least so far as Jessie was concerned. If "dazzled" by her women professors, she made no mention of them at the time, nor remembered taking any specific courses with them. Assuming equality rather than struggling for it, she instead exulted in the liberating, permissive atmosphere of the new environment.

The department that won her heart, intellectually and (as it turned out) romantically, was finally not English but sociology. As a freshman, Jessie first visited the class of Professor Luther Lee Bernard at Stanley Rypins's suggestion, appropriately enough given the problems inter-marriage would cause her as it caused him. The outcome was an exhilarating blend of new ideas, new experiences, and apparent libera-tion from the cloistered world of Eleventh and Lake Avenue. For four years, without her parents' knowledge, she carried on a clandestine affair with her professor while embracing the teachings of modern sociology with the passion of the convert, as one by one the apparently outmoded values of her youth crumbled.

F or the Jewish community of Minneapolis, the war years had brought dramatic changes. Older neighborhoods were relin-quished to blacks, while suburbs further out catered to the newly rich. East Europeans Jews from the South Side invaded the formerly German West Side. "The already well-established young Rus-sian or Rumanian Jews quickly acquired a veneer of breeding which made them quite indistinguishable from the onetime aristocrats of the community," Bernard later wrote in a thinly disguised account of her own relatives and their families. The socially ambitious left Orthodox synagogues for the Reform Temple, while the older generation branded these deserters "Deutsche Yehudi"—the "so-called German Jews." Homes and the people in them were redone so as to hide all traces of the Old World. Women no longer visited but "entertained." "Boyish forms became the rage and everyone dieted," Bernard re-membered. Summers were now spent at lakeside resorts. For the women, lacemaking and needlework gave way to mah-jong or bridge. Men pursued fishing, golf, and other activities earlier thought to be too frivolous or, worse, too Gentile.[10]

Although the David Ravitches were the poor relations in the eyes of their more successful relatives, Jessie shared this new prosperity vicari-ously, especially during visits with her rich cousins at their home (a "semi-mansion," she recalled) or at their lakeside retreat. Nor was the Minnesota undergraduate above these things. "I got the dearest little hat today—gray and blue felt," she reported of one new purchase. "It's most becoming too."[11] For her cousin's summer house she had even more lavish praise: "I never in my life have seen such a lovely place. They have a cottage with four bathrooms, eight porches, two fireplaces, accommodations for 14 people, electric stove, hot and cold running water—a gorgeous lawn and beautiful men in the water."[12] More socially active than she had been in high school, she now reported on dances and socials and the attention of a number of young men, one or more of whom periodically raised her parents' hopes for a marriage. Between times, she read voraciously. Like her sister Clara before her, she invited her favorite professor to the house on several occasions.[13] All in all, her parents had good reason to be proud of their intelligent, industrious third child.

What they did not know was that, by the summer of 1922, Jessie was also living another life. Read in their entirety, her reports of clothes, summerhouses, and socials told a further story. "Mother saw today's letter and asked if it were from 'the professor.' I said no, merely an 'ad,' so that you may write again soon," she began one such letter. The recipient was Luther Lee Bernard, her sociology professor.[14] By this time, she had a relationship with him that would please them not at all. Whether all this liberation would add up to true emancipation and personal fulfillment remained to be seen.

W hen Jessie arrived, Minnesota's Department of Sociology was entering its golden years.[15] F. Stuart Chapin, appointed chairman in 1922, had been director of social work at Smith and was now a major proponent of statistical, quantitative sociology. Departmental restructuring had begun five years earlier with the appointment of Luther L. Bernard, a rising star in social psychology whose *Instinct* (1924) would soon apear. Others included Manuel C. Elmer, a Chicago-trained social surveyist with an interest in the family and delinquency, and later an ally of L.L.B. in battles to reform the American Sociological Society in the 1930s (appointed 1919); Frank Bruno, a Yale Ph.D. and social worker who arrived in 1921 to replace outgoing chairman Arthur J. Todd; and two assistant professors. In Jessie's senior year, Pitirim Sorokin also joined the department. Graduate students included George A. Lundberg, a disciple of L.L.B. who would later outdo the master in the quest for "objective" knowledge.

Although Jessie took her first course with Elmer, he made little impression (student rap, as reported later to L.L.B. by another young woman, was that Elmer was "very funny indeed . . . but we felt he was nothing but a bluff").[16] Although Chapin interested her in statistical techniques and was a significant influence on her work in the thirties, he also did not immediately capture her imagination. She also took one course with the departing Todd, "whose first name I can't remember."[17]

But Luther Bernard was another matter. For Jessie, as for the author of the uncharitable comment on Elmer, he was the one sociology professor with whom one really *had* to study. By the time Jessie discovered him, there was already something of a Bernard cult. Two student fans styled themselves "neo-Bernardians"; another sent him a toy ape in thanks for a lecture on primate behavior.[18] "Every once in a while we come across most amazing specimens of instincts, which we chloroform and collect in bottles," one of the neo-Bernardians joked with reference to his scholarly hobby.[19] Jessie herself was quite literally swept off her feet. He "enthralled me—literally held me in thrall," she recalled. "He seemed to have all the answers a seventeen-year-old could ask for."[20]

Luther himself had made it to Minnesota the hard way.[21] As a youth, he grew up in shabby austerity in several parts of west Texas and the Southwest, where his father tried to earn a living by farming. In 1900 he took a B.S. degree from the less-than-prestigious Pierce Baptist College in southwestern Missouri and a B.A. from the state university seven years later. At the University of Chicago, where he earned his doctorate in 1910, he was perhaps the most brilliant of his classmates, but also (as he remembered it) consistently the worst dressed. In his final year he led a movement to reform the curriculum, which alienated virtually every member of the sociology faculty. These experiences, in turn, left their mark in a prickly personality, a monumental sensitivity, and an outsized appetite for affection and approval, especially female.

Despite his brilliance, Bernard's prickly personality exiled him to a succession of mediocre positions in the several years after graduation:

first at Western Reserve (1910), then the University of Florida (1911–1914), and finally the University of Missouri (1914–1917). One source of comfort in these trying years was his marriage in 1911 to Frances Fenton, a fellow graduate student, and the birth of a daughter soon after. But on the eve of his offer from Minnesota in 1917, his marriage was disintegrating. Falling back on his scholarly work, Bernard resumed the crusade that he had begun in his doctoral thesis: a refutation of instinct theory and the elaboration of what he termed "an objective standard of social control." In 1919 he published an important article in the *American Journal of Sociology*, and five years later he wrote *Instinct*, the study that won him a reputation as a leading proponent of sociological behaviorism. When Luther first met Jessie in 1921, he was forty, she seventeen.

Among this theories, L.L.B. also had some definite ideas about women. At their root in his case was the stuff of which psychology texts are made: an unhappy home life in his youth; a tyrannical, often abusive father who kept his mother in virtual bondage; a Baptist atmosphere longer on sin than forgiveness. The outcome was a complex of attitudes the twenties would call "puritanical," although "misogynist" would be as accurate. The pattern developed early. On one occasion, when his younger sister, then three or so, appeared in the yard without underpants on a very hot day, Luther ordered his mother to whip her. "She did not whip me," his sister remembered years later, "tho you stormed a great deal about it." Three years after, when this same sister asked the meaning of "the vulgar 4 letter sex word" she had just heard from a friend, Luther staged a repeat performance. "You stormed again, ordered [mother] to whip me and talked REFORM SCHOOL," his sister continued. "You actually did."[22]

During his graduate school years, Luther focused his ire on the "new" woman, much in evidence in Chicago when he arrived in 1907. In one classroom essay, he lamented the "moral motif" of the modern stage as illustrated by a current play, which exonerated a woman prostitute and drug addict on the ground that she had been seduced by a "rake." Luther instead blamed the woman entirely. In his doctoral thesis he inveighed against the "modern woman of fashion" who divided her time "between her clothes and fashionable functions or personal and sensuous gratifications." Some years later his first marriage dissolved, in part because he saw some of these qualities in his first wife.[23]

By the twenties, his theory concerning the sexes was appallingly simple: women were either angels or whores, mostly the latter, manipulating and undermining men ("sabotaging" was a favorite term) when not themselves the victims of emotions that assumed crippling proportions one week of every month. "If Jessie fails me there is no use trying to appeal to something finer in another woman," he wrote during a bout of despair three months before they were married. "I shall take them for what they are—slaves and prostitutes—and play their game with them."[24]

Men, in contrast, were the truly sensitive ones. "Strange things are men," he wrote Jessie years later, summing up this philosophy. "No wonder women do not understand them or appreciate them. Their loyalty and devotion, their longing, are so foreign to them. They *do* live in different worlds. Someone will—let us hope—discover the male some day and give *him* credit for the patient, long suffering devotion he has given women throughout the ages."[25] Imagined disloyalty often drove him to tears. "Why, *why* can't you control yourself?" one young woman exploded when she had had enough of this behavior. "You make me hate those things in you, your crying etc. But when you are a *man*, well, you're so fine."[26] But in more cases than not, the ploy was apparently unbeatable.

LUTHER'S streak of puritanism did not rule out womanizing on a grand scale. His affairs began even before he arrived in Minnesota. "She is eager sexually, and we struggle for 3½ hours for her to have orgasm, but she fails," he recorded dispassionately of one early conquest. "Neglect supper. Have baths together, then supper."[27] In Minnesota, he played the role of unhappy husband to the hilt (he was not finally divorced until August 1922). Charmingly paunchy, he possessed boyish good looks and piercing blue eyes. Of a potential rival Jessie wrote at the time: "She is crazy about him, as all women are who know him."[28] On campus, Professor Bernard was soon the darling of a coterie of female students and other women whose relations with him apparently ranged from flirtatious to considerably more. In 1920 a rumor that he had "been kicked out of somebody's home, apparently because of immorality with somebody's wife" (a rumor he later repeated but vehemently denied) caused the university temporarily to suspend his salary.[29]

Sometime in 1921, he began a semipermanent relationship with a young woman whom he hoped to marry, although scandal over the affair eventually led to his departure from the university.[30] At his insistence, his fiancée (as he called her in one version) signed an agreement to assure, as its prelude stated, "an adjustment which will be as happy and as loyal as possible on both sides." Then followed a list of *her* major faults: she allowed her family to dominate her; she was "absolute, irritable, irrational, and unjust" in the ten days preceding each menstrual period; she was selfish, fickle, and disloyal. To remedy these shortcomings, she promised to avoid dogmatism, obey him over her parents, and go to Chicago with him the following summer, if he wished.[31] The list, as it turned out, was a chilling forecast of later charges against Jessie. "You are acting now like a child," he scolded on one such occasion more than a decade later. "Don't imitate [Heather] so completely."[32]

Bernard's behaviorism and his personal dispositions were not unrelated. More remarkable than the conquests themselves was the careful detail with which he recorded his sexual encounters. For more than a decade, in diaries of varying size, he chronicled dates, times, and places. During his affair with his Minneapolis fiancée, he outdid himself in a journal that described the finest details from dress to undress, arousal to ejaculation. His aim apparently was not to stimulate passion but to reify it. In his developing behaviorist logic, no distinction existed between attitude and act, since the first was simply the second in the process of becoming. By chronicling guilty behavior, one somehow neutralized it, making it something to be studied and examined as if it were the action of another.

Although this interpretation is admittedly speculative, Bernard in his way supported it in a revealing letter he wrote to his fiancée at a time when she refused to have intercourse despite claiming she loved him. "It is your love I want," he wrote impatiently. "Of course I don't think one can separate love from the expression of it. You see I'm a behaviorist."[33]

In the meantime, his special blend of vulnerability and sensitivity made him a campus legend. His circle of female admirers—"groupies," Jessie later called them—discussed their love lives, poured out their souls, and generally gossiped with him. "Mildred . . . and I went to the Trades and Labor Assembly," Jessie reported to Luther of one of their mutual friends. "She says she misses you ever so much [and] . . . wishes you were here where she could talk to you."[34] Offering some "friendly advice," another warned him not to be tricked by an engaged young women ("a flirt and a vamp") whose fiancé was soon to return from big-game hunting in South America and "may not approve of the way she is carrying on in your office."[35] To her sorority sisters, an anonymous student reported: "If you don't like that man, you don't know what you are missing."[36]

Bernard's derisive attitude toward women, although sometimes an occasion for scolding, was finally only a minor nuisance. "What you say is unfair to women in general, and to the women in your class in particular," began a seven-page indictment of his biases from one married student. "Can't you see how unfair, how unmanly, it is to take such advantage of a group of fairly intelligent women?" she demanded. "You had me so angry I was trembling and I had to get out so as not to scream." Yet, six months later, this same student wrote to borrow a copy of Havelock Ellis's *Studies in the Psychology of Sex,* suggesting seductively that she come to his office on the weekend to pick it up. "Can you help me out? Think it over, will you." Then followed a lament over a miserable marriage and the "vicious violent tempered man" with whom she was forced to live.[37] Another woman student, who by Luther's own account very much wanted to marry him, did not even try to reform him. "There was an awfully good story in the *Saturday Evening Post* entitled 'Tyrant Woman'!" she wrote. "I know you would enjoy it immensely." "You are a woman hater," added another fan. "Always!"[38]

At the start of his relationship with Jessie, as he later recorded the details, Luther was the model of restraint and propriety. She "professed to admire [me] greatly" and soon made "her admiration personal," he remembered. "I was much pleased and flattered by it, but early in 1922 I came to the conclusion that our relationship should not become more personal"—probably alluding to his conclusion in May of an informal marriage contract with the fiancée whom he would also call his "common-law" wife. To keep Jessie from visiting his apartment, he refused to tell her his address. In the end, however, she prevailed. "After that," he added, in a gem of understatement, "we maintained a constant friendship."[39]

Just how much an understatement Jessie revealed in letters to her professor the following summer. Her salutations set the tone: "Hello Lover"; "Dearest"; "Very Dearest Abelard."[40] What followed might be read as adolescent fantasy, written but not sent, had Luther not responded to her letters and so carefully preserved each one. She would join him in Chicago (where he was teaching summer school) and be introduced to Jane Addams as "Mrs. Luther Bernard." They would travel abroad for ten years or so—to Europe, Asia, Africa, South America—and then have a son on whom Bernard could conduct his educational experiments. Above all, they would "play."[41]

Yet, on the matter of sex, the object of this reference, Jessie was still largely at sea. In her home, the topic was taboo, at least so far as her mother was concerned. When her first menstrual period arrived, it was her grandmother who told her what to expect and what to do, taking as a matter of course the whole world of sex, babies, and birth. Her mother, cut off from the female world of European village life (or so Bernard later explained it), found the whole business distasteful. When neighborhood children explained the facts of life, her reaction was the perennial disbelief of the sheltered middle-class child: "Our parents? Our parents?"[42]

What sort of woman would she herself be in the jazz age? As a child she had snuggled in hiding places with boys playing hide-and-seek, and piled body upon body while bobsledding. But her sexual inexperience now left her without an answer. In high school she had not dated at all. When she wore makeup and her sister's tightly fitting dress in the senior class play, the boys looked up. But by Monday morning, she later recalled, their interest had evaporated. For instruction she turned to one of her sister's textbooks, William McDougall's *Social Psychology*. Although his description of human reproduction was enough to put anyone off ("It is necessary that the organ of the male shall enter the antechamber of the woman, and that the emission of the sperm cells shall [not] take place until this is accomplished"), Jessie

memorized every word.[43] The Saturday afternoon movies offered
instruction of a different sort in the form of competing feminine
roles: one Mary Pickford, ever "sweet and charming"; the other
Theda Bara, the original vamp whose sultry sexuality made her a star
overnight following the appearance of *A Fool There Was* (1915).[44]
Pickford was the role the nineteenth century had automatically assigned nice girls like Jessie. But behind closed doors, before a mirror,
she tried out her Theda Bara.[45]

In 1922, Luther gave her a chance to practice the part. Early in
their relationship, her attitude toward sex was a tangle of convention
and calculation that added up to no so far as intercourse was concerned. "Women have power over men only through the fact that they
have something to bestow which men are willing to work for," she
lectured her professor, in the stilted language of convention. "But
when women are eager to give it away, men are no longer obliged to
work for it." Luther was apparently not satisfied. Her refusal, he
charged, was harming his health, physical and mental. Perhaps even
causing impotence. Most of all it was making him miserable, an appeal
he used with effect on virtually every woman he knew. "I asked for
bread and you gave me stones," he lamented.[46]

As the Victorian darkness gave way to the dawn of a twenties-style
Aquarius, Jessie struggled to explain her complex feelings. "Your letter
this morning was a most painful surprise," she replied. "If I don't give
myself completely you know it's because I'm scared and not because I
don't care. If it weren't for my parents, I'd do anything in the world for
you. I'd prove it." Were she living with him, she would feel differently.
"But when I come to your apartment, the idea of coming just for that is
revolting and offends my sense of the fitness of things." Were she to
give herself under present circumstances, she would "never be able to
marry anyone." She would, that is, "always feel immoral, unclean and a
'fallen woman.' " "I do even now at times with girls who are still uniniti-
ated," she added. The answer, that is, was still no.[47]

Then, in a curious about-face, and with reference to the puzzling
remark about initiation, she reminded him that no intercourse did not
mean no sex. Oral sex? Manual sex? All these would be his if she were
"not too bashful." In language as explicit and bold as her previous
sentiments were conventional, she detailed promises of how things

would be when next they met. If not bread, then "almost bread, say rye bread," she joked. Anything and everything, as she put it, to keep him "healthy, strong, and virile." Only at the close of this extraordinary communication did convention rear its timid head. "I'm too discreet to sign my name," she wrote, "but destroy this letter anyway won't you?"[48]

Thus entranced, Jessie quickly lost interest in the young men upon whom her parents pinned their hopes. "Tomorrow I am going on an all day party with a man I've never seen and know I won't like," she wrote Luther, still in August 1922. And of another suitor: "Going out with Henry just ruins my personality. I like the Jessie that you know best of all."[49] Almost two weeks later she added: "He is always the soul of propriety [and] doesn't seem to be much of a lover, you know—and rather paternal in his attitude."[50]

The pretended liberation of her contemporaries likewise lost its glitter. "Tonight I'm all powdered up and fixed—You know. I hate it, it isn't Jessie," she wrote. "I went to a Bohemian party the other night, not really Bohemian, you understand—pseudo-so. They'll never really amount to anything, but they like to play with the idea."[51] Even sex talk seemed stale. "Henry and I went out to Radisson Inn that night," she continued one report. "He bores me. He likes a very sophisticated type of woman—one who is very sex-conscious—one who will flirt with her eyes and attitude but be very naive in her speech. You know the kind. And I hate to do that. He wanted to discuss sex problems but I am so bored with sex—honestly. . . . I'm just plain tired of having it on all sides." To make matters worse, this same Henry had then lectured her on the evil influence of modern novels. "He asked me if I hadn't given myself lots of freedom, that I wouldn't have done had it not been for modern novels," she concluded with obvious sarcasm.[52]

Novels or not, Jessie' resolve had apparently crumbled by the spring of her senior year (1923). "You have given me more romance in one year than most women have in their whole lives and I love you," she wrote Luther in April. "I would rather have lost half my life than missed the wonderful experience of having had your love and loving you." Several months later, leaving no doubt, she added: "[I] wish we were together on your couch or bed don't you?. . . . What an immoral pagan I am, n'est ce pas?" To prove her emancipation, she

half-seriously suggested that she marry the beau her parents preferred, that Luther marry his mistress, and that they both continue to
be lovers. By this time, her letters regularly featured sketches of
genitalia and of stick figures making love.[53] Among its benefits, this
secret liaison also gave her subtle power over her older sister Clara,
who gradually suspected that something was up. "Clara has already
discovered that I'm merely your echo," Jessie wrote Luther sometime
late in 1923. "Have you had it lately?" she then asked him, with a
boldness that escalated with each letter. "I often talk to Clara about it,
to see how she reacts to it."[54]

Although events would later reveal that the old-fashioned girl was
not dead, Jessie's capitulation provided an early lesson of the power of
behavior over conviction, environment over heredity. To behave in
one way and think in another, according to Luther, was at best meaningless, at worst a sign of being "maladjusted." The proper and studious "Jess" of her parents, the powdered and painted "Jessie" of her
pseudo-bohemian contemporaries, and Luther's "Jessie" in some way
were all creatures of environment, to be referred to, as she did often
in her letters, as persons apart from an essential self, mired somewhere in the past. For the moment, the new Jessie was neither her
parents' Mary Pickford nor her classmates' flapper, but the person
Luther had helped create: sexy and brainy, sensual and intellectual.

D id sexual permissiveness mean freedom from sexual stereotypes or emancipation in any significant sense? For someone
determined to find evidences of feminism, Jessie's letters of
these years contain hints that she rejected traditional conceptions of
woman's domestic no less than sexual role. On vacation in rural Minnesota after graduation, for example, she wrote that the women in the
group bored her to tears. "Imagine mature women with nothing more
in their minds than [diets and fatness]," she wrote Luther.[55] To such
evidences of youthful feminism Bernard herself later added other examples. Her high school teachers, as she remembered, were "staunch
feminists." One in particular entertained classes with a story of one
antifeminist denouncing woman's suffrage. "Imagine your cook vot-

ing," he demanded. "I often think of it," his hostess replied. "You see he does."[56] At the university, she took the lesson to heart, refusing to major in home economics as Clara urged in a moment of discouragement over her own English major.

More importantly, however, Bernard tacitly but unmistakably accepted and even catered to her lover's unflattering view of women. At first it was teasing, almost playful. "I love to be dominated, and bossed, and mastered by the man I love," she wrote early in their relationship. "Ain't a female a funny animal." And a week later: "You are very selfish and domineering, but I love you anyway in spite of it all."[57] Although several months together taught her that he could be "mean" when he wanted to be, she still wondered provocatively what he might do if he really became angry: "Spank me? or scold me? or just loathe [*sic*] unspeakable things!"[58]

In time, this teasing mood gave way to one of self-accusation and apology. "Wasn't I a villain lots of times last year?" she asked in the summer of their second year. "But you forgave me, didn't you beloved? Hereafter I'll trot around like a little puppy dog."[59] "I always seem to be doing things that warrant scolding, don't I?" she wrote sometime after graduation. "I know I'm an irresponsible, lightheaded dumbbell."[60] In early 1925, nine months before their marriage, self-criticism reached a crescendo. "I failed you!' she lamented. "Instead of the wonderful person I used to think myself, I find that I'm a quarrelsome, pampered, self-centered little weakling—without wisdom, power, or ability of any kind."[61] (In short, precisely the things Luther had said about the "new woman" in his doctoral thesis a decade earlier.) Then, on New Year's Day a year later: "You will always hate me subconsciously, and I deserve it."[62]

Ultimately, if subtly, similar sentiments shaped Jessie's view of scholarship and science, and of her part in them. Her love for Luther from the start fed as much on ideas as on sex, perhaps even more so. In her letters, protestations of undying love competed with comments on Herbert Spencer, with reports of perusing an entire year of the *Reader's Guide* for bibliography, and with questions about his career. How was his scholarship going? Would he get a position at the University of Chicago? "In fact," she wrote in early 1924, "one of the reasons I am eager to marry you is . . . to make my brains available."[63] "I love our

work," she exulted soon after their marriage. "Books, books, books—
we must write dozens. . . . Work is the only thing. Work and you."[64]

But the question was whether, as a woman, she could live up to his
demands and to the standard she believed he represented. The earliest signs were innocent enough. "All of which proves," she concluded
a letter in August 1922, apropos of nothing, "that when a woman falls
in love she loses the calm impartiality necessary to scientific work. I'm
your sweetheart before I am a scientist, aren't I?"[65] In an attempt to
put her own situation in perspective, she decided to write a book on
the adolescent girl. At the library, she discovered one study that
seemed exactly to describe her situation[66]—"girls who longed to express themselves sexually, but were always restrained by scruples, religious or otherwise." From this same source she also learned that some
adolescents fall in love with older men, only to find that such unions
are invariably "unfortunate." ("We'll prove contrary, won't we?" she
asked Luther nervously). But the discovery that someone else had
already written the book burst her balloon. To her lover she wrote:
"Guess I'll have to content myself with being just your sweetheart."[67]
There were also hints of self-sacrifice, of subordinating her career to
his ambitions. "I'm not very ambitious for myself anymore," she wrote
with reference to the books they would write together. "I could drown
my abilities in yours."[68]

These sentiments proved little barrier to academic success in the
short run. In 1923, Jessie received her B.A., graduating magna cum
laude. The following year she completed an M.A. that won a local
prize and won its author a place on the program of the American
Sociological Society in 1924. But self-criticism, even self-denigration,
would increase rather than disappear with marriage during a decade
or more in which she ploughed through library archives largely for
Luther's benefit.

━━━━━━━━━━

While romance broke the tie of sexual convention, Jessie's marriage to Luther in September 1925 destroyed her relationship with her parents, shattering the nest of associations she
had known through her youth. By the time she took her M.A., Lu-

ther's situation at the university was precarious to say the least. Since his appointment in 1917, his combative personality and thin skin had brought him into conflict with most of the members of his department. The coup de grace was a scandal that attended the refusal of Heather to marry him in the summer of 1924, and subsequent pressure from her parents on university officials to prevent Luther from troubling their daughter.[69]

Since Luther initially had the support of department chairman F. Stuart Chapin, it appeared that he might weather the storm. But by January 1925, as he wrote in his diary, "it became evident that the president, urged on by the Dean, was determined to be rid of me." Although a temporary appointment at Cornell for September, followed by a fellowship to South America, allowed him to salvage appearances, the circumstances of his departure from Minnesota clouded his career for the rest of the decade.

Jessie publicly put a brave front on things, notably in a letter she wrote in April 1925 to a Bernard supporter at Cornell, where gossip threatened Luther's appointment. As his "student and assistant" for five years, as a friend of both Bernard and his lover, and as the woman who now planned to marry him, she claimed that she knew the whole story. Although Luther and the young woman had been sincerely devoted to one another, the girl's family and her physician ("without any manifest cause") influenced her to break off the relationship. The physician then announced his own engagement to the young lady and sought protection from the president of the university against Bernard for them both—an absurd request, as anyone familiar with Bernard's "mild and generous nature" would know. Since the physician's action was "not . . . very ethical," perhaps his action was the product of guilt, she surmised. Certainly, university politics of the shabbiest sort had also played a role.[70]

In private, Jessie apparently began to have second thoughts. Although her early talk of marriage sometimes smacked of fantasy, she was not entirely blind to her lover's psychological quirks. "I don't believe you want to marry me really," she wrote that August, when they were still sparring over their sexual relationship. "You just want me but not as a wife," she continued with more insight than she knew. "You'd rather have me marry someone else and be unfaithful, wouldn't you?"[71] She was also vaguely aware of his womanizing even before the affair with the disloyal lover had threatened his career. Juggling the affections of two women strained even Luther's resources, particularly on occasions when Heather would phone the office when Jessie was there. "I couldn't answer clearly," Bernard noted after one such incident. "Jessie was in the office and always asks who it is, looking rather troubled."[72] After reading Jung's *New Psychology* in the spring of 1923, Jessie wondered if Luther agreed that men constantly needed new sources of sexual stimulation. "If you thought I would never find out and if there was no social pressure against it," she asked in a question that should have come back to haunt her, "would you always be seeking new women for satisfaction?"[73]

Jessie's public loyalty during the difficult autumn of 1924 had, in fact, carried a personal price. "I told him of the almost unendurable strain his position had been for me," she wrote in her diary once Luther's fate was sealed. "It was awful to be tender and sympathetic and consoling to a man who thot of nothing but another woman." To console herself, she imagined "that as soon as he was out of trouble, he would love me again."[74] In self-defense she played up a flirtation with another young man. For several unhappy months during 1925, it was Luther who pressed for marriage while she dragged her feet.

Luther, in the privacy of his diary, not surprisingly had his own version of the proceedings. Only three persons had stood up for him during the crisis: one a colleague, one the most loyal of the Bernard groupies, and the third a fellow who had also once been engaged to the perfidious young lady. "Jessie, whom I had believed to be the perfection of womanhood and loyalty, proved unequal to the situation at best," he continued. Then followed a tortured catalogue of her failings that revealed more about Luther's neurotic personality and his personal insecurity than anything Jessie had or had not done.[75]

His charges were the now familiar litany of the faults of the "new woman." Jessie was more interested in finding a comfortable "nesting place" than in helping him fight the battle. Her concern for his career was financial at heart. Fearing the adverse publicity that marriage would bring, she backed away from her promises while clinging "to her chances with other men." As to the latter, he had consoled himself at the time that the would-be rival was "too effeminate" to take seriously. But in retrospect the flirtation was part of the package. "I know women well," he continued, in one of his bitterest denunciations to date. "I know how utterly conscienceless they are about such things—always ready to sell themselves to the highest bidder. But their subconsciousnesses do it for them and save them from realizing consciously what prostitutes they are by nature and training." He concluded: "I didn't want to believe that Jessie was like other women, . . . but slowly and painfully I came to see all this. Still, I couldn't bring myself to let her go in spite of my pride."[76]

Did Luther love Jessie as she obviously did him or was she simply one sexual diversion among several? Did he desperately need her love and loyalty, as he so often insisted, or had he merely a compulsive need to dominate and control women, preferably his juniors? Had the thought of losing her in early 1925 driven him to despair, or had he finally pressed for a marriage he had resisted in order to squelch scandal and rumor that threatened his career? Despite their soap-opera ring, these questions involve serious issues. Love or sex? Dependency or domination? Passion or propriety? Since thought and act were one in his behaviorist scheme of things, these questions would have seemed largely meaningless to Luther himself. Taken singly, none really explained him, but together they described him completely.

Whatever his motives in marrying Jessie (and his first wife, Frances, characterized them as "cold-blooded" without explanation), the union took place under circumstances designed to compound the trauma and, in the process, cut Jessie off from her past irretrievably. For starters, he had her sign a marriage pledge that promised eternal devotion and ruled out separation or divorce. "I asked her to think about this carefully and not to decide for marriage unless she was willing to make it final at *all* costs," he later explained, underlining *all* for effect. A second condition, also agreed to by both, was that the ceremony, which took place on September 23, 1925, in upstate New York near Cornell, should be kept secret from her family, at least until the couple was ready to sail for South America the following February.[77]

In the train on the way to the boat in New York, the accumulated tensions of five years—the strain of being torn between parents and lover, convention and liberation—burst to the surface. She did not love him, Jessie insisted, and wished to remain in the United States.

Aghast at her timing (tickets and passports were already in hand, the ever-frugal Luther protested), he finally realized that she really feared telling her parents, who were waiting for them in New York. After discussing the matter, they agreed that she should spend two days with her father, ample time to break the news, while Luther attended to last-minute business from a hotel room.

To add to the drama, Jessie in the end almost missed the boat, claiming that she had been delayed by her inability to locate Luther's name on the register of his hotel. But the distraught professor knew better. "I have always believed that she meant to give me the slip," he later wrote, "but at the last minute changed her mind." Finally, it was not he but her parents who were betrayed. Not only had Jessie not told them her news, but she had given her father the slip, leaving him at a post office while she escaped on the pretext of an errand. Not exactly Nora slamming the door in *A Doll's House*, but in her own way she had made her choice.[78]

Or almost. Within a few days at sea, radiograms arrived, and then letters, as one by one the bonds of family snapped. "Father is dying, for God's sake return," Jessie's sister cabled. "Don't throw Tragedies on us. Don't lie more." In a poignant appeal accented by his Rumanian past, her father wrote: "You have made a Old Broken man and shortened ½ of the balance of my life." It was signed "Heartbroken and sick."[79] At Barbados they received the message that her father had suffered a stroke ("which he did not, as I surmised," Luther later noted triumphantly). After they arrived in Buenos Aires, they were besieged by a private detective her parents sent to get her home.[80] When Jessie insisted that she must return, Luther forbade her to do so.

When Jessie's family discovered the two had not simply run off but were married, things got even worse. In New York, Luther had drafted a letter to her father, breaking the news, but he apparently did not send it.[81] When sister Clara learned the truth early the next summer, she feared it would kill her parents. In a new round of cables, her husband appealed to Luther man to man: "Jessie left without parents' knowledge. They are heartbroken. . . . We leave it to you." In a subsequent letter, he described the devastating effect of these events on Clara.[82] Two years later, Clara herself wrote to her sister: "Of course you have surmised what a shattered thing our so-called family has become. . . . All my illusions . . . have turned to utter bitterness and hopelessness."[83]

In the confusion in New York, Luther apparently failed to see how serious the matter was. "J. visited folks. Some opposition to going away," he recorded in the opening entry of his travel diary. Jessie also seemed to take things in stride. After a touch of seasickness, she tucked into a steak luncheon the first day at sea. By the summer, however, not only did the family know of their flight, but also a fair proportion of the sociological community, including former chairman Chapin, whom Clara asked to intercede.[84] "Domestic difficulties," Luther scrawled in his diary sometime in July. "March, April, May the darkest moments in my life. . . . Dumb powerlessness. . . . Hopelessness."[85] By this time, reputation more than affection was the issue. Luther could see it all: her parents would persuade her to file for divorce and to testify to goodness knows what, causing a scandal against which he could not defend himself from South America. Jessie replied that he couldn't stop her from seeking a divorce, and that she could testify as she pleased. "This was my second lesson in the real character of the woman I had married," Bernard observed ruefully.[86]

Although Jessie did not record her feelings at the time, some stories she wrote two years later probably told more that she intended. One favorite theme was the betrayal of fathers, who then sought revenge. Two fragments, one a short story, the other a play, dealt with Joshua March, a patriarch who marries a girl half his age, only to have her run out on him and their baby. Although March adopts the child, he seeks revenge on her mother by finally disinheriting the daughter. Janet March, the daughter in the play version, then defiantly attends a country club dance while her father lies dying, but not before recalling an incident when, as a child, she had slipped naked into his bed only to be thrust out for mentioning her mother. "But I'll get even with you, old Joshua March," she screams at scene's end. "I'll get your money yet."[87]

In another piece of fiction, Jessie revealed how the events of 1926 had affected her relations with her idol Clara. The story was "Little Sister," which began with Ruthie's (Jessie) youthful adoration of her sister Helen (Clara). As the story unfolds, however, another tale is told. Seeking a career as an artist, Ruthie plods unsuccessively for years while her glamorous sister is married in a lavish ceremony and then pursues her own artistic career. After ten years of trying, Ruthie at last paints a truly beautiful portrait of a young man, only to find that her sister has abandoned art for interior decorating. When, on top of this, Helen criticizes her, Ruthie suddenly sees Helen in a new light. She will paint this tarnished sister, she decides. She will call it "A Portrait of Disillusion."[88]

In real life, Jessie sought neither money nor revenge. But these stories suggest how deep had been the break with her past. Although she was soon back on good terms with her sister, contact with her parents ceased completely for half a dozen years. When it resumed it was largely through weekly letters, written, as she confided to Luther, only because they were old and sick, not for anything it "did" for her.[89] In yet another fictional self-portrait, Jessie painted her own situation with devastating clarity, this time in the words of Vaughan, a biology professor who has lost his university position in circumstances much like Luther's. "No home. No family ties," says Vaughan of Castel-Leigh, his student mistress. "Practically nothing at all. That's what's the matter with her. That's why she is so restless. Everything knocks her over."[90] Reflecting on the real-life events a decade later, Jessie put the point more directly. "The violence of the break with my past was extremely traumatic," she wrote Luther, "and I suppose I will never really recover from it."[91]

WHAT LEGACY did the tumultuous twenties leave Bernard's later feminism? Writing of the 1960s, Barbara Ehrenreich, among others, has argued that the sexual permissiveness of this decade worked ultimately against the emancipation of women, as hippies and *Playboy* readers joined in a "flight from responsibility," leaving women worse off than before.[92] Superficially, something similar might appear to have been the case here. The heady mix of sex, books, and new ideas was certainly freedom of a sort. But from what and to what was less clear. Jessie had traded old-fashioned parents and a Jewish heritage for a behaviorist sociologist and his creed that environment made the person. Although her husband's demands for scholarly assistance may have slowed her career, this same sociology became her ticket to a professional career and a degree of personal autonomy.

There was a catch. For Luther, their romance was anything but a flight from responsibility, as the forced promise of lifelong fidelity alone attested. A behaviorist Henry Higgins, he was dedicated to converting his Eliza to his faith in objectivity and science. Objectivity in this Bernardian version meant the denial of feeling, emotion, and most other qualities conventionally deemed feminine. In Jessie Bernard's early professional work, this creed would mean a style of sociology more concerned with behavior and control than with intentions and self-fulfillment—a style she would later brand "agentic." In her private life, as she was already discovering, it meant doing more or less what Luther said.

3

Research Assistant
(1927–1935)

Of course [Jessie] is daughter, sister, wife, secretary, housekeeper and many other persons in one to you and . . . certainly keeps your armor plate polished.
            —Helen Bernard to Luther Bernard, December 14, 1932

Although marriage was forever, jobs proved less permanent. The Bernards moved almost annually during their first decade together. After Cornell (1925) and Argentina (1926), Luther went to Tulane (1927–1928), to the University of North Carolina (1928–1929), and finally to Washington University in St. Louis (1929), where he remained until his reluctant retirement sixteen years later. At each institution, the story was slightly different: at Cornell (where he reapplied unsuccessfully), they needed someone to do fieldwork in group behavior; at Tulane, there were only funds for an appointment in social work; at North Carolina, he quarreled with Howard Odum and was finally bested for the position by a rural sociologist; at Washington University, the department chairman was out to get him. The result was the same in any case: his talents were no longer required.

At each stop, departmental colleagues did their best to make Jessie feel at home. At Tulane, the wife of departmental head Jesse Steiner befriended her and later offered advice concerning the Chapel Hill social scene. Odum also did his best. In hiring Luther, he knew he might be borrowing trouble, but was almost as concerned about the new Mrs. Bernard. "Before [Bernard] should consider Chapel Hill," Odum wrote Steiner even before the Tulane appointment, "his wife ought to learn whether she minds what people like Mrs. B [unidenti-

fied] and others say about her." New Orleans, he added, would probably "be city enough for Mrs. Bernard."¹ Once the Chapel Hill appointment was offered, Odum put southern hospitality into high gear,
arranging for rooms in the picturesque Carolina Inn, offering assistance, and trying to stay calm in the face of endless demands (Luther
should choose the institution, not haggle about stenographic help, he
lectured at one point).²

For Luther these years were the most productive and successful of
his career. By the time he published his *Social Psychology* (1926), he was
already a frequent contributor to *Social Forces* and other scholarly
journals. In the late twenties he launched an ambitious project on the
history of his discipline. With Jessie's help he began collecting archival
material on the nineteenth-century roots of American sociology in the
Comtean tradition, work that finally resulted in their magisterial *Origins of American Sociology* (1943). He also circulated requests for bio-
graphical sketches to everyone who was anyone in the profession, an
effort that brought more than a hundred responses and, in the process, did him no harm so far as name recognition was concerned. At
the annual meetings of the American Sociological Society in December 1931, he was elected president for what became one of the stormi-
est years in the association's history.³

Working around the edges, Jessie pursued two quite different careers. One, of course, was sociology. At Chicago in 1927, she studied
with Ellsworth Faris, Robert Park, and George Herbert Mead. At
Tulane, she virtually finished her course work for the doctorate. In
1929 she contributed a long piece to a collaborative study entitled
Trends in American Sociology with some of L.L.B.'s disciples.⁴ From 1930
until she received her doctorate at Washington University in 1935, she
collected historical materials for what was meant to be a thesis on
Comte's influence in the United States, but ended up being the jointly
authored *Origins of American Sociology*. Her dissertation was finally a
statistical study of patterns of settlement within neighborhoods.⁵

A second Jessie, however, wanted to be a writer. For several years
after her return from Argentina, she poured energy, and more hope
than she would later admit, into short stories, essays, and several
novels. With titles such as "Puritan's Mistress," "Purple Prose," and
"Other People's Sins," these fictional pieces, as already noted, were

often revealing, as in them she attempted to sort out the tumultuous events and tangled feelings of the previous years.[6] But as literature, the results were not happy. Declining to serve as literary agent for "Other People's Sins," one critic faulted its bookish dialogue, weak story line, and overwhelming central thesis—effectively ending her dreams of a literary career by mid-1931.[7]

Jessie's personal life in these years was also a study in contrasts. At home, fights and recrimination alternated with fits of reconciliation. On the road, she assumed the role of unpaid research assistant, while Luther nagged at her lack of efficiency in doing work for which he inevitably got the lion's share of credit.[8] During 1930 she made extensive forays into the South looking for materials, while continuing course work at Washington University. In 1932 she talked of going to the University of Chicago for her doctorate, but finally stayed in St. Louis. After receiving her Ph.D. there, she spent four months alone in Paris in the fall of 1935 transcribing a manuscript journal the English positivist Henry Edger had deposited there and which the Bernards hoped to publish.

Soon after her return from Paris, however, a decade of marriage took its toll. The issues, as will appear, were ones that had divided them from the start: Luther's bullying and abuse (as she saw it), her uncontrollable emotions (his claim); Luther's unreasonable demand for total loyalty (her version), her parents' opposition to her marriage outside the faith, compounded by countless other faults rooted in her Jewish background (his); his endless string of affairs, her incurable flirtatiousness. In Jessie's case, these tensions at first produced, not self-assertion, but a self-deprecation that combined sexism and anti-Semitism in equal measure. By the spring of 1936, however, she had had enough. On April 8 she wished her husband goodbye, apparently all smiles, as he left for a trip to Fort Worth. Two days later, she filed for divorce.[9]

What followed was as curious as it was complicated. To all appearances, Jessie at age thirty-three, with Ph.D. in hand, had finally asserted her independence. After much discussion and some professional counseling, she agreed not to press for divorce. Nonetheless, for the next four years she remained in Washington (where she had fled), working in a series of jobs in the federal government, refusing her husband's pleas to come home.

In later years, Bernard occasionally alluded casually to her "stormy" marriage. But this simple characterization fails to convey the depths of a troubled relationship that meant manipulation and control, on the one side, subordination and self-denigration on the other. In one sense, their story was unexceptional, if colorful in its details: two gifted but temperamental individuals who could not live together or apart, perhaps even (as the text on the adolescent girl had predicted) the probable outcome of May-September unions. What makes it worth examining in detail, however, is the role in their many quarrels of two elements that had shaped their relationship from the start: Luther's views of women and Jessie's ambivalence concerning her femininity; Jessie's Jewish background and his anti-Semitism.

———

Although outsiders take sides in marital disputes at their peril, Jessie would appear to have had far the worst of it during her first years of marriage. "You humiliate and degrade me unmercifully," she began an extraordinary indictment of Luther's behavior in the eighteen months since they had sailed from New York. One issue was money, or rather, Luther's insistence that she account for every penny she spent. "In Argentina I once bought some candy without your permission, and you went into a depressive tantrum," she wrote of their stay there during 1926. Although she had actually spent less than two hundred dollars on herself, "you make me feel guilty every time I spend a penny." Even worse, he forbade her to mention money matters, on the grounds that his first wife had given him a "complex" about the subject.[10]

The case illustrated the feminist contention that men's control of money is at the root of female subjugation. Significantly, however, Jessie voiced this argument, not directly, but in the words of the central character in her novel "Puritan's Mistress," using fiction to express half-formed sentiments. "Vaughan's description fits my case exactly," she wrote, quoting her own character: " 'Her economic dependence upon her husband has been a torture to herself. . . . The married woman has been penalized by economic slavery for the privilege of a home.' " This fictional speech over, however, she quickly retreated: "I am making no demands now. I would accept no concession I had to fight for."[11]

The worst was yet to come, as in best academic style she outlined his "methods" of coercion: "(a) Manic temper tantrums—You become violent and use your superior strength to bully and bulldoze me." She had stopped keeping track of the dates, she added, noting that he would not have dared hit his first wife because she was bigger. And so the list continued: "(b) Depressive Temper Tantrums. . . . (c) Verbal Logic. . . . (d) Vituperative tantrums." The last, although short of violence, involved calling her a "God damn fool." "Or else you merely shake your head and condemn all women." Between the lines, a history of their arguments emerged. He talked of the importance of "breeding" ("but well-bred people do not make scenes . . . as you do"). He complained that he could not appeal to her pride or self-esteem ("Of course not, because you have robbed me of any"). He could not forget some unspecified infidelity of two years before ("I have equal grounds for resentment and antagonism but I do not throw them in your face as you do"). "You have said and done things just as bad as I have," she added, as this letter drew to a close, "—worse, for I have never said I felt like killing you."[12]

Although she did not again level such devastating charges, her research efforts on his behalf from 1930 onward produced continuing nagging and hectoring on his part. Sometimes his tone was almost paternal. "I'm sorry you always write as if you disliked the work you are doing," he lectured in 1930, on one of her early trips to locate materials on American positivism. "It is discouraging. What *would* you like to do? . . . Everybody, almost, has to do some hard work."[13] More often he nagged: "*Please* [underlined four times] carry out my instructions about the college. Can't you take the business I give you to do seriously and do it well?" Occasionally he outright bullied: "I'll tell you when to start. I am not through telling you what to do. . . . Now do it!"[14]

More than her scholarly accuracy, the issue underlying these outbursts went to the very core of their relationship. At stake was control—his of her, and by extension, of the entire universe of untrustworthy and unpredictable human behavior. For Luther, life was potential chaos, with him at the center, automatonlike, preserving order

with the help of "science." This he made clear in an unusually revealing letter written to Jessie in early 1932, shortly after the last outburst.
"My life is complex and I have to keep it ordered," the behaviorist told
his wife-assistant. "If any part of the system fails to respond the whole
is more or less crippled. I, being the coordinating mechanism, am
damaged by the failure of the system to react properly."[15]

During a four-month research trip in the fall of 1935, her first trip
overseas alone, Jessie learned that even oceans did not diminish this
desire to control. Her job was to read and transcribe twenty volumes
of the journal of Henry Edger, an English positivist whom the Bernards later termed the John the Baptist of Comtean positivism in the
United States. The journals at that time were in the possession of his
son, M. Paul Edger, who had taken up residence in France. Jessie's
mission combined scholarship and diplomacy, since it was important
both that the Bernards obtain literary rights for future publication
and that the journals not be read by anyone else.[16]

Among familiar themes, Luther's nagging now took on some new
twists. An innocent comment that beer was on a shopping list brought
immediate rebuke—"You know quite fully my attitude about your
drinking alcoholic drinks. It is perfectly definite, irrevocable, uncom-
promising." Her fondness for a local Jewish restaurant meant, predict-
ably, that she could not break from her Jewish past. Above all, she
must beware of all Frenchmen, and of Edger *fils* in particular. Her
report that he had brought some materials to her apartment and
kissed her hand ("twice") triggered lectures on French national character and the positivist personality ("I think it quite possible that Paul
Edger is not so unlike his father in sentimentality about women and
sex, and perhaps just as incapable of facing himself objectively"). In a
delicious but unintended irony, Luther's mistress, although still unknown as such to Jessie, joined the chorus. "Don't fall in the Seine,"
she counseled in one of several breezy letters. "Don't get any fat-
ter. . . . Don't let the prostitutes' customers get you."[17]

Jessie's reactions to Luther's nagging (if not to his amorous activities) at first combined good-humored resignation with the subordination she had displayed in her undergraduate days. "What's the matter
anyway?" she responded to one of his outbursts during an early road
trip. "All you do is attack me for something or other in every letter."[18]

Otherwise she took his outbursts without comment, reporting back her research findings in obedient detail. During the Paris trip, however, a new tone crept into her letters; not rebellion exactly, but a new sense of independence and self-esteem. In reply to his warning about Frenchmen she joked that her gray hairs (three of them), wrinkles, glasses, and poor dress made her an unlikely candidate for seduction. "I would still be safe," she added, in a comment she would doubtless not endorse today, "for, as you know, nothing can happen to a woman without her cooperation." In early November, in reply to his comments about the Jewish restaurant, she wrote: "Won't you please try to treat me as tho there was an occasional ounce of something besides malice and stupidity in my make-up?" Later that month she complained that she had had only two letters in four weeks, "and one of those almost hysterical (i.e. you were sick because I had not obeyed you, or had forgotten instructions, or something like that)"—the final phrase indicating how trivial she now thought his complaints. In December she included long samples of his complaints, in effect throwing them back in his face.[19]

Just as Luther in his comments on the younger Edger seemed almost to describe himself, so Jessie, most revealingly, found the same qualities in both son and father, and in describing them, appeared to attack Luther, as it were, by surrogate. "I can see how these Positivist husbands would get their families down," she reported of Paul Edger. "[He] lectures and preaches at me till I can hardly bear it." When she suggested that positivism was handicapped "in offering nothing concrete to its adherents," Luther responded with a windy lecture on the Religion of Humanity. "These people who love Humanity so intensely," she concluded, "are very likely to hate human beings, I find." The old man, in his way, was even worse. "[Henry] Edger gives me a pain . . . advising Metcalf [a disciple] to have relations with any woman who will be good enough to oblige him," she exploded. "Wasn't he a degenerate person at this time? If he was ever anything else!"[20]

Barely hidden in these comments were her feelings toward Luther's own behavior. Although she rarely faced the issue directly and even today is reluctant to discuss details, his philandering was a major factor in these emotional ups and downs, behavior she found less easy to ignore as the years went by. Letters carefully saved, and still preserved in the Bernard Papers, however, tell much of the story. For almost a year after his departure from New Orleans, his betrayal was recorded in meticulously typed, unsigned messages from a graduate student at Tulane (the first arriving almost on the day of Jessie's earliest outbursts quoted above). By 1931 it was handscribbled notes from another woman coyly signed "Me," one with the plaintive appeal: "Won't Jessie divorce you, maybe?" This time Jessie indeed threatened to leave him, but instead lapsed into what he later termed "a prolonged temper tantrum." For a time, she signed her own letters to him rather stiffly, "Your wife." During 1934 and after, it was yet another lover (or apparently so), this one an assistant at Washington University.[21]

By the time she left for Paris, their married life was becoming intolerable. Luther's compulsion to save everything had filled their apartment to bursting: canned foods, bottles, string and boxes in the kitchen; books and manuscripts in the living and dining rooms. "Socially my life was equally barren," she reported. Even had she a place to entertain, he was critical of any woman with whom she made friends. Since he deliberately invited no colleagues to their home, their entertaining consisted of a monthly meeting of the Alpha Kappa Delta honorary sociological fraternity and weekly Sunday-night readings attended by four to six persons at most, "including his mistress, who always came." In the summer, Jessie added, they often had picnics, also with the mistress. "The chief function I performed," she noted with bitter sarcasm, "was to prepare the food and act as chaperone." For almost two years, from April 1934 to March 1936, sex ceased between husband and wife, presumably on his initiative.[22] When she returned from Paris to find Luther lecturing again on the need for discipline and self-control, she had had it. "It is very hard on the personality to repress one's natural affections," she exploded. "Why do you insist on doing it?"[23]

I f things were not bad enough, religion could always be counted on to make them worse. Clara, in this matter as in others, was the first to cause trouble. In the Ravitch home she had openly criticized Jewish traditions and practices. Although she married a Jew, Noah

Lambert, she named her first child Robert (Bobby) and frankly confessed that she wished him to "lose his Jewishness." Even her commitment to progressive education (she worked at Columbia in the Dewey
tradition) contained an implicit protest against what she saw as a Jewish tendency to seek "superiority in obscure fields of erudition rather
than writing or doing things for their [students]"—a tendency she
labeled (following Veblen) "conspicuous scholarship." Although she
had some second thoughts about her child's Jewish upbringing by the
end of the 1920s, the Lamberts continued to celebrate Christmas,
Jessie reported a few years later, and said they "didn't care" when
their younger child "sang songs about little Jesus in his manger."[24]

It was also Clara who noted, in what appears to have been a heated
discussion with Jessie and Luther in mid-1925, how central to Judaism
was the doctrine of "endogamy"; that is, marrying within the faith. At
its root, she explained, was the fact that Jews considered themselves
superior to other peoples. Although she did not necessarily endorse
this position, the cards were on the table. The reaction of Jessie's
parents to their marriage the following year seemed to leave little
doubt on this issue, at least in Luther's mind.

Jessie herself continued to see the issue of Judaism and its enemies
through the protective lenses she had worn as a girl. Planning a
follow-up to her M.A. thesis, she applied a strict environmentalism to
understand anti-Semitism historically. Basically, it was an expression
of economic rivalry, she decided. While nations are primarily agricultural, little anti-Semitism exists; an example being the early United
States. When they industrialize, economic rivalry leads to group hostility. Rural Russia was an exception of sizable proportion, she admitted.
But, "there must be some other force there." Among its advantages
this theory allowed her to undertake precisely the sort of study that
Luther would approve: mapping and tracing "physical environments"
and then correlating them with different cultural traits.[25]

Although not unaware that her husband harbored some anti-
Semitic feelings, she downplayed them. Since he blamed the hostility
of her parents toward their marriage entirely on religion, she recalled,
"his attitude became one that would ordinarily be called anti-Semitic."
But, she added, "It wasn't that in the usual sense, but it was a quasi- or
pseudo form.[26] In reality, of course, the roots of anti-Semitism go far

deeper than economic rivalry, as Luther himself would demonstrate. The "bit" about her Jewish background, accordingly, was one of the darker clouds in a marriage not known for its sunny days.

NOT that something in Luther did not want to like Jews, as is probably the case with many non-Jews who expend vast energies worrying the issue. "I am so glad she is Jewish," he wrote of Jessie in one of his most positive moods, but then somewhat pompously added "for I think much that is so wonderful in her attitude toward me is due to her Jewish training."[27] In the letter drafted but not sent to Jessie's father as they sailed from New York, he also stated his position in positive terms. "To be sure I am not a Jew," he observed, "but neither am I a member of any sect opposed to the Jews, so there will be no barrier between her and her family ever, unless her family raises it...."[28] Crude anti-Semitism, especially among Jews, could offend him. "She speaks depreciatingly of the Jews, even calling them Kykes [*sic*]," he wrote of a Jewish landlady in St. Louis in the early thirties. "I told her Jews were as nice as anybody if they were nice."[29] But among countless other comments throughout their married life, these were the exceptions. If Luther's anti-Semitism was of the "quasi" or "pseudo" variety, he could have fooled a lot of people.

Clara's comments about endogamy triggered one of his first diary reflections on the matter. She had not realized that "such a statement was a declaration of war against the other peoples whom they maintain persecute them." Moreover, her own attitudes undermined her position. "I noticed also in the conversation of the evening, that Mrs. L[ambert], like many other Jews I know, wish to avoid too close identification with Jewishness, wanted her child to look non-Jewish [and] disliked the mores of the Jewish people, especially regarding family domination and community gossip and snooping," he continued, citing several examples. "Yet she wouldn't want to break the Jewish charmed circle, or get out of the Intellectual Ghetto (as Jessie calls it)." The arrival of one of Jessie's Jewish friends from New York prompted more hostile comments, as he warmed to the theme: "The European ghetto still dominates most of them and it is still a question in my mind whether they can be civilized, or will perish as barbarians barbarously, and die Kosher." But his most savage comments he now reserved for Jessie herself, then resisting his entreaties to marry him. "She must make her choice," he wrote angrily, "between becoming a Jewish brood sow and small-talk artist or my wife."[30]

During the early years of their marriage, most discussion of the issue focused on the hostile attitude of Jessie's parents to their marriage. Despite Bessie Ravitch's "matter-of-fact" dislike of all Gentiles, religion may not have been their major cause of concern. Clara insisted that it was rather Luther's age and that Jessie had deceived them. But Luther would not listen. By the time Jessie actually left him in the mid-1930s, he had a full explanation in place: she had chosen her "tribe" over him "because your tribe outlawed me for the crime of not being of God's Chosen People."[31]

Luther's family, in the person of his sister, Helen, did not make things any better. Although she suppressed openly anti-Semitic sentiments in the early years, something of her true feelings about her Jewish sister-in-law appeared in a report to Luther of a visit by Jessie to the Bernard homestead in Missouri during 1932. During this stay her sins included gossiping with neighbors, milking cows "with the various men in the neighborhood," "waiting to watch pigs and cows suck," and a general officiousness in minding everyone's business. During a flap over some research notes that same year (she was then working for a degree at the University of Kansas), Helen added that she had never met "anyone who violated one's sensitiveness as much as Jessie does." But it was after a disastrous stay as live-in-auntie with the Bernards and their children a decade later that Helen finally stopped mincing words. In dealing with Jessie, she lectured her brother, he must "remember always that she is a Jew, wholly so and completely so, and that it is as a Jew that she will react and behave."[32]

By the mid-1930s, Luther himself could find Jews anywhere. When Huey Long was assassinated in October 1935, he reported to Jessie that the killer was "the son of a Jewish politician" (as it turned out, the killer, one Carl Weiss, was not a Jew, despite his German name). "The report," he continued, "is that they took 60 bullets out of the Jew's stomach after the guards got thru with him."[33] Whether from sympathy for Long (whose populist politics appealed to him), or because

Jessie at this same time was feeding him anti-Jewish stories from Washington, he could not get the issue out of his mind. Deceptive advertising on a "clearance sale" triggered a cluster of prejudices: the prices were too high even for FDR and Hugh Johnson (a swipe at the National Recovery Administration, which he deplored), while the salesman "had the typical Jewish 'pulling attitude.'" A few days later it was the charge that all but one of eleven cheating cases he had encountered at Washington University involved a Jew (and in that one "the passive party was non-Jewish"). "It is part of their community ethics, I suppose," he opined. Two weeks later it reached proportions that would have been almost comic, had it not been for the seriousness of the issue. "I was awakened from a good sleep by someone honking his horn," he again wrote Jessie. "I can't say it was a Jew, but I have my suspicions."[34]

Reports from Jessie concerning her troubles with Jewish co-workers at the Railroad Retirement Board in Washington, starting even before the Long assassination, fueled this fire. "J's becoming more and more disgusted with the favoritism and intrigues of the Jews in her department," he noted in his diary in the summer of 1936. "It was unfortunate," he added, when she had decided she could stand the situation no longer, "that you had to be thrown with such a bunch of swine as some of those swine-haters were."[35]

It was his relations with Jessie that invariably brought his feelings toward Jews to a boil. In December 1936, her allegedly flirtatious behavior during a party in Washington set off another round of philosophizing. "I guess the main difference between Jewish and Christian women," he lectured after returning from Washington to St. Louis, "is that Jews retain their sex by-play but are restrained from complete expression so long as they are within the orthodox fold." When after three years in Washington she decided to stay another year, it was "to be the mistress of 'Hector,' the Jew" (a reference to an alleged relationship, although whether real or in Luther's imagination remains unclear).[36] Behind it all was Luther's fear that Jews, her parents or others, had turned her against him. "Do not let the New York or Minneapolis or any other Jews distort your valuation of me," he pleaded in the spring of 1938. "I have sometimes wondered if the Jewish concept of a chosen people also meant that they do not feel it necessary to keep faith with a gentile, even when married to him," he added the following summer. "Yet, I think I have known honest Jews." When, a year later, Jessie speculated whether their differences were due to personality or culture, she being Jewish, he replied that the two could not be separated.[37]

All this may have been simply another burden for Jessie to bear had she not herself come subtly to share his outlook, like a child led into something it doesn't like, but doesn't quite know how to get out of. As with her self-deprecation of feminine weakness, her earliest comments were almost whimsical. When on one occasion, while still a graduate student, she annoyed some movie patrons by repeatedly dropping her umbrella under the seat, she wrote Luther that she could hear him saying ("with the clear-blue chuckle in your eyes"): " 'Just like the rest of your tribe.' "[38] Other comments showed a serious young woman attempting to come to grips with issues that clearly bothered her. Observing Jewish passengers on their voyage to South America, she catalogued those Jewish "traits" she most disliked, from a tendency to enter "petty and parasitic businesses" to aggressive behavior (such as displayed by a six-year-old whom she saw literally grab some books from a Frenchman's hands) and even questionable loyalty ("would they fight for American principles if it involved fighting against Jewish ones? I doubt it"). Jews must take more responsibility for their collective behavior, rather than provide protection to any and all members of the group, she lectured herself (probably also for Luther's benefit, since they shared this particular diary).[39]

After a decade together, Luther's cruder stereotypes became part of her world view, subtly but unmistakably. On occasion, this came out in almost causal comments. He "is a sweet child," she remarked of her nephew, "but alas he looks like an east side slum child with extremely Jewish features of the receding chin and forehead type." Her parents, she confessed, had always felt that she "made fun of them and Jews." Sometimes it could be half in sympathy for Luther and the Jews he caricatured. "I get a terribly sad picture of you from your letters," she wrote from Paris in the fall of 1935; "the sort of thing you once said old Jews gave you." On at least one occasion, it was casually cruel. "There have been some dumb passengers—Jews, I think, tho they don't admit it," she wrote while crossing the channel in early 1936, when Jews were already fleeing from a terror of which she was yet only dimly aware.[40]

Nor was it only Luther. The worst thing about prejudice, as W.E.B. Du Bois wrote of the African-American situation, is the constant seeing of oneself through the eyes of the dominant culture, a sort of soul-destroying double-consciousness.[41] So it was for Jessie, who could not avoid seeing Jews as she imagined others saw them. On one occasion, it was a party of Jews playing cards, laughing, and joking on a Great Lakes steamer. "Jews seem to enjoy themselves more than other people," she commented innocently to a girl next to her. "And you haven't seen anything yet," came the reply to what was taken as sarcasm. "Wait till you get to New York." Another time, it was a well-dressed Jewish family waiting for the Library of Congress to open. "Presently they became playfully impatient, knocked on the doors, saying 'Tell 'em we came a long way, to open the shack,' " she recalled. They then talked boisterously of the mint and the burning of old currency ("such a fire in the summertime too"). Bernard watched them with amusement until she spied the look of disgust on the face of another bystander. "Wait till you get to New York," she thought.[42]

Jessie's reports of office politics during her first autumn in Washington (1936) seemed almost to be playing to Luther's prejudices, as if critical comments toward Jews would raise her in his esteem. "Interesting statistics," she reported of a nightmarish tea she had just attended. "There are 18 people on our staff at present time, of which 6 are non-Jews. There were 12 at the tea, 2 of whom were non-Jews." She continued: "And with no checks it was pretty awful. I mean Mary F——told dirty stories and so did some of the others. I was quite embarrassed and I think C——was, too, she couldn't say anything. . . . I didn't get a chance to say much because you have to work so hard to get a word in edgewise when there are J's around, and talk too loud to make it worth the effort."[43]

In yet another report, she complained of the aggressive manner and high salary of a Jewish co-worker and of the boorish social behavior of her Jewish colleagues ("cocktail drinking, dirty-story-telling, you know the kind"). "You said I would learn a lot about Jews on this job," she reported to Luther, "and I certainly have." Through it all was her dislike of the "aggressive personality" one had to have to get ahead. "I wonder if it would be the same if my bosses were not Jews." Nor was it just to Luther. "The place [Washington] seems to be over-run with Jews," she wrote T. V. Smith, then editor of the *International Journal of Ethics*, "many of the disagreeable sort, and, characteristically enough, in the research and publicity departments." "Many, of course" she added, "are of the very best sort."[44]

The fate of a lengthy manuscript dealing with Jewish life added to her bitterness.[45] "Macmillan's returned my ms. regretfully declining to make a publishing offer," she wrote Luther in late February 1937, "tho they recognize that it is an 'unusual piece of work.' " The probable cause? "[They] are afraid of Jewish reprisals. Which, in turn, means that no publishers will touch it." Her best hope was publishing houses outside New York. "I'm afraid all of the New York houses would be too cowed by their propinquity to Jews to dare take it." Then, in a moment of self-doubt: "Or am I just rationalizing?"[46] And so it went throughout her first autumn and early winter in Washington.

These stereotypes notwithstanding, Jessie was always more ready than Luther to balance the good against the bad in Jewish culture. Her qualification in the letter to T. V. Smith, coming when it did, was particularly significant. In early 1937 she was finally turning a corner in her thinking about Jew and Gentile, if only in confronting the issue openly and intellectually. Perhaps one reason for the change was Luther's rhetorical excesses of the previous fall. More likely, the confrontations in her office forced her to come to grips with an issue that could no longer be ignored. The decision to quit the WPA job, a difficult one since Luther opposed the move, was directly tied to the composition of the personnel—almost entirely "the worst type of disagreeable Jew."[47]

In an unsigned article in the *International Journal of Ethics* the following summer she attempted to put these experiences in perspective. "Some of my best friends are Jews," she began, quoting a common Gentile refrain, "but when they get together. . . ." Rather than something to condemn, this reaction revealed an important dimension of anti-Semitism and what she now termed "the compulsiveness of culture." In fostering adjustment, culture supplied "inner security." But the price was a blindness and hostility to competing cultures. "It is hard, therefore—almost impossibly hard—to see one's culture and its personality type objectively, as they appear to those on the outside; to be relativistic in one's viewpoint, in other words, and tolerant."[48]

Was this thus a plea for tolerance and cultural relativism? Only in part, and finally not the most important part. In placing anti-Semitism in the "culture as environment" framework (although tilting more than ever to the coerciveness of culture), Bernard rejected religious, racial, and even economic interpretations of anti-Semitism, although she had previously endorsed the latter. Her characterization of Jewish culture showed insight into and sympathy for its complexities: its emphasis on personality and its stifling "tribalism"; its Einsteins and Freuds and its vulgar move moguls. "If the intensely personalistic, literate, individual yet clannish, sensuous culture of the Jews produces . . . the ostentatious, spectacular, boisterous model of the new-rich sort," she observed, "it produces also . . . the understanding and sympathetic model of the poet." Her final plea was that Americans prize "excellent models of all cultures," creating a sort of "intercultural fellowship."[49]

Yet, in other ways the logic of the argument undercut the tolerance it appeared to preach, probably explaining why she asked the editors to break their rule against publishing articles anonymously. Her emphasis on the coercive character of culture, whatever her intention, ruled out a genuine pluralism, and seemed almost to make anti-Semitism (as one cultural response) as legitimate as Jewish "tribalism" (as another) and the movie censorship of the Legion of Decency as acceptable as the "exotic unreality" that prompted it. Implied criticism of Jewish culture barely hid her personal concerns: that Jewish culture did not value "self-sacrifice" (and its attenuation in Emily Post's dictum that "good manners consist in toning down one's behavior so as not to offend others"), for example, or the tribalism that allowed disaffected Jews no decent exit or recourse other than "a sort of feverish, neurotic anti-Semitism." Little wonder that writing the essay "had not been easy," as she noted in a prefatory footnote.[50]

Philosophically, the quest for excellence also raised problems. Since cultures presumably define the good for its members, there is presumably no standard by which one may be valued more than another. What, then, was the basis for stating that some cultural forms "may be" absolutely inferior or inferior? Or, indeed, for deciding what is

excellent in different cultures? In the absence of answers, her intercultural fellowship looked less like modern pluralism than an undated
version of the Enlightenment "scientific" (WASP?) ideal of a universal
standard.

Whatever the problems, the exercise helped her find peace of sorts
on the issue. In her letters and her personal dealings, she expressed
greater sympathy and tolerance for the situation of her fellow Jews
and growing dissatisfaction with her husband's anti-Semitism. Ponder-
ing a job at Hunter College in 1938, she stressed the advantage of
being able to help lower- and middle-class Jewish girls navigate outside the ghetto. Her aim, of course, was to help them escape the
"worst" (as she still saw it) in Jewish culture. "Contrary to what you
think," she told Luther in this same letter, "I react very strongly
against the Jewish prejudices of my family, and cling to you partly as a
protection against being a Jew." And she would no longer retail crude
stereotypes, or take her husband's abuse on the subject. Explaining
why she could not return to St. Louis, she wrote a month after the
foregoing: "I positively would not have you nagging me about my
family and about my Jewishness."[51] When in the fall of 1938 he
warned her not to accept a job with "the two Jews" at the Federal
Writers' Project, she replied matter-of-factly that only one of the two
was a Jew.[52] Sometime that year, she also found "intercultural fellowship" by associating herself with the Society of Friends, thus making
permanent a break with her childhood religion.

WHAT CONDITIONS in the interwar United States had produced such
attitudes, with all the consequences for Bernard's marriage and happiness? In broad outline, Luther's anti-Semitism, call it "quasi" or whatever, was as old as western civilization. But in its particular shadings, it
was very much a product of his personality and of the age. An undeni-
able factor was his fear of losing Jessie. But there was more. For
L.L.B., as his tirades against the "new" woman revealed, the delights
of modern life were at once a temptation and a challenge. Shabbily
dressed through graduate school, he observed the stylish clothes, the
social lives, and the leisure activities of contemporaries with censori-

ous envy. The perfect puritan, he condemned drinking, smoking, and loose morals, however much, in the latter regard, he may have violated conventional norms. When, in private, he indulged the pleasures of the flesh, he often recorded the activities in exquisite detail, making of them data, as it were, to be analyzed objectively rather than judged morally. Viewing behavior as more important than intentions, he devoted his professional energies to the study of environments and the way individuals do or do not adjust successfully.[53]

Judaism, as he understood it, bothered him precisely because it would not make a problem of worldly pleasures. As Jessie put the matter in the *Ethics* article: "Jewish culture . . . is sensuous—good food, fine clothing, a fine home. No theory of the depravity of human nature stands in the way of the Jew's enjoyment of these pleasures of the flesh. He need not, therefore, be apologetic even to himself if he gloats over them." The Protestant, she continued, in what could easily have been a reference to Luther, "might—human biology being everywhere the same—seek pleasures of the flesh, but he can never naively enjoy them, without conflict, however subtle, as Jews do."[54]

In Luther's attacks on Jessie and her family, it was precisely these qualities he could not stand. For one thing, sex without guilt: despite his complicity, she remained in his eyes a "pagan, n'est-ce pas," a woman, as Jessie herself saw, whom one would rather have as a mistress than a wife. He was always "trying to be helpful to her," he wrote in one of their periodic downs in the late thirties, "even though I cannot respect her with her sex habits and lack of loyalty to me."[55]

For another thing, the goodies of consumer capitalism offended him. Behind his compulsive penury lay a deep distaste for the good life. A workaholic in the classic mold, he neither wanted nor enjoyed social life—one of her many complaints against him by the mid-1930s. Instead, as Jessie once noted, his desire to compensate for the deprivations of his youth manifested itself in an obsession with keeping everything he ever possessed. Nor did he ever get over these feelings. "She has a theory that the Jews have never had any conception of sin, having a philosophy of self-indulgence," he wrote three years before his death. "She is a perfect illustration of it."[56]

Judaism, moreover, prized personality over mechanism, in effect challenging the basic premise of a behaviorism that saw the individual as a bundle of responses to stimulus. In 1937, Jessie again was the expert: "From Jesus to Spinoza to Freud, and through them all, has run this intense interest in personality. In the family, in the community, in social life, in the arts and sciences, in economic life—everywhere the emphasis is on the relationship between persons."[57] If one is a Jew, who needs behaviorism? Who, come to think of it, are the Jewish behaviorists? If the questions were not that blunt, the undertone was there.

In discussing Jewish characteristics openly (or almost, since she had insisted on anonymity), even if remaining critical of some aspects of it, Bernard's "Analysis of Jewish Culture" marked another small step away from her husband's control. As with her attitudes toward women and femininity and her critical comments concerning the positivist Edger, these straws contained hints of things to come. Although the results were not all in, 1936 and 1937 had been momentous years. In the meantime, however, the events of the previous decade left their mark on her scholarship, which now deserves attention.

4
Runaway Wife (1936–1940)

I love the order that my correlations inject into disorderly data.
—Jessie Bernard, "Lucy Page"

A job in Washington meant financial independence and an introduction to a real world Bernard barely knew. Starting first at
the Railroad Retirement Board (May–November 1936), she
interviewed families of laid-off workers, helping them cope with the
traumas of dislocation. A less satisfactory stint with the Works Progress Administration (November 1936–February 1937) was followed
by a position as analyst for the Bureau of Labor Statistics (1937–
1940), one she described at the time as "the feebleminded job" but
later remembered with enthusiasm.[1] Washington also meant a social
life of her own, while a serious affair let Luther know she meant
business. Still interested in a career in sociology, she pursued her
passion for measurement and quantification in articles in the *American
Journal of Sociology* and other journals. After seeking an academic post
unsuccessfully for some time, she finally obtained a job at Lindenwood College in St. Charles, Missouri, in 1940.

Although Jessie agreed to call off divorce proceedings, the future
remained uncertain. To her friend George Lundberg she wrote of her
hopes of obtaining a job that would allow her to return to St. Louis.[2]
For the first six months in Washington, Jessie's letters to Luther were
lavishly affectionate, his supportive and loving once the initial shock
of her departure had passed. But his nagging would not quit. After
spending time together in Washington over the holidays in 1937, it
was her "coquettishness"; two weeks later it was her "wastefulness and
fear reactions"; still later that spring it was her refusal to resume
sexual relations.[3] By the spring of 1938, the strain of separation was

taking its toll: she charging him with raising obstacles to her return; he replying that she dragged her feet because having children, in ratifying their marriage, would permanently separate her from her parents (an absurd charge since it was he who resisted having children). By the end of the year, he was openly critical of her irresponsibility in money matters.[4] To a former student six months later, he confided that, after careful observation, he was convinced that Jessie was "a schizophrenic of a decided type."[5]

Outward appearances told only half of the story. The price of calling off the divorce, or so Jessie understood it, was Luther's agreement that they have children. In letter after letter she pictured the joys of motherhood and family life with a determination that recalled her initial campaign for his affections, although the sketches in the margins this time were of herself and her future babies. In this plan, "career" was a means to an end that for many woman spelled its opposite—namely, children and home—since Luther's terms were that financial security must precede parenthood.[6] The job at Lindenwood, conveniently near St. Louis, did the trick, even though Luther held out until the contract was actually signed and delivered.[7] In July 1941 their first child was born.

Marriage, Bernard later insisted in *The Future of Marriage*, is always a double thing, a *Rashomon* affair in which there are always at least two interpretations of everything. Her own marriage had proved the point with a vengeance. In a more general sense also, her life for a decade had revolved around a series of polarities: between science and art, scientific objectivity and temper tantrums. To these she now added career and motherhood. In one of his countless attempts to straighten her out, Luther thought he saw a direct relation between the public and private selves. It was the collapse of her dream of being a novelist, a collapse that coincided with his own loss of considerable money to a stockbroker in 1931, that started their real marriage troubles. Literary success meant security, just as did his anticipated fortune. With both gone, she looked for security through having children (reversing her previous position) and in getting a job. Within a few years her priorities shifted so that children, job, and her parents and siblings all outranked her husband.[8]

Additional reflection, however, convinced him that there was more to it, as he looked again at the relation between her Jewish background (as represented by her parents), her literary ambitions, and her quest for motherhood. Unlike her sister Clara, she had not been able to break the Jewish tie and hence make a clear choice between her parents and her husband. Literary success might have saved her by allowing her "to integrate your personality around something that could have been all absorbing to you." Children also might serve the same function, although during 1938 (when he wrote these remarks) Luther continued to drag his feet on this issue.[9]

Although self-serving, Luther's analysis as usual was more right than wrong. There *was* more to it than a desire for economic security. For Jessie, her novels and stories were a way of coping with events that had been chaotic by any standard, a means of ordering experience with the help of feeling and imagination. If art would not serve, then perhaps science, with the emotional life now having an outlet in mothering. Such was the key to her apparently paradoxical behavior in the late thirties, churning out correlations in one breath, celebrating domesticity in the next. If the stormy details of her own marriage provided a subject for later analysis, her distress helped dictate the style this analysis would take. Like her fictional Lucy Page, Jessie found that her correlations indeed helped order the messy data of human relations, although at the price of denying the subjective and affective dimensions of social experience. Eventually, through motherhood, she would begin a long rediscovery of her emotional, feminine self.

———

Jessie's professional debut at the annual meeting of the American Sociological Society (ASS) in 1924 was every graduate student's dream. Chairing the session was William F. Ogburn, then of Columbia, author of *Social Change* (1922) and soon to be the profession's leading proponent of objectivist sociology. Also attending was her own Luther, perhaps second to Ogburn in his field. Both Luther and Jessie were pleased with the convention, although, characteristically, each remembered a slightly different meeting. "I was very proud of her being on the program," L.L.B. noted in his diary. "Ogburn suggested her, saying she did well." In fact, for reasons of appearance, he deliberately had seen very little of Jessie during the meetings. "At this rate I shall soon have only Ogburn for a rival," he observed after being elected chairman of a national honor society, "and him only on the personality side."[10]

Jessie was also pleased, but far less competitive about the whole thing. "I was the only girl on the program, and I received applause both before and after my talk," she wrote in her diary. But somehow, approval did not fire ambition. "Strangely enough," she continued, "despite my susceptibility to flattery, I wasn't moved by my reception." She also noted that she hadn't seen much of Luther during the meetings, but attributed that to his being busy and important. His performance during his session, in any case, was genuinely thrilling. "Cheetah," as she called him in this diary, "was as always, brilliant."[11]

For more than three decades, sociology had guided college-educated Americans through the maze of mysterious forces transforming the social life of the nation. But why, in Jessie's case, her husband's particular brand of objectivist sociology and the quantitative statistical approaches of Chapin, Ogburn, and other mentors? To Bernard, the explanation later seemed obvious. Awed by her husband's learning and (for a time at least) overwhelmed by her affection for him, she adopted objectivism willy-nilly.[12] Nor was she alone. Young women, as we have seen, flocked to L.L.B.'s classes in droves, attracted by his personality, but also by a creed that so-called instincts (including the traditionally "feminine" one of maternal love), were made, not born.

Sociological styles were also changing in other ways, as armchair evolutionary theory gave way to emphasis on empirical investigation, preferably statistical in nature. Ogburn's *Social Change*, one of the most important books of the decade, had just appeared. As department chair, F. Stuart Chapin lost no time putting his particular stamp on Minnesota sociology. Suddenly, the prewar giants seemed old-fashioned. "Gee, it seems funny to read articles in a magazine by Spencer, and Huxley and Darwin et al. and L. F. Ward," Jessie wrote Luther in her senior year, after perusing back issues of *Popular Science*. "I sort of hesitate to use that old material because I imagine most of it is antiquated by now."[13] There were, of course, varieties of Chicago sociology, notably the urban ecology of Robert Park and his school and the case-study method of W. I. Thomas. But when in doubt, as graduate students forget at their peril, best to stick with the home-grown product.

Despite some obvious truth in this commonsense of the matter, the reasons for Jessie's choice of sociological style were finally more complex. In the first place, objectivism projected a mixed message at best, so far as women were concerned. On the one hand, its image of sexless intelligence, its attack on gender-specific instincts, and its stark professionalism promised escape from Victorian stereotypes and related constraints. But on the other, as she herself would later see, it introduced its own gender biases in making power and control the end of social science; in promulgating the cult of expertise that intruded increasingly into domains of life previously the preserve of women; and in excluding women, de facto if not de jure, from the new world of team research and foundation grants.

On the personal side, she had also had ample exposure to the darker side of the behaviorist personality. For Luther, as we have seen, the reification of behavior was part of a complex psychology of public asceticism and private sensuality, outer control and inner emotional chaos. Behaviorism made external "things" of potentially guilt-producing impulses and behavior. Feelings, being mere responses to stimuli, were thus subject to "scientific" analysis and control—no matter that the behaviorist was on occasion his own subject. If intention and act were out of phase, so much the worse for the former. "An attitude is an uncompleted or suspected or inhibited act," Luther wrote in one of his scholarly expositions of the issue. Where a conflict exists between two "behavior tendencies" or between the organism as a whole and its environment, a crisis occurs, the unstated assumption being that the truly adjusted individual has no troubling feelings, no unfulfilled acts, no burden of self-consciousness.[14]

For Jessie, who rarely if ever theorized about the matter, quantification, more simply, was a way of making messy, unmanageable issues less threatening, and in the process, of pretending certainty without making up her mind. "It was emotionally easy," she wrote years later, "to escape troubling kinds of research implications by translating human beings into sets of variables and running multiple regressions."[15]

Her master's thesis—a study of Jewish assimilation to American life—was an early example of this strategy. Although the issue was intensely personal, she insisted that the choice of topic was "a matter of technic [*sic*] and expediency," to be treated with cool detachment. The framework was behaviorist, heavily indebted to L.L.B. and, to a lesser degree, to Ogburn's theory of cultural lag. Social environment rather than "physical [biological] or anthropological facts" were the important ones in Jewish history, she insisted. Her aim was "to state in mathematical terms [these] psycho-social relationships, as physical and chemical relationships are."[16]

The method was quantitative. Twelve hundred questionnaires were sent to Jewish organizations, mostly in the Minneapolis/St. Paul area, of which some 369 were returned. Questions ranged from languages spoken to belief in the theory of evolution—the hot issue in the Ravitch home. Stripped of its many charts and arcane rhetoric, the thesis weighed two conflicting theories concerning change within the American Jewish community: the first, that the "disintegration of the psycho-social environment" meant the ultimate "annihilation of the Jewish people"; the second, that changes were a sign of "a dynamic vigor which adapts itself to meet the exigencies."[17] Her specific findings supported those of the sociologist E. A. Ross, but even more, of her own experience: belief changed more quickly than observance or custom, the greatest amount of change in the Minneapolis area being in her own Lake Street district. But what did her findings suggest more generally? Would Jewish culture survive and thrive in the United States or would it disappear? Here, scientific impartiality suddenly intruded. There are "not enough data to decide the issue," she concluded. "With the limited information we have at present . . . both views are theoretically defensible."[18]

By the late 1920s, Jessie was even more firmly a disciple of her husband, so much so that it became almost impossible to distinguish the work of the two. During the spring and summer terms of 1927, while Luther taught summer sessions at the University of Chicago, she took courses there with Robert Park and George Herbert Mead, whose theories would eventually surface in her work as it became increasingly eclectic. She also studied with department chairman Ellsworth Faris, a social psychologist known for his opposition to all forms of behaviorism. But even this made little impression. On the exam for

Faris's course, she argued that various approaches to sociology, seemingly at odds, yield the "same generalizations." As proof, she drew up two parallel columns, the first containing statements by Faris, and the second excerpts from Luther Bernard, John B. Watson, and Edward A. Ross. "With apologies," she scribbled in the margin, "knowing your attitude toward behaviorism!"[19]

In her essay ("History and Prospects of Sociology") in the collaborative *Trends in American Sociology* (1929), Bernard placed Luther and herself within a sociological tradition going back to Comte. Among earlier American sociologists, their favorites were Edward A. Ross, author of *Social Control* (1901); William Graham Sumner, whose *Folkways* (1906) she pronounced "a marvellous contribution"; and Charles Horton Cooley, a "trained statistician," though his major contributions lay elsewhere. Since the war, she continued, a number of theoretical innovations had transformed the field, among them the decline of instinct theory; the influence of Freudianism and its opposite, behaviorism; the battle of the methodologists (case study versus statistics, inter alia); and the rise of cultural anthropology. Institutionally, the growth of the educational foundations and the emergence of Chicago and Columbia as major centers of sociology also shaped the discipline.

Assessing these developments, Bernard played the impartial observer almost to a fault. Debates over methodology ("sometimes acrimonious and emotional") were giving way to a realization that different problems required different methods. The appointment of Ogburn at Chicago two years before was evidence that even the Chicago school might be softening its opposition to statistics. Whereas prewar sociologists expended vast amounts of energy differentiating themselves from other social scientists, there was now a move toward integration, the formation of the Social Science Research Council in 1923 being one manifestation.

Only when discussing dangers posed by the educational foundations—an issue that agitated L.L.B. considerably in these years—did some passion intrude. Although she did not believe that the foundations could make unpopular fields popular, she worried that projects and conclusions might be tailored to suit the donors. Of major foundations, only the Laura Spelman Rockefeller Fund took sociology seriously. The Guggenheim Foundation (to which Jessie had applied unsuccessfully a year before) had renewed a project on the authorship of *Tale of a Tub,* but had not funded a single sociology project among its seventy-five grants. With large-scale cooperative research there was also a tendency toward "formalism or ossification." This issue was of special interest to the Bernards since they were executing and financing their history of sociology on their own. Four years later, this theme was the central one in L.L.B.'s presidential address to the American Sociological Society.[20]

A second early piece, although also a footnote to Luther's work, provided another view of the relation between Bernard's sociology and her personal concerns.[21] At issue was the contention of the Columbia anthropologist Franz Boas and his followers (Robert Lowie, Clark Wissler and others) that the physical environment serves as a limiting but not a determining factor in culture. Culture, in turn, was coercive rather than permissive. As proof, they cited instances of different cultural forms existing contemporaneously or successively in identical physical environments: the Eskimo and the Chukchee in the Arctic, for example, or the Algonquins, Iroquois, and white settlers in Manhattan. Moreover, some of these anthropologists maintained that culture is sui generis—distinct from physical environment, on the one hand, and from human beings, on the other.

Bernard, in reply, argued that exactly the opposite conclusion could be drawn if one reversed the situation, varying the environment while holding the culture constant. Of course, options must exist in a culture before they can be used (one doesn't make the raising of boa constrictors a major industry in New York even if the climate would support it, since such activity is not part of our culture). But the choice of a cultural pattern (commerce, hunting, agriculture) will depend on a physical circumstance, a large harbor in the case of Manhattan and overseas trade. Environment, not culture, is thus finally determining. Nor is culture something unique. Rather, as a creation of human beings, it is simply another type of environment. Bernard knew from her own experience that those elements called "cultural" packed a greater emotional punch than those termed "natural": the "cultural environment," as she put it, was a "much more voluminous, much more direct, immediate, coercive source of stimuli than natural environment."[22] But these differences were of degree, not kind.

Although an outsider might judge these distinctions to be quibbles, the issue cut deeply in several ways. At the level of theory, the anthropologists' premise was a direct assault on the stark environmentalism of L. L. Bernard. Professionally, it gave cultural anthropologists primacy in deciding what stimuli should count as more important than others, and hence, as more legitimate objects of study. Personally, for Jessie, the issue went to the heart of her concern with the vitality of Jewish culture, and by extension, its hold upon her. If the cultural anthropologists were right, then perhaps so also were her parents. Although she never put it in these terms, of course, this issue would resurface in various forms in later years, including what sometimes seemed like a running battle with Margaret Mead, soon one of Boas's best-known students.

During the 1930s, Bernard's work assumed a new direction, as she developed what she later termed a "mania" for measurement.[23] By 1930, the interwar passion for statistics had reached flood tide. Chapin, following the publication of his *Cultural Change* (1928), escalated his demand for behaviorist and quantitative definitions of social institutions, while devising scales to measure everything from social status to the civic contributions of former Boy Scouts. Ogburn, in his presidential address before the ASS in 1929, predicted that the future belonged to the statisticians. From the University of Pennsylvania, Stuart A. Rice preached a similar message in various articles and his soon-to-appear *Methods in Social Science* (1931).

Sometime in 1930, Jessie caught the bug. Whatever Luther's merits as a theorist, he was neither interested nor skilled in the techniques of measurement. In the fall of 1930, she thus enrolled in some noncredit classes in freshman math and statistics at Washington University. "Also," she wrote to an old graduate school friend, "I have been working on a course book in methods of social research," adding that she hoped that Rice's forthcoming book would not overlap. "Have you mastered statistics yet?" she asked.[24] In a survey of methods in social science she prepared for a collection Luther edited four years later, she concluded with praise of statistics.[25]

The result was two series of articles that appeared during the 1930s, the first dealing with the measurement of success in marriage, the second with social patterns of neighborhood behavior. Technically

interesting, if almost unreadable, the marriage studies were really
more about numbers than people. After describing her questionnaire
and scoring scale at length, Bernard applied this scale to measure the
success of 146 marriages in St. Louis, Seattle, and Los Angeles, the
latter from the files of a local institute of family relations, and hence
termed "clinical." When all the tallies were complete, she concluded
that 13 percent of women were unhappy with their marriages, even
though squaring this number with the findings of other investigators
required some arbitrary (or at least unexplained) distinctions between
"clinical" and "normal" groups, not to mention between "sexual malad-
justments" due to marriage and others attributable to the subjects'
"own sexual peculiarities." Although Bernard had initially assumed
that the same percentages would be true of men, more rigorous calculation showed that men tended to rate their wives higher than vice
versa ("whether due to greater generosity, chivalry, or fear of reprisal
we cannot say," she added in a whimsical aside) and that a slightly
higher proportion (18 percent) were nonetheless unhappy in their
marriages.[26]

For the total group, Bernard's findings showed a "negative skewness" of approximately .759 in the distribution of "marital satisfaction"; that is, instances of unhappiness showed more extreme values
in the lower half of the scale than of happiness in the upper half. But
did this say anything about the population as a whole or the institution
of marriage? After testing for possible skewing effects of age, income,
education, and the absence of children (four respects in which the
sample was known to be non-normal) she concluded that the fault lay
not in ourselves, but in our scales; that is, it simply was not possible at
the upper end to ask questions that would discriminate between "the
not-quite adjusted, the adjusted, and the well-adjusted." This was not
the only problem, she continued, since our concept of "adjusted" was
so framed that it was easier for people to answer yes than no, thus
skewing replies in the opposite direction. The conclusion? "A negatively skewed curve is [thus] probably normal for distribution of marital satisfaction, but this skewness is exaggerated in the present study
by the instrument used and by psychological selective factors." Translated: marriage seems to produce greater extremes of unhappiness
than its opposite, but we can't be quite sure.

Although common sense might have suggested a similar conclusion, what makes these marriage studies interesting is the questions themselves and the way Bernard chose to handle them. What makes for a good marriage: age, income, education, children? These were the questions of vital concern to her in the years when her own marriage was coming apart. What was "normal": more happiness than unhappiness, or the opposite?

The neighborhood studies also masked a personal agenda. In the first, she found that the presence of children increased neighborhood interaction among women, again hardly startling, but a significant index of her isolation from female companionship in these years and of her desire for children. In a second, the question was the old one of when and why children break away from their parents into a wider peer-group world of functional relationships. As in her M.A. thesis, she found that activities more quickly reflected changed circumstances than attitudes: a twelve-year-old is more likely to act like his peers, but to see the world as his eighteen-year-old brother does. As in the marriage studies, technique again eclipsed substance. And there was the inevitable final caution: since the evidence was "not unequivocal," all conclusions were tentative.[27] But this fact did not keep these articles from serving a more personal need for emotional detachment from problems in her own past. It was this she had in mind when she later spoke of "translating human beings into sets of variables and running multiple regressions."[28]

ASIDE from these publications, Bernard hung in the shadows for several years so far as other professional activities were concerned. Despite her success at the ASS meeting of 1924, she stopped attending the annual conventions after her marriage. "The reason I don't go," she explained of her failure to attend the 1930 meeting, "is that L.L.B. would think he had to take care of me and so he wouldn't get a chance to talk to people freely if I were there."[29] By 1932, however, she changed her mind. One probable reason was that Luther was now president of the society, with reputation presumably immune to a competing Bernard. Another, perhaps, was his announced policy of opening up the society, including more women on committees and on the program (although when Susan Kingsbury, a Bryn Mawr professor and feminist, challenged him to follow through, he replied with a list of women who had let him down when asked to serve).[30] But a third may also have been an early stirring of Jessie's professional ambition, perhaps related to the recent collapse of her literary hopes, despite her later denials that she was pursuing a career in these years.

Such indirectly was the testimony of Luther's sister, Helen, who finally clashed openly with her over the 1932 meeting. Although Jessie's recent visits to the Bernards in Missouri had caused strain, this particular flap began that spring when, according to Helen, Jessie badly mangled some tables she (Helen) had prepared for her dissertation at the University of Kansas, and later made other errors in revising the introduction. On top of this, Jessie then advised her sister-in-law not to send her materials to the Social Work Division of the ASS for presentation at the annual meetings, even though Frank Bruno (L.L.B.'s colleague at Minnesota and now Washington University) urged her to do so, and even offered the railroad fare to the convention. Jessie's reason, again according to Helen, was "that a second Bernard on the program would injure [Luther] very much." When she saw Jessie's name there, she rather naturally felt betrayed. To Luther, well after the deadline for the conference, she exploded: "I was a fool to listen to Jessie regarding the paper." As the memory festered, her bitterness grew. "My resentment, still alive, is that Jessie *cheated* to help Jessie," she wrote a full decade after the fact, "and *meddled* where she had no business."[31]

Since we unfortunately have only one side of this story—and Helen's deepening bitterness suggests that a lot more was at issue than one missed opportunity—charges of "cheating" and "lying" must be treated with considerable skepticism. Whatever Jessie's motives (her replies, if there were any, no longer exist), feminine solidarity was not apparently among them. Nor does it seem unreasonable to assume, if she indeed still believed that two Bernards on the program were one too many, that professional ambition helped her make an exception in her own case. With her presentation at the 1932 meetings and another a year later,[32] her career as a sociologist, in any event, was on its way.

If this incident provided a minor lesson in academic politics, Jessie's exclusion from the newly formed Sociological Research Association (SRA) four years later introduced her to the big leagues. A self-selected group of one hundred, the SRA was organized in the spring of 1936 as part of an ongoing struggle between those who wished to make the ASS more "democratic" (led by L.L.B.) and others who wanted it to be more exclusive. Its membership was to be limited to those sociologists "who have made a significant contribution to socio-logical research other than in the doctoral dissertation." Although biased toward "scientific" (i.e., quantitative) sociology, its membership finally ranged from hardball quantifiers to theorists of various persuasions. But one thing soon became perfectly clear: the Bernards were not welcome. Although George Lundberg and Read Bain nominated Luther for membership, he failed to get a necessary second (thanks to Chapin, Lundberg reported). With Luther out, their further attempt to include Jessie also failed, since it would not do to have one Bernard in and not the other.[33]

If Jessie knew the details concerning her nomination at the time (which is likely, since she was an old friend of Lundberg's and still saw him occasionally), she confined her comments to sympathy for her husband. "Now at least you know how things stand," she wrote in January 1937, after he had received a blow-by-blow from Bain:

> Very obviously they have a grudge against you. But if people like Bain get in and you don't it will reflect so glaringly on the society that it will lose whatever prestige it might otherwise have had. It is clear that the reason they don't want you in is that you foiled their efforts to dominate the A.S.S. and they are afraid of you.

"Don't let their society get you down," she counseled. "You are going to be the person who evaluates and judges American sociologists and puts it [*sic*] into perspective."[34] But another lesson was not lost on her, as she made clear in recounting this episode several times in later years.[35] For perhaps the first time, her marriage to her "famous" sociologist (as she still thought of him) had proved more liability than asset.

S ometime after she had stopped divorce proceedings, Bernard again looked to fiction in hopes of a literary career, as well as to make sense of things, this time in a story called "A Runaway Wife."[36] Boyd Hemming, the husband in the piece, was clearly L.L.B. "I can't stand your temper any longer," his wife, Ruth, screams as she leaves him. "You're a mean, nasty, disagreeable old thing." Like his real-life counterpart, Hemming is most impossible when in the throes of creation, in his case "something or other about the insides of an automobile." As the tale wends its wooden way, Ruth takes a job in St. Louis, has an almost-affair with an old flame Henry (a carbon of the passionless Henry of Jessie's youth), and finally returns to her husband. "Oh, Boyd darling, I love you," she exclaims as the curtain falls. "Kiss me a million times." When Boyd appears to be leaving, she panics. "Where are you going?" she asks. "I was going crazy, darling, but I don't have to now," he replies. "And he made a good beginning on the one million kisses."[37]

In real life, however, things were not quite so easy. After discovering Luther in another affair, Jessie had filed for divorce in April 1936. After Luther heard the news, he almost did go crazy—or crazier, as some of his colleagues by then would have put it.[38] "I have just returned and found this last horrible thing you have done to me," his neatly typed note began.

> Please come back. I must see you. Your interpretation is all wrong. The person you mention was not here. There will be no substitution. There can be none. It was cowardly and unjust beyond measure for you to do this. You can't dispose of my life in this way merely because you wish to and because always you have sabotaged me in the past. Come back at once before it is too late, and let this horrible nightmare end.

The note was brief, he observed, because he had "to keep my work going."[39]

In pleading letters, written almost daily for six weeks, he then chronicled the world according to Luther. She had been threatening divorce ever since they had married, the first time being in 1926. Five years later, she again threatened to leave, this time staging a "prolonged temper tantrum" of several months ("which I believed was due to an attachment for L," he added).[40] In early 1932, the plan to get her Ph.D. at Chicago was part of the same strategy. After that, "threats came pretty heavily and thickly." In the autumn of 1934 she outdid herself with a "terrific tantrum for two or three weeks," while she refused to register for the final term at the University—a performance he characterized in a second letter as an "irrational demonical possession of shouting your hate for me."[41]

More than once, he had thought of death as the only way out. The thought began in 1931. Two years later, he drafted a "Statement of Motives" detailing her perfidy, "to be published upon the death of L. L. Bernard from any but natural causes." Her latest news drove him to the brink. In Fort Worth on his most recent trip he planned to buy a revolver (for reasons not clear, since he thought they were getting on well), but finally couldn't find the shop. "I gave up the search, thinking that I probably would not need it now, for I believed we were going to be happy." But, he warned, if he had had the gun when he returned to discover her plans, "I should not have gone to class, but would have left a note for you to read when you came to say good by to me."[42]

In the attempt to win her back, Luther tried everything in his bag of tricks, no less transparent for being totally sincere. First pathos: once vigorous and strong, he was now "old, broken, deserted, quite alone"; he was "begging for life here."[43] Then principle: "You sought me out as a child and I introduced you to a new world. I guided your steps thru the mazes of the new science."[44] And prejudice: "Send my letters to your family so they can gloat over my suffering. Let the Shylocks triumph over the 'Goy,' as your father has called me. Tell them of my humiliation." For good measure: "Only women could do that." And the bottom line: "I almost forced you to get a Ph.D., which now enables you to betray me."[45] In the end these letters covered dozen of pages. But, for all his passion, Luther's pleading this time did not work, since Jessie returned most of them unopened, as they remained for more than four decades, leaving history alone to know his desperation.[46]

In June the Bernards sought professional advice. Although Jessie had urged Luther to seek help earlier, he characteristically resisted. "He was very annoyed that I had gone to you," she explained to the doctor they finally chose: "did not want our private affairs bruited abroad, etc., insisting that he was the best adviser for me, etc." This choice was one Sidney I. Schwab, whose study *The Adolescent* (1929) the Bernards had reviewed jointly six years before. A behaviorist rather than a Freudian, Schwab was their kind of psychiatrist. Adolescent conflicts, he wrote in his book, were the result of the need to adjust to a multiplicity of new "social environments" in the teen years (rather than unresolved Oedipal or other complexes). In her review, Jessie praised him for giving primacy to the environment, for handling instincts "with care," and for providing a "classification of environments" similar to one that L.L.B. had proposed independently some years before.[47]

Although the doctor insisted at the start that he nad no preconceived outcome in mind, he prescribed massive doses of objectivity. Both Jessie and Luther saw their difficulties as evidence of some sort of schizophrenia (unfortunately, not further explained since no copies of these particular letters exist). But Schwab believed that their conflicts required "a much more objective and unprejudiced analysis" than either was able to give. If there were differences in "personality traits," these need not be "insurmountable" barriers to "mutual adjustment" once they understood those elements in their environment causing the difficulty. Urging Jessie to return to Luther, at least temporarily, he hammered home the need for objectivity, especially on her part. "I strongly advise you to accept this compromise rather than to make your decisions solely upon your feeling [n.b.] and your understandings," he wrote in his first communication. In a second, he praised the "very detached and objective way" that she viewed matters in her scholarly writing (a sample of which Luther had given him), and wondered if she might not use this "objectivity and analytical skill" in understanding her marital difficulties.[48]

Jessie's response, like this advice itself, is especially interesting given later feminist attacks on male "expertise" and on psychiatry in particular, whether Freudian or behaviorist. Hey, wait a minute, one can imagine Bernard saying forty years later. What is this "objectivity" that boils down to going back to a husband, exactly as he wants? Was

it not "well-documented," as she put it in the early 1970s, "that psychiatry has an anti-female bias"?[49] At the time, however, such a response was beyond her: not only did faith in "experts" run at flood
tide, but more importantly, the vocabularly simply did not exist. Replying to the doctor, she was appropriately contrite. "Objectivity and
unprejudiced analysis," she agreed, repeating his words, should have
preceded her decision to leave her husband. In letters to Luther
throughout the next fall, she repeatedly promised to view herself
"objectively," which invariably meant to see her emotions and feelings
as "childish" and "immature."[50] But in her heart, she knew she had
been right. Although Luther spent a summer of reconciliation with
her in Washington, she steadfastly refused to move back to St. Louis,
despite his entreaties, for another four years.

If not feminism, then what? For these four years Jessie argued, not
for independence as might a modern feminist, but for self-fulfillment
through having children. Her letters to Luther, accordingly, soon read
like the stage version of Betty Friedan's *Feminine Mystique* (1963). By
October 1936, it was stick drawings of a father, mother, and two children, labeled "Bernard family 1940." In November it was elaborate
descriptions of the house they would have. "The matter of having a
baby," she began one attempt to explain her feelings, "keeps coming
up in my mind all the time, like an obsession. . . . I'm sure if you really
understood how I felt you wouldn't be so opposed to it. I know it
would involve a reorientation of my whole life. But that is what I want.
I want the relaxation of it." Continuing, she added later that month:
"I shall certainly learn to make pumpkin pies! Although I doubt if
they are good for the children." As Luther piled objection upon caution, and as the warm glow of the summer faded, Jessie retrenched
but did not give up. By December, the stick figures were reduced to
parents and one child, and the date moved to 1945. But the message
was the same.[51]

Although their continued discussion of the issue and their emotional ups and downs of the following three years would fill many
more pages, a full account would add little to the conclusion that
Jessie gradually displayed a growing confidence in her independence
and in her womanhood, just as she had in facing the issue of her
Jewish past. "I must . . . beg you not to continue harping on my

supposed neuroses," she wrote in one especially forceful letter in the spring of 1938. "Sometimes it looks as tho the only thing that will satisfy you is for me to capitulate completely to your interpretation and analyses, regardless of my own understanding of the situation. I do not think I am lacking in self-understanding as you suppose. And I do not think it good for my morale to have you hammering away at it with your insistence on my abnormality as a prerequisite for becoming normal." She particularly objected to his references to her " 'feverish, constant struggle for literary success,' " she went on to say, since in her view it had been neither feverish "nor, unfortunately, very constant." Then the crux of the matter: "You seem to forget that I am no longer a little girl, but a mature woman whose hair is beginning to turn gray. You treat me as though I were just a child, to be reformed, reprimanded, and made over." If he wanted her, it would have to be as she was. "Marriages," she concluded, "cannot be made reformatory institutions and remain marriages."[52]

By 1940 her campaign for children finally paid off, even though Luther made things as difficult as possible until the bitter end. "Still no mention of children or even of sex relations," she wrote early that year, in a diary apparently created solely to monitor progress in this area. "It is almost three mos. . . . It is beginning to tell on me physically." Three months later, things were no better. "Tuesday, I broke down and said I was dying for love/affection," this diary continued. "He . . . patted me and said he was afraid of me for I . . . wanted to receive but not to give affection."[53]

As the childless years ticked by, their advancing ages had inevitably been an issue. Arguing for delay, Luther noted that Jessie's mother had had a child when she was Jessie's age, to which Jessie replied that there was a difference between having a third or fourth child and a first. But the problem in any case was not her age. "Not because I am too old," she had argued two years before, "but because you are too old." With unnerving frankness she then went to the heart of the issue: "You have ejaculations very rarely and at your age the number of spermatazoa is not great." To this she added an appropriately statistical lesson in the demographics of fertility, noting that the probability of a woman thirty-five to thirty-nine having a child with a father fifty-five to fifty-nine was only 7.6 percent.[54]

When the decision was finally made, it appeared that there might indeed be a problem. When several months of trying produced no result, Jessie consulted a doctor ("a woman doctor," she told Luther), who informed her that there was no apparent reason why she could not conceive. "She said once or twice a month was not enough to ensure conception," Jessie continued, with the clinical detail she brought to the entire project. The doctor also advised that Luther have a sperm count, that they both "eat whole wheat breads instead of white," and that "it was better to do it at night." Whether because or in spite of this advice, their concerns soon proved unfounded when their first child was conceived soon after.[55]

When at last she was pregnant, Jessie gloried in the experience. Despite what she called its "touched up phoniness," a radiant photo taken in January 1941 for the Lindenwood College yearbook told much of the story. On its back she penned: "To my beloved child, for a wedding present. Taken when I was carrying you. Your loving mother." In the months before the birth in July, she wrote adoring letters to the unborn baby into which she poured her dreams and fears for its future. For the time being, however, she remained the academic. "Your father was reluctant to bring a child into this kind of world," she lectured her unborn in one characteristic passage. "He felt that in this day and age parents had so little chance against the outside world of commercialized amusements, propaganda, and other forces competing for the mind and attention of children."[56]

To Luther, meanwhile, she plotted the baby's development in best behaviorist fashion. "Maybe it will be good for you to be near when he nurses so he will associate you with good food," she wrote in April. "And maybe he can lie on your lap when I fix him up after a bath and pour orange juice down his throat. Those will all be good ways for him to get conditioned to you, and I want him to be as close to you as to me. It is a mistake for children to have too much association with their mothers and none with their fathers." She would need lots of help with this "personality" development, to assure the child's "integration and integrity," she continued, particularly in view of her own problems in overcoming her "bi-cultural heritage" as a Jew in a WASP world.[57]

Despite these confident plans, the birth itself was more difficult than Bernard had imagined. "My metabolism is generally quite stepped up," she wrote her sister Clara a month later, describing a seemingly endless pregnancy. "I matured very young, my menstrual cycle is 26 days etc. etc., and so I figured that it would take me only about 8 months to have a baby." When the doctor advised a cesarean because of the size of the infant's head, she had nightmare visions of "a hydrocephalic idiot or a mongolian idiot, or some kind of Monster." If such were the case, she "preferred a normal labor even if it meant sacrifice of the baby." Re-assured that the baby was entirely normal, she agreed to a cesarean, which went ahead without incident. "The first thing I asked was What kind of baby is it?" Bernard recalled of her first waking moments. "Then I asked L.L.B. if he were disappointed."[58]

While Luther's obvious delight in his new daughter quickly an-swered this question, the newborn taught other lessons in the months to come. I feel "overwhelmed by my inadequacy as a mother and wife," she wrote to Luther a few days after the birth, temporarily relinquish-ing whatever small gains in self-esteem she had made in the previous two years. "I don't know why motherhood should bring such humility. I seem to want to make up to you all the disappointments I have caused you."[59] A second lesson concerned the futility of rational analysis. A month of feeding, fondling, and changing the newborn made her let-ters of the spring seem suddenly "academic and remote." Since being absorbed in daily physical care, she wrote her daughter, "the more abstract values in your development are crowded out." In another she added: "I had to learn everything from the beginning. And yet you baffle me completely. You are not at all a scientific object." "They cer-tainly are not scientific objects," she repeated to her sister Clara. "The behavior is not the same under identical circumstances."[60]

In personal terms, the dilemma was whether or when to return to work. But on this point Bernard finally had no doubts. "You advise against teaching so that the baby will have a relaxed mother," she continued this report to her sister. "I assure you that getting back into the academic routine will do more to relax me than staying home. I find myself tempted to handle the baby too much. It gives me such intense pleasure that I find myself making all sorts of excuses to pick her up. I believe that getting away from her several hours a day will be good for both of us." "My main problem now," she concluded, "is to snap back into the ordinary routine of living."[61]

In later years, Bernard would have occasion to rethink this entire sequence of events. Had she hugged and fondled the children enough? she wondered in letters to them, some published in *Self-Portrait of a Family*. Had she fully appreciated the birth of a daughter rather than a son? "Preferred or not, many a little girl is born to women who have a strong underlying preference for sons," she wrote in *The Female World*, "although the chances are good that that in most cases the child's intrinsic appeal will soon win welcome and considerable attention and affection." By this time, personal experience and a wealth of feminist scholarship had convinced her that the relationship to daughter "is probably going to be the closest" a mother will ever have. But in the early 1940s, career still beckoned.[62]

A lthough Bernard dedicated *American Family Behavior,* her first book, to her daughter and husband ("my best teachers"), it showed the behaviorist and quantifier still very much in command, partly because it was in a series edited by Chapin (and hence subject to certain specifications), and partly because the events that would finally precipitate significant changes in her assumptions and sociological style still lay in the future. Her starting point was the theory of Ogburn and others that the modern American family increasingly served affective rather than productive functions, serving less as an economic unit than (in the recent phrase) as a haven in a heartless world.[63] Bernard's aim was to measure its success in serving various functions; specifically, reproduction, protection, socialization, affection, and regulation. In each of these areas she found the family to be considerably less than a success. Moreover, there was significant nonconformity to accepted marriage norms, showing a distribution that followed a J-shaped curve (a concept she adapted from the psychologist Floyd H. Allport) rather than a bell-shaped one.

Although the substance of the argument best bears analysis in relation to her later feminist writings, the study, for present purposes, reveals refinement and development in technique, particularly in her use of sociometric studies, but no major departures. In most regards she remained wedded to her husband's behaviorist assumptions (maternal love, for example, is conditioned, not instinctive) and the related faith in scientific expertise ("married couples who find themselves locked in conflict [should] seek . . . professional advice"). Family sociologists ask what are successful marriages, she observed in an engineering analogy often used by the objectivists, "just as industrial technicians ask, What are the conditions that make for maximum production in the plant?"[64]

A concluding section, expounding a "shock theory" of marriage and the benefits of "disequilibrium," suggested how she herself had come to terms with Luther. Marriage, she now saw, is a series of shocks, as couples cope with one unpleasant reality after another. As a "framework" or "vise," she noted, changing the metaphor, it is characterized by a seesaw struggle for domination between the partners. While sentimental types might wince at her Hobbesian view of nuptial bliss, she went on to insist that this struggle is not necessarily to be regretted. "Perfect equilibrium is by no means necessarily always a good thing," she continued. "The teetering up and down of the status of husband and wife, giving now superiority to one, now to the other, may be a normal process that is useful in preserving some sort of equilibrium." Marital strife was thus not evidence of the decline of the family. The "surprising fact" was that the American family during the 1930s had proved to be "amazingly tough, resilient, and resistant to disintegration," she noted, working to an almost obligatory conclusion in family textbooks of this generation. "No substitute for the family is even remotely advocated."[65]

American Family Behavior also revealed Bernard's continuing ambivalence on at least three points. The first went to the heart of L.L.B.'s behaviorism. The fact that maternal love was not instinctive did not lessen its reality, power, and utility, she continued, again citing the work of the cultural anthropologists. This equivocation, as one reviewer noted, was in turn symptomatic of a tendency to duck the nature-nurture controversy entirely. "The author seems to try to avoid the problem," wrote Clifford Kirkpatrick of the University of Minnesota, "cannot quite escape, and then inclines to an environmentalist position without a systematic justification of her stand."[66]

A second concerned conflict and nonconformity. Despite the conclusion that neither was to be regretted, a countercurrent revealed a desire for "adjustment," even "normality." "We cannot carry too great a load of dishonest, un-cooperative, maladjusted individuals," she noted at one point. An increase in the number of average-sized families, she speculated further, would produce more cooperative, helpful children. "The weight of the evidence," she added, "seems to lead unequivocally to the conclusion that personalities which have been shaped in well-adjusted homes to fit the institutional patterns of our culture will tend to have the best chances of success in marriage."[67]

A third ambivalence concerned the objectivity of science. Although she still insisted that sociologists as social scientists should not impose values on their materials—and had charts, graphs, and statistics to prove it—she also indicated that she was beginning to take the issue more seriously. Events of the war years would soon move this issue to the top of her agenda.

BERNARD's voyage into motherhood and family life was not all smooth sailing, as she later made painfully clear in *Self-Portrait of a Family*. Within four years, Dorothy Lee, as she named her daughter, was followed by Claude, and later David, thus fulfilling her long-held dream of having, not just a child, but a family. But, despite her emotional return to L.L.B.'s arms, their relationship soon returned to its old pattern. During 1941 and after, a new unsigned, feminine hand was addressing him as "Darling" and suggesting times and places for a rendezvous ("Words can't express how wonderful it would be to see you").[68] A plan to have Helen Bernard live with them and help care for the children ended in an emotional bloodbath. Within two years, Jessie's own letters also had a familiar ring. "No woman would remain affectionate in the face of that kind of beating," she wrote in the spring of 1943 concerning his mistreatment of her. "It is better for both of us to find an adjustment in our separate lives."[69]

Despite another separation and more arguing about children, Jessie remained Luther's wife, as she had promised years before, until his death from cancer a decade later. But in the five years since she had filed for divorce she nonetheless had loosed his grip on her activities and, more importantly, her thinking. She had not openly challenged his faith in the powers of science, nor had she resolved the tensions that drove her back and forth between statistics and art, objectivity and tears. Although she would soon question whether science was inherently a force for good, her devotion to statistics, now augmented by new interest in sociometry, continued unabated.[70] If anything, the gap between the public-professional and the private-feminine self had widened. But into the equation now entered a new variable, as she might have put it, to add to her earlier doubts about Henry Edger's positivism: her growing confidence in herself as a woman and her continued ambivalence concerning the power of culture. If her baby was "not at all a scientific object," then what about grown-ups? When in the forties and fifties new issues arose—fascism and the Holocaust, the limits of science, domestic affluence and international cold war— she would continue to ponder this question.

5

Loss of Faith (1941–1950)

Twenty years ago a good many of us agreed with you 100%. And I believed we got much of what we thought from L.L.B.'s *Transition to an Objective Standard of Social Control.* But the last 20 years have considerably shaken my confidence in the inherent beneficence of the application of science.
—Jessie Bernard to George Lundberg, July 12, 1949

After toiling for seven years at Lindenwood College, Jessie and Luther received appointments at Pennsylvania State University starting in the fall term of 1947: she as assistant professor at $3,600 per year; he as lecturer at $600 for one course of his choice per year. These appointments capped more than a year of searching for a university that would take them both. Initially, they hoped for something at the University of Washington in Seattle, where George Lundberg was now department chair. Advertising their credentials, Luther reminded Lundberg that Jessie was at the "top of sociometric work in sociology" and he himself known "in every country of the world." Together, they "could easily make the University of Washington the chief graduate center in the country."[1] But nothing finally opened up.

A carefully worded appointment letter from Penn State suggested that his new colleagues knew what they were getting. Since they were crowded for office space, the then-chair of sociology explained, they had arranged for a private study for L.L.B in the library. "Also," he continued, "I should mentioned that it is our policy for visiting professors and part-time staff members not to be included in the working out of departmental policies." Concerning the appointment, Jessie later claimed for public consumption that neither came "on the other's coat-tails" ("the Chair was delighted to get two 'names' "). But in her heart she knew that by this time she was the chief attraction.[2]

When the Bernards arrived, Pennsylvania State College, as it was still called, was in the process of transforming itself from an agricultural and technical school to a modern university. Its student body consisted of some ten thousand students: seven thousand at the main campus at State College, and the rest dispersed in a network of state teachers' colleges. A few years earlier, an accrediting committee had suggested that the liberal arts faculty be strengthened and its courses no longer viewed primarily as serving the physical and biological sciences.[3]

The conflict between old guard and new faculty was accordingly predictable. "To some of the old-timers we were strange, foreign beings," Jessie remembered. "Our ideas seemed far out to them." The issues, she further recalled, were mostly political, concerning loyalty oaths, McCarthyism, and the House Committee on Un-American Activities. "I had problems, but nothing personal," she later wrote, before reconsidering and crossing out this last statement.[4]

Among Penn State departments, sociology was neither large nor particularly distinguished, certainly not by the standards of Minnesota or many other large state universities. In 1947 the department consisted of only five members, with a projected increase of several additions within the year. Among her senior colleagues were Seth W. Russell, a product of the University of Pittsburgh (Ph.D. 1939) with an interest in the rural church and community; and Walter Coutu, a Wisconsin Ph.D. (1935), where he wrote a thesis on the professions. The rural sociologists, virtually a separate department, included William G. Mather, a clergyman (Rochester Theological 1927) turned sociologist (Ph.D. 1936), who eventually chaired a combined department of Sociology and Anthropology from 1954 to 1962; Samuel W. Blizzard, a recent Cornell graduate (Ph.D. 1946); and, for a brief time, Otis Dudley Duncan, a Chicago Ph.D. (1949) and later a distinguished human ecologist whose publications included an edition of the writings of William Ogburn. By the time Bernard left the department, however, the number had grown to almost twenty, plus several part-timers.[5]

Among her colleagues, Bernard was soon known for her boundless vitality. When she failed to show up at a faculty meeting the day after her third child was born, as she later told the story, a male colleague

looked around and asked "Where's Jessie?" Told of the birth, he simply repeated the question, to the amusement of all. Informally, many
called her "Jet" Bernard as she rushed from classroom to library to
committee meetings.[6]

Bernard found the teaching demanding, but satisfying. As she
began her second year, she complained to Lundberg that the department was understaffed, the classes too large, and the load—twelve
hours a week—heavy by university standards. But she was also pleased
to report that the work of some of her undergraduate students would
soon appear in print: one a study of fashion based on changing
lengths of women's skirts 1929 to 1947 in the *American Sociological
Review* ("if Davie doesn't renege on Angell")[7]; and another of the
dating and drinking habits of college women ("coeds," Bernard still
called them) in the *Journal of Alcohol Studies*. "The caliber of these
undergraduate studies has been commented on as of M.A. thesis quality," she continued, noting that several others sat on editors' desks for
consideration. "I seem to be able to make the students feel enthusiasm
and do good work."[8]

Graduate students were few, however, and somewhat longer in
coming. During Bernard's tenure, the department granted relatively
few M.A.s and even fewer doctorates, most supervised by other members of the department. Although she eventually directed a handful
of doctorates, at best tangentially related to her major interests, she
increasingly directed her professional energies to the wider world of
conferences and professional organizations.[9]

If somewhat less stimulating intellectually than they might have
been, the early Penn State years (1947 to 1951) were nonetheless important in Bernard's intellectual development. The beginning of her transformation, as she later reconstructed it, was her gradual recognition at
this time of the nature of fascism and eventually, of the atrocities of the
Holocaust. From this followed her disillusionment with science—a "loss
of faith," she termed it—and a public debate with George Lundberg,
L.L.B.'s disciple and her longtime friend. Of these, she remembered
the first as being basic. "It was a troubled time," she wrote of her
discovery of the Nazi degradation of science, "in which, almost day by
day, I was learning about the underside and the vulnerability of scientists." The denominator common to both was her questioning of the

objectivist faith of her husband. It was a measure of the power of this faith, she later wrote, "that it took a catastrophe as overwhelming as the Final Solution to challenge it."[10]

In reality, the situation was more complicated since her realization of the full horrors of nazism and the Holocaust eroded a faith in science that was already weakening, an erosion that began in the early 1940s. Like many educated Americans, and particularly sociologists in the objectivist camp, Bernard saw the evils of fascism only gradually, in part because of Nazi success in hiding the truth, in part because her world view simply could not accommodate the reality of evil. As confirmation of the Holocaust splashed across the headlines, she was stunned and sickened, as were most Americans of this generation. However, the result was less an abrupt about-face than the quickening of an ongoing process.

Moreover, as was later the case with her conversion to feminism, more important sources of change lay closer to home in her professional and personal life. One was her ongoing debate with Lundberg; the second was the death of her husband in 1951. Related only symbolically, these two events marked the beginning of her intellectual emancipation from the creed of her youth and her coming of age as a sociologist in her own right.

———————

Although the story of American sociology's reaction to fascism and the Holocaust remains to be told, most in the profession were blind to the essential evil of Nazi policy through the 1930s. This was especially the case with leading objectivists, including William F. Ogburn of Chicago and such younger men as Read Bain of Miami University and George Lundberg, who by the end of the decade was teaching at Bennington. One reason for their myopia was their special interest in propaganda and social control, techniques that the fascist leaders seemed to have raised to an art. Attending a meeting in 1942 at which the Associated Press correspondent in Berlin described Nazi propaganda, Ogburn found himself marveling at their skill ("not admiration for the end, but for the means," he noted in his diary). Another reason was their belief that social science was or should be politically and ethically neutral. "I have already been run out of 2 or 3 households almost for saying that I believe I could get along in Nazi Germany as a scientist, about as well as here—some better," Bain wrote Lundberg soon after Munich. For his isolationist views and comments at the 1942 meeting and elsewhere, Ogburn found himself the victim of whispers that he was soft on fascism. Bain and Lundberg meanwhile compared notes in these years as to whether this or that statement would appear pro-fascist.[11]

An apparent exception was Luther Bernard, who by the late 1930s was vocal in opposition to "fascistic tendencies" at home and abroad. Shortly after Munich, he condemned the "effete 'democracies' " of Europe for not calling Hitler's bluff. "[War] would have been the best thing," he wrote Jessie, "war now—for it will certainly be war in earnest in a few years, after Hitler has fully armed, and after Fr. and Eng. are ruined by armament races. Only Russia, Germany, and Italy will survive (in Europe) this cowardly policy."[12] Yet Luther, finally, did not see the full nature of the evil much more clearly than his fellow objectivists. As the reference to "effete" democracies suggests, his own version of democracy was something other than actually practiced in Britain, France, and the United States, and was closer to a populist authoritarianism than he cared to admit. When attacking "fascists" he was more likely to be referring to his enemies within the American Sociological Society (the "Heil Hitlers," as he labeled them) than to the real thing. This battle, which he waged in earnest from 1938 onward, was tangentially rooted in world affairs insofar as the ASS at its 1937 meeting defeated a Bernard amendment that would have blocked affiliation with the International Federation of Sociological Societies, and through it to the French International Institute of Sociology (IIS), then (or soon to be) subject to fascist influences.[13] But the ostensible basis of Bernard's objection was that the IIS was a self-perpetuating clique, not its political complexion.[14] He may also have suspected that some of his colleagues were actually soft on fascism, although here also he provided no details. In any case, as applied to Bernard's own exclusion from the Sociological Research Association—the occasion for most of his name-calling—the epithet "fascist" merely trivialized the reality.

Since Jessie Bernard rarely commented on national politics or world affairs, her early reactions to fascism are sketchy and appear mostly in the context of helping Luther prepare his new book *Social Control* (1939). In the fall of 1936 she read John Strachey's *Menace of Fascism* (1933), a left-wing attack widely criticized by American reviewers as communist propaganda, in order to provide Luther with a thumbnail summary. But she did not otherwise comment upon it.[15] "I listened to Hitler this afternoon," she wrote to Luther two years later, at the height of the Czech crisis. "The speech was a declaration of war. But it was consummate publicity. The man has convinced himself that he is the protector of the Germans, not the aggressor. It was painful."[16] After reading Stephen H. Roberts's *House that Hitler Built* (1937) and another work by a "British journalist," she again commented on the power of German propaganda. "Both authors point out that they themselves were influenced by the Nazi propaganda," she wrote Luther a week after Munich. "It is simply compelling; you haven't got a chance against it. Isn't that interesting? I mean that even foreigners should succumb when they know better and that not until they leave the country do they regain their critical faculties? That's efficiency with a vengeance, I should say."[17]

Jessie's references to Nazi treatment of Jews were even scarcer. By the fall of 1938, when the treatment of the refugees was becoming a public issue, she cared enough to ask Luther for advice: "What do you think of the Nazi situation with reference to the Jews? Do you think it legitimate to give money to the fund to move the refugees?"[18] But otherwise she ignored the issue until the war was well underway.

If rumors of German atrocities filtered through by the eve of the war, they did little to change the views concerning Jews that she had developed several years earlier. Of two chapters she contributed to *Jews in a Gentile World* (1942), the first was a barely revised version of the *Ethics* article of the summer of 1937, while the second was a semiautobiographical analysis of "Biculturality." The revisions boiled down to a tortured restatement of the view that there was a need for change on both sides, as Bernard cautiously split the difference between one contributor who blamed anti-Semitism on the Jews (the sociologist Joyce Hertzler of the University of Nebraska) and another who called for changes in non-Jewish culture. Non-Jews must view Jews "sympathetically," she lectured, while Jews must "modify those aspects of [their] culture which do most violence to the standards of [their] cultural hosts." The essay on "Biculturality," in turn, concluded with a rhapsodic account of how one Jew (presumably herself), after discovering Christ, realized that the worst thing Christianity had done to her people was to make it impossible for them "ever to reverse their traditional attitude toward Jesus."[19]

Jews in a Gentile World won few friends, and indeed had been a source of controversy between its two editors and potential contributors since the project was conceived three years earlier. The editors deliberately included essays by non-Jews "in the interest of tact and effectiveness"—the reason, presumably, for inviting Hertzler to contribute. But, in the case of Talcott Parsons at least, they were soon at loggerheads over proposed revisions and unauthorized changes.[20] Nor were reviewers pleased with the result. "A disappointing book," one concluded. "Here, of all places, the old moth-eaten slogans and shibboleths mouthed by the antisemites are brushed off and paraded." Hertzler was the worst, but other contributors also seemed almost to make a case for anti-Semitism "by explaining it in the palaver of the social sciences."[21]

Bernard's association with the volume was also an unhappy one. "I certainly had some disagreeable experiences in this connection," she recalled to Lundberg somewhat later. "The editor promised me faithfully that he would not change my copy. Yet low [*sic*] and behold, he changed a number of things, omitted telling data, etc." As a result, she had not been able to bring herself to write to him since. Although the hostile reviewer did not mention Bernard by name, her contributions also came in for their share of criticism. "Religious gentiles and Jews alike," she wrote Lundberg soon after, "have agreed that my two chapters are the worst in the book, that they should not have been included, etc. etc."[22]

Bernard addressed the issue once again in *American Community Behavior* (1949). Although the fact of the Holocaust could no longer be ignored, she added little if anything to her earlier position. A textbook in the you-decide-the-issues tradition, the study provided few conclusions concerning Jewish-Gentile relations or any other matter. Her few references to the Nazi atrocities remained curiously restrained. "Hitler tried to get rid of the Jews by expelling them or simply by

killing them," she stated in one of two passing references to this tragedy. Otherwise, Nazi policy was simply an example of negative scape-
goating or social control.[23]

Anti-Semitism was the product of social no less than economic
competition, she continued, modifying her earlier emphasis on economics. A major source of Jewish-Gentile tension was the rise of Jews
in social status, education, and occupation to a point where they might
expect to associate with "upper-class non-Jews," but could not because
of the intricacies of class definitions. However true, this way of stating
it not only appeared to condone such discrimination ("Some sociologists maintain that discriminatory behavior . . . is inherent in the very
structure of society"), but also to suggest that anti-Semitism was of
greater concern to a social elite. As before, she was fair to a fault. Anti-
Semitism and "anti-gentilism" were both problems: Jews must be
aware of and eliminate the behavior that antagonizes Gentiles, just as
the latter must curb their overt antagonism to Jews.[24]

If this evenhandedness suggested a change, she set the record
straight in a letter to Lundberg written as the book went to press.
Although the publisher (Dryden) had made her redo her treatment of
Catholic–non-Catholic conflict "at least ten times," they had not mentioned her handling of Jews at all. "Then, believe it or not," she
continued, "when the entire MS is in galley, they send me the galley of
this chapter with changes I had not authorized. They then insisted on
further changes so that instead of a straightforward statement of the
issue, it has become a conventional Jewish apologia, the usual stuff—
it's all your fault, we are more sinned against than sinning, our faults
are all explainable, yours are not, etc. Just straight propaganda." The
publishers were Jews, although they insisted the firm was not, she
added. "Not that I want to say anything bad or wrong about Jews. It is
precisely because I believe that this kind of tripe is bad for Jews that it
worries me so."[25]

To note that Bernard's public reaction to the Holocaust was late in
coming and relatively subdued is not to say that she was less than
sympathetic to the plight of European Jews or in any sense soft on
fascism. Quite the contrary. But, from her writings, it would appear
that a number of factors restrained her response, among them her
personal religious agenda, a generally aloof attitude toward public

affairs, scholarly canons of objectivity, and pressures to avoid gratuitous controversy in textbooks. The result was that the experiences of world war and fascist totalitarianism produced, not a fundamental intellectual change, but a somewhat narrower attack on one aspect of her earlier thought: the uncritical, often naive faith in science and scientists that she had imbibed in Minnesota three decades earlier. Although reports of the Nazi abuse of science finally figured in this controversy, there was a good deal more to it.

———————

By the late 1940s, Bernard's principal target, in fact, was not Nazism but George Lundberg's *Can Science Save Us?* (1947), originally lectures at the University of Washington in the spring of 1945. Lundberg's message was vintage positivism, coupled with a lament that social scientists get no respect. Without benefit of a scientific approach, the postwar settlement was doomed to go the way of the disastrous Versailles settlement of two decades before, Lundberg warned. Although he never defined the term *science* (nor, significantly, did Bernard challenge him on this point), his model was essentially that of the engineer or technician, stressing method and results over theory and truth. Scientific statements, so conceived, had a similar formulation whether dealing with disease or social problems: if you want this, then do that. Statements of any other sort— whether political, ethical, or aesthetic—were not scientific even when uttered by scientists. "[Social] scientists, like other people, often have strong feelings about religion, art, politics, and economics," he wrote. "That is they have their likes and dislikes in these matters as they have in wine, women, and song." They often form pressure groups to advance these preferences. But neither the likes, the dislikes, nor the organizations were thus scientific.[26]

Stripped of Lundberg's colorful, often vitriolic prose, his argument boiled down to three basic points. First, science had nothing to do with values: the "is" and "ought" were totally separate. As citizens, scientists might urge this or that cause, but "no science tells us what to do with the knowledge that constitutes the science." Second, science should not be identified with any particular social system—whether "democratic" or "communist"—since historically it had thrived under quite different regimes. Lundberg himself preferred democracy ("the democratic way of life with all of its absurdities," as he put it) and, by implication, the uses to which science would be put in democratic society. But this was also a purely personal preference, and perhaps evidence of his "unfitness to live in a changing world." Finally, although he stressed that science could be put to good or evil purposes, he appeared (to Bernard at least) to assume that the use of "scientific method" was invariably a good thing, current hysteria over the atom bomb notwithstanding.[27]

By the time *Can Science Save Us?* appeared, its author was a well-known and controversial figure in sociological circles. Born in Fairdale, North Dakota, Lundberg (1895–1966) was the son of Swedish immigrants. His mother was the orphaned daughter of peasants and had been a servant from childhood. His own youth was one of hard work and plenty of food, "but a dearth of reading matter." Since there were no high schools in his area, his secondary education consisted of a college preparatory course from a Chicago correspondence school. From there it was a degree in education at the University of North Dakota, an appointment as superintendent of schools in a place called Hope, North Dakota (1920), and finally an M.A. under E. A. Ross and others at the University of Wisconsin (1922). Together, these experiences left him with a deep if convoluted faith in the people and a passion for the sort of certainty that better-educated folks know is impossible.[28]

A fifteen-month interruption to serve in the First World War shaped Lundberg's attitudes toward politics and world affairs more or less for life. "I escaped most of the irritations, indignities, and absurdities of the military routine," he later wrote with characteristic hauteur, "and felt more than adequately repaid for the inconvenience by a three months' period of study at the London School of Economics."[29] Whatever patriotism he may have felt yielded quickly to the post-Versailles disillusionment. To the end of his days, he remained a foe of internationalism in all its forms.

Were his convictions not problem enough, Lundberg had a way of putting things that was offensive or amusing, depending upon one's point of view. Although a self-professed champion of the people, his statements concerning democracy and dictatorship seemed to many to be profascist. "I know you are quite Fascist in speech," his friend and fellow objectivist Read Bain lectured him the spring of 1937. "But I imagine you wouldn't like it if you had to live under it—because you dearly love your 'inalienable right' to shoot off your mouth." Although Lundberg denied the charge ("I am not for a damn thing but Roosevelt at present, and share his views fully in democracy"), he proceeded to dig himself in even deeper. Sure, he liked ridiculing "the communists' criticism of fascism—most of it is idiotic." Further, he wasn't "at all sure that the Italians aren't as well off as they would have been under any other regime." And the Germans? "Somebody had to repudiate the treaty etc., etc. And if Hitler should take back some of his colonies, it might help the world situation, if it wasn't too expensive." As for "the freedom of speech stuff," as he termed it: "how important is it to those who have nothing to say, i.e. about 99%?" Since such freedoms were a "correlate or function of the security of a regime," one could expect their gradual return once the new rulers were firmly in the saddle.[30]

Lundberg also had an unfortunate way of talking about Jews; not anti-Semitism exactly, but it made you wonder. "I am breakfasting with two of the fairest Bennington Hebrews," he wrote to Bain in late 1936, adding: "They have insisted on meeting me at the train with the family limousine—I wouldn't get out to meet Jesus Christ at a Chicago station at such an hour of the morning." To Bain's remark about his fascist tendencies he replied: "Whence came this idea that I am 'quite Fascist in speech'? I hate the bastards as much as any Hebrew."[31]

From 1939 to 1941, with war raging in Europe, Lundberg supported isolationism and such America Firsters as the aviator Charles Lindberg. "I call your attention to the testimony of Lindberg these days," he wrote Bain in early 1941. "A genius, as well as a man of courage."[32] In public he could be biting enough, but in private he was even worse. While visiting the sociologist Roderick D. McKenzie at the University of Michigan in the summer of 1940, he boasted—as Jessie heard the story—that he "had enjoyed [the war] and grown fat on it," a statement particularly offensive to Mrs. McKenzie, who had lost a brother in the war. For "intellectuals" he had nothing but contempt. He hoped to do an article on their "stupid behavior . . . in the face of the war," he wrote Jessie that same July. "I'd like to accuse them of selfishly looking after what they think is their own interest—a vested interest in talk—and selling the masses of the people in every country down the river by inducing them to fight for symbols which aren't worth fighting for, except for journalists, preachers and professors, who live by them."[33]

Nor did American involvement in the war change Lundberg's mind, as he revealed in his presidential speech to the ASS in 1943. Although the subject was "Sociologists and the Peace," he lost no time getting to religion, the source of those moral and ethical views that had consistently frustrated true social science. A "minor illustration," he noted, were "large numbers of organized and articulate Jews in their unhappy predicament devoting themselves to legalistic and moralistic conjurings so that their attention is entirely diverted from a realistic approach. They demand legislation prohibiting criticism and they demand international action outlawing anti-Semitism, instead of reckoning with the causes of the antagonism." These "firebrands" would probably attack his remarks as anti-Semitic, he continued, as his lengthy harangue concluded. But this fact merely showed "how a primitive, moralistic, theological, legalistic attitude obstructs a scientific approach." As it happened, Lundberg did not have to wait. "I am compelled to report," he later wrote of the reception, that the talk "was interrupted with some hisses and boss—not a usual recognition at this annual occasion." In fact, he had not seen such "an accolade" in thirty years of attending scholarly meetings.[34]

───────

The Bernards had known Lundberg since the early twenties. As a graduate student, he was one of L.L.B.'s prize pupils, one whom he was later pleased to claim as a "disciple" whether or not it was quite true.[35] His first published paper was a study of the demographic and economic basis of political radicalism prepared for one of Luther Bernard's seminars. *Social Research* (1929), his first book, was spiced with quotations from Bernard and references to his work.[36] By the time Jessie had finished her third year at the University of Minnesota, he knew her well enough to retail a rumor that their favorite professor (L.L.B.) was seen kissing his lady love at the train station. When she did poorly on her M.A. exam, she noted, he let her "weep on your shoulders."[37] During her postgraduate year, he admired her master's thesis enough to propose a study of his own using the same approach. At the end of the decade, he invited her to contribute an essay on the history of sociology to his *Trends in American Sociology*. Although she disagreed with one or two points (unspecified) in the paper he contributed, they were sufficiently friendly to gossip about their mutual interests within the profession. "Ellwood's discomfiture . . . delights me greatly," he wrote concerning Ogburn's election as president of the ASS for 1929, Ellwood being one of the chief opponents of sociological behaviorism. "We shall see that he gets much more of this."[38]

During the early 1930s, if Luther is to be believed, Jessie had hopes that she and Lundberg might be more than good friends. "Did I not know of your correspondence with L[undberg], and how you used to be afraid that a letter would come some time that I might see?" he wrote angrily in the midst of their divorce crisis, charging her with maneuvering to keep sole possession of the mailbox key. He saw also "how bitterly disappointed" she had been in late 1934 (December by his calculation) "to see that he greatly preferred another person to you," someone described only as "the Yale woman." "After that you were much nicer to me for many months," Luther continued this accusation, "and hated your rival in his affections."[39]

Whether this alleged disappointment existed in reality or in Luther's imagination remains a matter of conjecture. On one reading, a letter that Jessie wrote to Lundberg in mid-1934 would appear to support Luther's suspicions, at the least of coquettish behavior. In it she complained that she has not heard from Lundberg in some time, and was afraid she might have "offended" him. Then, in a postscript: "Do you ever play your violin? I sometimes think I shall take up the piano again. . . . Why don't you fiddle again? I think it might be very nice. Maybe sometime we'll be able to develop into an orchestra!"[40] Several years later, after months of bitter discussion concerning divorce proceedings, however, Jessie affirmed that Luther could take as "absolutely correct" her statement that she had not been romantically interested in Lundberg ("or for that matter . . . any of the other men you have accused me of being interested in"). Nor was she coquettish.

"As a matter of fact, I utterly detest the whole theory and practice of coquetry because it is indirect, insincere, and exploitive," she continued. "As you know, I believe that if a woman is attracted to a man she should be as candid and direct about it as he."[41] In reply, Luther said he didn't care what she called it, "it is the thing that bothers me," whether expressed toward Lundberg or others.[42]

For whatever reason, Jessie's friendship with Lundberg cooled from the mid-1930s on, at least so far as she was concerned. In a letter to him from Paris in the fall of 1935 she described the local scene, still friendly, even mildly flirtatious: "Paris is a nice place for women, and the nicest thing is that one doesn't have to be young or beautiful or chic or bright or anything else just so she is a woman, in order to be loved, or least treated as tho she were loved, which to a behaviorist isn't so awfully different."[43] But a year later, their friendship showed signs of strain. Although she had asked Lundberg to meet the ship on her return from Paris in January 1936, he did not show up, leaving her to fend for herself in what turned out to be a horrendous trip to her hotel. Although she recovered enough to call him for dinner ("after a good cry"), his continual talk of job prospects and general demeanor put her off ("Lundberg is more and more self-satisfied and conceited," she reported to L.L.B.).[44]

During the next two years, Bernard nonetheless sought Lundberg's help in obtaining jobs—also to no avail. Although Lundberg had mentioned the possibility of an opening at Bennington in 1937, he failed to follow up, pleading that he was abroad when the appointment was finally made.[45] The next year it was a plea for help in obtaining a position with the Works Progress Administration. Before Lundberg could answer (he took two weeks), she poured out her frustration to Luther: "He is a louse. He has not even replied to my letter. I never appeal to him except when it is absolutely essential. He always fails me, without exception." When Lundberg's reply finally arrived ("Dear Mrs. Bernard"), it was cool and noncommittal.[46]

The flap over L.L.B.'s nonmembership in the Sociological Research Association probably also did not help, although Jessie expressed no opinion concerning Lundberg's role. To be sure, he and Read Bain had originally nominated Luther, and he expressed his disgust when his professor was excluded. But he remained active in the organization

through the late thirties, at a time when L.L.B. was trying unsuccessfully to find out who was in the thing in the first place. When in early
1938 a Bernard ally, at Luther's request, attempted to get him a membership list from Lundberg, the latter reportedly replied that "it was
printed on the program, but I could not get one." This same ally
suggested further that he write the president of the ASS for a copy
(Bernard by this time had quit the society). Although only another
teapot tempest, that Bernard had not written Lundberg himself, and
apparently finally got the membership list without his former student's
help, suggested less than cordial relations.[47]

When in the 1940s Lundberg was busy making enemies throughout the profession, Jessie offered some advice of her own. In the first
of two letters in September 1940, she warned that his antiwar sentiments, Olympian objectivity, and apparent disdain of democracy were
harming his reputation. "I wonder if you will let me say a number of
things to you without becoming offended," she began the first of these
letters, adding that their years of friendship gave her this "privilege:"

> It has occurred to me . . . that in the past decade or so you have allowed
> yourself to become a bit too removed from the ordinary human values.
> Having given no hostages to fate in the form of a family [Lundberg re-
> mained a bachelor], you are particularly invulnerable. You have acquired a
> sort of Jovian disdain of the way of all flesh. Right? Are you not a bit too
> Olympian? pontifical? unsympathetic?

And so it continued. Although Bernard made no reference to their
own relations, a hint of her frustrations came out as she further attacked Lundberg for his treatment of Stuart Dodd. Dodd, later a
colleague and close friend of Lundberg's at the University of Washington, was at the time in a somewhat desperate search for an academic
position to get out of Lebanon, where he had been teaching at Beirut
University for a decade. Simply saying that Dodd should be at a "good
university" was not enough, Bernard charged, echoing her own dealings with her old friend. "It seems to me that it would be the part of
friendship to do something active to see that he is placed."[48]

In a heated response, Lundberg chronicled a lifetime of charity
and caring toward others; damned college presidents, professors, and

"the boys from Groton and Eaton" [*sic*]; and asserted that southern sharecroppers would probably be better off under Hitler. Jessie then apologized, after a fashion ("I understand that you cannot go about broadcasting your philanthropies and frankly I was surprised to hear of them"). But she stuck to her guns so far as his attitudes toward Hitler and the war were concerned. As a "mere citizen" she knew only what she read in the papers, but she could not believe that "our present program" (Congress passed the lend-lease bill in March) was "based on air." Although she too would like to see "the rotten class system . . . knocked into a cocked hat," she was "not willing to let Hitler do it." "As between two evils," she concluded, with a characteristic display of wry common sense, "I prefer the ones I am used to and accustomed to and have plans for meeting."[49]

During the next two years, the Bernards' relations with Lundberg continued to wend their convoluted way. In 1941, Luther rang in the New York with a blast at Lundberg for refusing in a "discourteous" manner to subscribe to the *American Sociologist*, the one-man periodical in which L.L.B. published his increasing animus toward most of the sociological profession ("Perhaps you were not aware of the manner in which you acted, or possibly you think that you are privileged to behave in such a way because of some special attribute or quality," Bernard lectured). Yet two months later, he served his former student some juicy snippets concerning the opinions a dean at the University of Michigan held toward Lundberg—"your origins (brought up in a prairie shack), had queer notions about scientific method, didn't get along well at [Bennington], etc." All this "not as a matter of gossip" but because he hoped that Lundberg would look out for his old professor's interests should similar rumors concerning Bernard reach his ear.[50]

When Lundberg was elected president of the American Sociological Society the following year, Jessie added a twist of her own in what must rank as one of the more curious letters of congratulation on record. "Of course I think you deserve the honor," she wrote, accepting an offer to serve on the research committee. But she could not help but feel "that it was not yet your turn" since many men in sociology's "second generation" had not yet been so honored (among them, Howard Woolston, later Lundberg's colleague at Washington; Albert

Keller of Yale; and Manuel Elmer of Pitt, an ally during the "Bernard rebellion" within the ASS the previous decade). "And then there is this to be considered too," she added. "That once you have been president people begin to think of you as an older person." Among the younger men, he perhaps deserved it more than any. But she regretted the demise of the older men. "I know that your hard-boiled philosophy does not leave room for such a sentimental attitude, but that's how I feel." Excessively ambitious, prematurely old, and hard-boiled to boot. Not surprisingly, Lundberg's reply was stiffly cordial at best.[51]

In the aftermath of Lundberg's presidential speech to the ASS in December 1943, he again turned to Jessie. In May 1944 he sent her copies of some responses to his address, including some favorable ones from the president of the Hebrew Union College in Cincinnati and other "prominent Jews." The latter were "probably in the minority," he conceded. All this would cause him to be seen as an anti-Semite, he noted nonchalantly. "Well, if they can afford to call me one, I can afford to be called one. All I wish is that they would consider what is best for themselves a little more carefully."[52]

Almost immediately, their differences resurfaced, anticipating the public exchange half a decade later. The issue, however, was not Lundberg's anti-Semitism (now the subject of public criticism), since Bernard generally shared his views that one problem with Jews was excessive sensitivity to criticism and a resulting tendency to charge anti-Semitism at the slightest provocation. At one point, for example, she noted that the creation of an Anti-Defamation League in her native Minneapolis was a disastrous mistake ("nothing could have been worse").[53]

Rather, her target was Lundberg's allegedly "unfavorable" attitude toward democracy and his general "snobbishness." The first came out in his renewed insistence that his preference for this or any form of government was simply a personal, not a scientific one. "That personal feeling on my part seems to me no reason why, as a scientist, I should claim that democracy is destined to succeed or remain forever as it is. . . . [For] a social scientist to arrive only at such analyses and conclusions as he himself happens to like is merely laughable." The more basic problem was his entire attitude—not economic or social snobbery exactly, but "rather a kind of intellectual snobbery." His earlier claim that he had helped more students and friends than many so-called humanitarians was beside the point. What Jessie had in mind was "a sort of fundamental contempt you seem to have for those who can't keep up with you intellectually or who do not share your rarified atmosphere and belief in science."[54]

Although the Bernards' *Origins of American Sociology* was, in effect, a plea for the continued marriage of science and democracy, Jessie by that time (1943) had already began seriously to rethink the issue, considerably before the full horrors of the Holocaust were public knowledge. Her reaction to these revelations, in turn, was more product than cause of her rejection of the notion that science was or should be value-free.

B ernard attempted her first published formulation of the value issue in *American Family Behavior,* appropriately enough a text in a series edited by F. Stuart Chapin, chairman of sociology at Minnesota since Bernard's days and now one of the elder statesmen of scientistic sociology. "Many social scientists declare that science as science can make no value judgements," she began cautiously. "This point of view, sometimes only a rationalization of timidity, does not seem to be warranted by the facts. No one is better prepared to make value judgements than the scientist. . . . Given a specific function or a goal to be achieved, the only reliable way to evaluate procedures is by scientific methods. Of course, as Dr. Chapin has pointed out . . . value judgements should not enter into scientific methods."[55]

This attempt at a middle ground had serious problems, one reviewer decided. Could one really hold the views contained in the second and last sentences in this selection? asked Robert Winch, a professor at the University of Chicago and philosopher of science of some distinction. "If value judgements should not enter into scientific method, then they must be derived by some non-scientific methods." In fact, Winch continued, Bernard displayed a general confusion concerning normative judgments and finally let readers down by not stating explicitly the nature and source of the societal "goods" she was assuming.[56]

Returning to this question after the war, Bernard focused on three issues: (1) did science contain normative values within itself? (2) did the application of science depend on the action of the "masses" or must it be imposed by some benevolent elite? (3) could one assume that science would inevitably, or even usually, be used for good rather than evil ends? In contrast to Lundberg (as she understood him), she entered a qualified yes to the first, a plea for "men of good will" to the second, and a no to the third.

The question whether value has inherent in science gave her the most trouble. In her first article on this issue (January 1947) she argued that inherent aspects of scientific method were "humility" and "sacrifice," the same values that were also necessary for societal well-being. "Whatever evil use it may be put to, science is, within itself, the most profoundly moral of all institutions." The Religion of Humanity, that is, was implicit in scientific method, not something imposed arbitrarily on it (as Comte's critics had maintained). In apparent contradiction, however, she also implied that those applying scientific method would be guided by values that lay outside it--in this particular formulation, the utilitarian standard of the greatest good for the greatest number.[57]

In subsequent installments, Bernard continued to have it both ways, the object of Winch's earlier criticism of *American Family Behavior.* On the one hand, science by its very nature could not escape morality. Lundberg's stark distinction between the normative "if" of the policy maker, and the nonnormative "then" of the scientist ignored the fact that the latter was no less part of the implied ethical injunction than the former, she insisted. On the other hand, she increasingly emphasized that external values in fact guided the application of science, and that conflicts among these values were the chief obstacles to this application—a position that appeared to assume the very dichotomy she denied. "The incompatible values may be held at the same time or serially," she explained in a 1949 article. "The impasse they offer to science is equally sharp." In a second piece that same year she added: "Men can be persuaded to submit everything to the judgment of science except their values."[58]

Now skeptical of the inherent goodness of science—she rejected the notion (which she also attributed to Lundberg) that it would invariably, or even generally, be put to good rather than evil ends. Recent history (Nazi Germany, but even more, the Soviet Union) offered examples of the latter. Nor, finally, was the power of the "masses" any guarantee that it would be different in a democracy, where "special interest groups" sought to put it to their special purposes. Lundberg's entire notion of the "masses" was anachronistic given modern social science's emphasis on the interplay of dynamic groups within society. That she distorted Lundberg's position on this point—a fact he noted in his rebuttal to this attack—merely highlighted her own pessimism.[59]

In the thicket of clarification and qualification that followed, it was hard to pick a winner. However, the sociologist Harry Alpert (although a protégé and friend of Lundberg's) thought that Bernard had the best of it on at least one major count. Lundberg's "nostalgic" faith in democracy itself appeared to contradict his statement that he accepted the "more sinister totalitarian implications" of his conclusions. Nor was the inconsistency removed by the questionable assertion that "dictators are gentlemen with popular support" (Alpert's paraphrase). The sincerity of his "nostalgic" bias toward democracy and minority rights was further suspect given the statement that a "rising generation" would find "integrated behavior" increasingly necessary. "Good grief, George!" Alpert exploded. "Aren't you saying that democracy is incompatible with the requirements of technologically advanced society?"[60]

Whatever Lundberg's faults, Bernard's alternatives were unfortunately vague. Ambivalent concerning the issue of values in science, she spoke sometimes as if the conflict of extrascientific values were the sole cause of the failure to apply scientific method to social affairs; at others, as if the problems of application were financial and logistical; and at still others, as if something in the role of the scientific investigator made scientists incapable of dealing with power. At no time did she seriously ask whether Lundberg's "natural science" method (his preferred term) was the appropriate one for the study of human affairs. Nor could she finally decide who should serve as the "men of good will" to act as social saviors.[61] In a final article in this series (1952), men of science and of power viewed one another across an impassable divide. "Policy-making can never be reduced to a science," Bernard concluded inconclusively, "and the role of the scientist probably precludes his becoming an action man." This "paradox," as she termed it, remained unresolved.[62]

For present purposes, however, winner and loser are less important than the factors that underlay this exchange and its significance in Bernard's development. One dimension was philosophical, rooted in a deep if rarely articulated split between what might be called "nominalist" and "realist" versions of objectivism. For the first (which included Ogburn, Chapin, and now Lundberg), a scientific sociology was nominalist and advisory; that is, concerned with regularities rather than realities, means rather than ends. For the second (Luther Bernard, preeminently), sociology was realist in that it dealt with a reality behind appearances and was thus able to finally to prescribe as well as to describe. Luther Bernard's lifelong goal was to provide an objective standard for social behavior, not simply to take a poll to discover how people in fact behave. This normative function, moreover, was intrinsic to all scientific investigation. Just as the scientist must postulate a "perfect vacuum" never found in nature in order to study the laws of falling bodies (L.L.B.'s favorite example), so social scientists must postulate ideal social states in order to study the actual workings of society. Although Jessie did not state the matter in these terms, her reluctance to abandon the notion that science was somehow intrinsically moral was a vestige of the realist position. At the same time, her ambivalence concerning the source of ultimate values (whether intrinsic or extrinsic to science) undercut this position.

The result was a growing interest in the sociology of knowledge, one of several departures in her thinking in these years. For both the nominalist and the realist, there was no issue concerning what aspect of the scientist's role unfitted him/her from making policy; that is, no need for a sociology of scientific knowledge. For the nominalist, policy matters were not the business of science in the first place; for the realist, they were preeminently the concern. Caught between the two, Jessie turned to the sociology of science, as presented in such works as J. D. Bernal's *Social Function of Science* (1939), precisely because she could accept neither the nominalist nor realist position entirely. From this new perspective, the issue was not the presence or absence of an inherent morality in science, but the nature of the scientific "role."

A second dimension was more personal. Although Bernard and

Lundberg ostensibly remained on friendly terms, his arrogance, coupled with the ups and downs of their earlier relationship, forced her to see a dimension of objectivism that she had previously ignored, much as her association with the Edgers in Paris in the fall of 1935 had done. Lundberg's politics, particularly his apparent disdain for democracy, were not irrelevant. But his words were doubtless more galling given his past association with the "scientific" elitists within the sociological profession. In a more general sense, their quarrel was a final chapter in a long-developing split within the objectivist camp, one dating back to L.L.B.'s early rivalry with Ogburn, his efforts to "democratize" the ASS in 1932 against the wishes of those who wished to make the organization more narrowly scientific, and his exclusion from the SRA. Closer to home, Lundberg's insistence on the inherent amorality of science may well have evoked memories of his personal unwillingness to be there in a crunch. Had Lundberg not existed, Bernard might have been forced to invent him. But his actual existence made things a lot easier.

Was Lundberg also a surrogate for Jessie's half-suppressed resentments against L.L.B.? Was he par excellence the man of science she had in mind in supporting the feminist charge that agentic science has a masculine bias (just as for C. Wright Mills Lundberg was the epitome of "abstracted empiricism")?[63] Were these attacks on the arrogance of excessive objectivity really an assault on the male world of Lundberg and her husband, a protofeminism still lacking a vocabulary? These questions unfortunately must remain matters of speculation. But the personal dimensions of Bernard's quarrel with Lundberg and, by 1950, the coincidence that Luther was dying of cancer clearly gave the issue an emotional edge that their differences on the surface did not alone merit.

And Luther was part of the issue, although rarely mentioned as such. Just as Jessie was beginning her quarrel with Lundberg, she leveled virtually the same charge of elitism against her husband. "In spite of your strongly environmental theory of personality, in actual practice you deny it," she wrote in 1941. "You feel that no matter what the early environment of these proletarians is they ought to be able to overcome it when they are told by university professors what they ought to do."[64] By the late 1940s, L.L.B. himself was aware that a

Matriarch: Bessie (Jessie's mother) with Bettsy Kanter, (maternal grandmother),
ca. 1900.

University of Minnesota undergraduate: Jessie, ca. 1922.

Professor: Luther Lee Bernard, *early 1920s.*

Couple: Luther and Jessie ca. 1926, shortly before their trip to Argentina.

Doctoral candidate: Jessie at Washington University, ca. 1934.

Mother: Jessie and Dorothy Lee, ca. 1942.

Single Parent: Claude, David, Jessie, and Dorothy Lee, Ostende, 1953.

Feminist: Jessie, mid-1980s. Photograph by Raphaela Best.

reaction against his lifelong faith was setting in. "Jessie [and others] joined the argument as to whether science could set standards and goals or only assist in their realization, and whether Comte was fascistic," he reported in his diary concerning a discussion at Penn State in early 1948, but with no further comment.[65] Jessie herself felt that her dissent might be taken for apostasy. "I never discussed the matter with him," she later noted. A protracted quarrel with the dean at Washington University to forestall an unwanted retirement earlier in the decade, and now his illness, had taken their toll. "By the end of the '40s he was already a spent man, too ill to care."[66]

But apostasy it nonetheless was. On the eve of the public exchange with Lundberg, she identified L.L.B.'s *Transition to an Objective Standard of Social Control* (1911) as the source of their once-common faith. Several years later, responding to a comment Lundberg made concerning this work, she confessed that for many years she had been "afraid to look at it" for fear "that it is fascistic or totalitarian or what-ever in orientation."[67]

Although Luther's death in January 1951 was ultimately emancipating, this fact was temporarily obscured by the suffering and tragedy of his final months. "He has been magnificent, in fact, heroic," Jessie wrote Lundberg in the fall of 1950 when the illness was already well advanced, expressing affection for the man whom, through it all, she continued to love and to revere. After teaching three-quarter time that term, Luther had finally given up one course, but met the others until he could no longer stand. "The students have been very nice," she continued. "They bore with him when he could scarcely make himself heard. They wept when he turned the course over to other teachers. As you know, there was never a greater teacher than he. Students love him. It has been heartbreaking to watch him vanish before our sight during the last few months." For the moment, she could not keep her mind on their controversy. But, she added, resuming her professional demeanor: "When this crisis is over I will [be] glad to resume our perennial discussion in re science, etc."[68]

The personal dimension probably also explains why Bernard somewhat exaggerated her "loss of faith" (since she was the first to admit that her differences with Lundberg were much less than they appeared) and its effect on her sociology (which continued to feature charts, scales, and other "scientific" paraphernalia through most of her career). But her questioning of science nonetheless left its mark. One legacy was her interest in the sociology of knowledge, an area that would assume new importance following her discovery of the work of Thomas Kuhn in the late sixties, and which, in turn, led her further to reconceptualize her view of the scientific enterprise and ultimately to charge it with a masculine bias. A second was her realization that sociology would foster social welfare only if sociologists deliberately placed it at the service of society, not because of some inherent property of science, an opening wedge for the feminist activism she later espoused. A third was her concern with the sociology of conflict, to which she now turned.

6
Marginal Man
(1951–1963)

I have been the prototypical marginal man.
    —Jessie Bernard, "Twentieth Century Seen through the Life"

For the United States and Jessie Bernard, the 1950s were years of transition. In world affairs, an uneasy peace replaced the tensions of the early cold war and the fighting in Korea. At home, abundance and prosperity gradually blunted memories of McCarthyism and loyalty oaths. The result was the ascendency of what one historian has termed a "liberal consensus"—a mood born during the war, nurtured by the prosperity of the Eisenhower presidency, and reaffirmed with the election of John F. Kennedy.[1]

In the social sciences, Bernard's professional world, this consensus took a variety of forms. In political science Robert Dahl's *Who Governs?* (1951) proposed one of several pluralist models of American politics. In sociology, Talcott Parsons's structural functionalism turned attention from social conflict to social order, blunting (so his critics said) the potentially radical edge of the "action theory" he had proposed before the war. In anthropology, Clyde Kluckhohn in *Mirror for Man* (1949) was one of several scholars to survey the character of a prosperous, diverse, and secular United States. In history, one version of consensus translated into the assertion that the United States from the start had been liberal, democratic, and capitalist; while another reduced the past conflicts of farmers, workers, and capitalists to pseudostruggles based on concern with status rather than real economic exploitation.[2]

In calling for a sociology of conflict, Bernard at first appeared to resist this current. During the late forties and early fifties, she saw conflict, not consensus, as a permanent factor in national and world affairs. While taking on George Lundberg publicly and privately, she also stepped up her earlier battles with cultural anthropology, Clyde Kluckhohn in particular, charging the entire discipline with being socially conservative ("One looks in vain for meaningful analysis of conflict or competition in anthropological literature," Bernard lamented concerning this perennial bugaboo).[3] During these same years, she defended academic freedom against the threat of McCarthyism. In 1951 she was a moving force in the formation of the Society for the Study of Social Problems (SSSP), a dissident group some considered the radicals of the profession.[4]

Her publications meanwhile grew apace. Following *American Community Behavior,* she published *Remarriage* (1956) and *Dating, Mating, and Marriage* (1958, with Meahl and Smith), a continuation of her interest in marriage and the family; *Social Problems at Midcentury* (1957), a general survey of American society for classroom use; and a substantial installment on her lifetime total of more than seventy-five articles.

Thanks in part to these publications, Bernard also gradually joined the academic establishment and in the process substituted an eclectic blend of 1950s academic liberalism for both her earlier faith in an objectivist utopia and the incipient radicalism of the early SSSP years. In *Social Problems in Midcentury,* she temporarily set aside her conflict model to analyze the problems of American abundance in terms of "status" and changing "roles," an important theme in consensus history. In the early 1960s, her interest in conflict and its resolution led, not to a continued attack on consensus theory (as her earlier comments on Kluckhohn appeared to forecast), but to participation in Project Camelot, a government-sponsored investigation into Latin American insurgency that to its many critics combined the worst of cold war meddling and consensualist naiveté. To this she added a brief involvement with a second government-sponsored scheme, the so-called Iron Mountain Project to study the social and economic effects of permanent peace.

As a theorist, Bernard was neither a system builder nor a systematic thinker. Whatever the issue, she raised more questions than she

answered, leaving her position on key points frustratingly inconclu-
sive. Nowhere was this more the case than in her treatment of values
in science (the subject of the previous chapter) and the prospects of
conflict resolution (the focus of the present one). Her work, as a
result, defies precise categorization. "Although a dedicated sociologist, I proved to be an undisciplined one," she later wrote, citing her
tendency to violate discipline boundaries. Just as in the thirties she
"caught the fever" of statistical sociology, so in the early fifties it was
conflict sociology. Later in the decade her framework was closer to the
structural functionalism of Talcott Parsons. Although she was never a
Parsonian, indeed thought he was overrated, she adopted his terminol-
ogy because "it [was] coin of the realm."[5] When game theory came
along, she was again the ardent disciple, even though she soon saw
that she knew too little to keep up with the big boys.

"I have been the prototypical marginal man," Bernard observed,
using Robert Park's term this time to describe not her position between Jews and Gentiles, but her peculiar status within the discipline.
Although she had no clear theory on the subject, she believed that this
position had something to do with being a woman. She had not
wanted success in the usual sense, she insisted, nor even pursued a
career as the term is usually defined. For these reasons she was freer
than male colleagues to indulge her interests as they developed. If one
price of being a woman academic was not being taken quite seriously
(as she would explain in *Academic Women*), the benefit was greater
indulgence when one strayed from the paths of orthodoxy.

This insistence that she had not been "running a career" was partly
hyperbole, of course, tailored to fit her post-1970 hypothesis that
"career" was essentially a male concept. Many women academics of
her generation felt even more pressure than their male colleagues to
conform to professional orthodoxies, and Bernard in many ways was
no exception. By most of the usual measures—ambition, desire for
prestige, open-ended commitment to work—she was a full-fledged
professional.

Her self-image as "marginal man" nonetheless contained an important truth: she had been protected, even privileged in her early professional life (just as, in a way, she had been in her youth as "third child"),
whether the issue was places on the program of annual meetings,

access to journals, or job applications. Perhaps also as a woman she *had* been taken less seriously, but for this very reason was less worried that inconsistency might somehow damage her career. Whatever the issue, as she once put it, she could "get away with it."[6]

More importantly, her position as insider-outsider often enabled her to see things and to articulate issues before others did so. Thus, she attacked Lundberg's scientism a decade before the neo-Marxist sociologist C. Wright Mills (a "Texas Trotskyite," some called him)[7] labeled it "abstracted empiricism" in *The Sociological Imagination* (1959). She called for a conflict sociology when her younger colleague Lewis Coser (to mention only one conflict sociologist) was barely in graduate school, and early saw that abundance brought its own special problems. She turned to game theory when it was virtually unknown in the social sciences, just as she later explored the implications for her discipline of Thomas Kuhn's theories of scientific revolutions before many of her colleagues in sociology. Although Bernard in the fifties was no radical—indeed, quintessentially conservative by later standards—she thus voiced a number of concerns that would move to center stage in the 1960s.

In her overall development, the years from the early 1950s through the move from Penn State to Washington to 1961 were in several respects a necessary interlude in her journey from positivism to feminism.[8] For one thing, she was now "Professor Bernard" rather than the "wife of Professor Bernard," and probably one of the best-known women within sociology. For another, whatever the perils of eclecticism, she felt free to experiment with different sociological theories, including notions of role and status that would ultimately serve as one matrix of her feminism. If vestiges of Luther's objectivism continued to color her sociology, she came more squarely to see limitations in this scientistic creed.

B ernard made her debut as a conflict theorist just as the controversy with Lundberg was winding down. Personally, of course, she was no stranger to the subject, as the details of her marriage alone attested. Intellectually, she was early introduced to an

American version of conflict theory in a course with Robert Park at Chicago in the late 1920s. A belief in the reality and inevitability of conflict informed her debate over values with Lundberg ("Can you imagine strong interest groups accepting a scientific verdict if it went against them?" she demanded early in their exchange).[9] She had already emphasized its social role, including its positive functions, in *American Family Behavior* and in *American Community Behavior.* Now she launched what amounted to a crusade. In the process, she effectively resolved the issue of science and values by further widening the gap between them.[10]

A call to arms, her first article in this series reviewed the reasons why conflict theory in American sociology remained more or less where the German sociologist Georg Simmel had left it half a century before. In a second, she contrasted a sociological view of conflict with the more popular psychological analysis of Theodore Adorno and colleagues, *The Authoritarian Personality* (1950), a soon-classic product of the émigré sociology of the Frankfurt school. At the policy level she attacked a current UNESCO "tensions project" and similarly misguided efforts to create international peace. After discovering game theory in the early fifties, she incorporated it into her analysis.

Among conflict theorists, Bernard represented a minor wing of a neglected branch of the discipline. Unlike C. Wright Mills or the "classic" conflict theorist Ralf Dahrendorf, each of whom looked to European traditions, Bernard turned to the guides of her youth: Albion Small, Edward A. Ross, and, in particular, Robert Park. Whereas Marxists rooted conflict in class and economics, and the classic theorists in any interest that engenders group solidarity, Bernard's approach, as one commentator has described it, was "little distinguishable from Park's process cycle . . . where conflict is intertwined with custom, cooperation, equilibrium, dissonance, innovation and other mechanisms." All conflict theorists opposed mainstream sociologists who (following Durkheim, Weber, Mead, or Cooley) viewed conflict as temporary misunderstanding to be addressed by institutional or similar adjustments. But Bernard, in particular, saw the conflict of values as the central issue.[11]

Familiar themes now appeared in a new context. Still basic was a distinction between objective and subjective analyses, although she conceded that disciplines ranged themselves along a spectrum in this regard, from ecology at the objective end of the scale to psychology at the subjective. In treating social conflict, psychologists erred in locating it in the minds of individuals, rather than in the objective interests of groups. Individual members of different groups may loathe or love one another, but loathing is not the source of nor loving the solution to group conflict." A thousand quarrels between American tourists and French taxi-drivers [do not] add up to Franco-American conflict," she wrote, illustrating this point, any more than "a thousand love affairs between soldier and enemy women . . . add up to friendly group relations." Among conflict theorists, Bernard was virtually alone (or so Coser noted) in attacking all psychological analyses of conflict, including interpretations of the "authoritarian personality" by Adorno and his colleagues.[12] Although the Adorno portrait of the "prejudice-prone" individual offered insight into "certain personality configurations," it told us nothing about "intergroup relations."[13]

Sociologists instead "should be able to tell us something of the 'real' or 'objective' relations between groups, regardless of how they may appear subjectively within the minds of the members." Unfortunately, however, what constituted these objective relations was initially unclear. At one point Bernard hinted that demography, technology, and economics were among them. But her greater concern was so-called national value hierarchies as opposed to "subjective attitudes." Reified as "value hierarchies," that is to say, the attitudes and opinions of individuals were as "real" as material factors.[14]

Underlying this insistence that values were objective were one old issue and one new one. The first was the perennial question of Jewish-Gentile relations and Bernard's doubts that conflict between the two, however often analyzed, could be resolved. Just as Jews and Gentiles would never resolve their differences, however hard they tried, so conflict seemed a permanent aspect of the human condition more generally. Values, so to speak, were as tangible as things. Each group had value hierarchies that were as real as the quest for good housing and higher wages.

The new issue was the cold war and Bernard's feelings about communism. Despite a basic disinterest in partisan politics, her distaste for left-wingers was longstanding. In the late thirties, politics had reinforced her dislike of certain "Jewish behavior" among fellow workers at the WPA. He "judges people almost wholly in terms of their ideologies," she wrote L.L.B. concerning one of her bosses. "If their attitudes about the class struggle coincide with his, they are all right, regardless of technical or professional competence or efficiency. Otherwise not. My ideology is not his at all."[15] Jewish radicals especially bothered her. In her analysis of "Biculturality" several years later, she described the passage from Judaism to communism as the most "disintegrating" of all ways out of the faith. "To be impelled . . . by an inner daemon, to destroy in order to solve an inner conflict is a sad destiny," she wrote of two Milltown radicals who attacked the Gentile world in the name of revolution in order to expiate their guilt over abandoning Judaism. "Along the path these tortured souls trod lay only spiritual desolation." Fortunately, she added, there were not many of them.[16]

Although the cold war did not explicitly enter the exchange with Lundberg, it added a political overtone to an apparently apolitical debate. Not that Lundberg cared for communism any more than did Bernard. He often ridiculed communist ideological pretensions as just more theology; for example, in passing references to "Marxist or other evangelical journals."[17] True to his creed that scientists as scientists should remain politically neutral, he opposed a motion to put the American Sociological Society on record against a California loyalty oath—thus, in a sense, condoning the worst of cold war attitudes.[18]

But in his abrasive way Lundberg also demonstrated the fatal weakness in his particular combination of objectivism and isolationism when faced with political systems now lumped together as totalitarian. Although *Can Science Save Us?* appeared before the iron curtain had fully descended, he quoted approvingly a statement of wartime vicepresident Henry A. Wallace to the effect that the United States had no business meddling in the political affairs of Eastern Europe. With the help of science, moreover, one might better understand how and why such regional spheres of influence develop. "Current attempts of Russia to consolidate their territorial position on ecological lines and to advance their 'way of life,' " he explained in the fall of 1947, "may be regarded sociologically as examples of the same phenomenon as the expansion of the United States." Social scientists should thus recognize "that it is their business as scientists to look for general processes in social life as distinguished from agitating for one or another social policy." Science, in short, reinforced an isolationist attitude that effectively condoned a Soviet sphere of influence.[19]

Bernard, in contrast, saw mounting tensions between the United States and the Soviet Union as evidence, not of the need for detached scientific analysis, but of the fact that incompatible values made its application difficult if not impossible. "The one thing science could do for us at the present time is the only thing we will not permit it to do," she wrote. "That one thing is to determine whether or not the mutual fears of Soviet Russia and the United States are justified and rational."[20] But did she really propose that such analysis would prove the cold war to be groundless? Given her own attitude toward communism, there was always an implied assumption that the values of the two were irreconcilable and the cold war thus justified.

The international struggle of communism and democracy dominated her conflict writings. "Did the sociologists have anything creative to offer in the Cold War?" she demanded in her opening article of 1950. The answer, of course, was no. Compared to the Communists, Americans were "mere babes in the woods" when it came to understanding conflict and developing techniques for exploiting it to advantage. Whereas a cursory analysis of an English translation of Stalin's writing to 1940 revealed forty-two references to "conflict" or similar concepts, comparable ones by FDR contained only thirteen, she continued, conveniently overlooking the problems that translation posed. To remedy the situation, she called for an Institute for Conflict Analysis comparable to the pre–World War II Institute for Propaganda Analysis.[21]

Although *American Community Behavior* and *Social Problems at Midcentury* were relatively restrained in their criticisms of the Soviet Union, Bernard left little doubt where she stood. "The techniques used by Communists in waging political warfare are manifold," she wrote in the first of these books. "They travel under aliases, forge passports, make false declarations, perjure themselves, engage in espionage, and use character assassination to destroy the careers of persons they wish to remove from public life." A recent instance was their success in obtaining a "powerful position" in Henry Wallace's Progressive party during the 1948 election. After cataloguing the many social ills in the Soviet Union in the 1957 volume, she concluded that the Soviet failure to achieve the promised social reconstruction was as disillusioning to "men in the 20th century as [was] the similar failure of the French revolution . . . to men in the 19th."[22] One reviewer of the book, noting a "certain animus" in denigrating references to the Soviet Union, concluded: "Mrs. Bernard is a good patriot."[23]

T hus entered game theory as expounded in John Von Neumann and Oskar Morgenstern's *Theory of Games and Economic Behavior* (1947), in J.C.C. McKinsey's *Theory of Games* (1952), and in numerous other books that appeared during the fifties and early sixties.[24] At the level of theory the game approach provided Bernard a way of dealing with the problem of values, while in practice it promised to minimize the resort to violence as a way of resolving conflict. Pared of technicalities, the theory, as she interpreted it, involved six basic concepts: rational behavior, strategy, the "pay-off matrix," "rules of the game," coalitions and alliances, and solutions. The first was basic since the assumption of rational behavior distinguished the sociological from the psychological and cultural approaches. Players, that is, were assumed to pursue an optimum course with respect to a goal, not simply to bicker or to quarrel for psychological kicks or to sacrifice gains voluntarily because of some cultural norm (as in the case of a mother deliberately losing when playing checkers with her child).[25]

Values entered game theory in three ways: in the formulation of strategies (a process she now likened to artistic creativity); as aspects of the "rules of the game" (which included institutions such as existing family patterns); and in the choice of solutions (since "accepted social standards" would presumably govern a choice when two or more were equally acceptable). But game theory itself was entirely separate from values. "It begins with values," she wrote, but it neither assigns values in the "pay-off matrix" nor creates the strategies it evaluates mathematically.[26]

Its virtue as an approach to social conflict was that it "fits human beings as they now behave."

> It makes no demands on human nature that present-day conditions do not make on it. It does not ask for a change in attitude, a refashioning of human nature. It does not, furthermore, involve in its application any manipulation in the sense of changing people in the direction of goals set by others. What manipulation there is, is in terms of rationality.

"It does not envisage an end to conflict," she added; "it accepts conflict as a continuing fact." However, it might "conceivably help in minimizing the use of violence as a strategy in conflict."[27]

Bernard knew that this latest solution to the value problem was not without its own difficulties, even leaving aside the massive mathematical calculations required to evaluate different strategies for obtaining goals. One was conceptual, especially when one attempted to measure tangible gains (monetary) against intangible losses ("status" or "honor"), or when units of gain and loss were "non-transferable" (white economic gain from discrimination, for example, against black loss). A second was ethical in that the entire thing might appear to some observers to be merely a "modernized, streamlined, mathematical version of Machiavellianism"—although here Bernard took refuge in the indirect entry of values, as noted above.[28]

Had she really solved the problem of science and values? As in her debate with Lundberg, she could insist that the scientist-as-game-theorist operated within a value context insofar as values shaped the creation of strategy, determined the rules of the game, and affected the choice of solutions. Applying game theory to marriage counseling, she even suggested that the counselor might impose these values; for example, in refusing to show the player how to maximize goals based on feelings of "revenge or hostility," or other ends judged not to be "normal."[29] But the point in any case was that these values were extrinsic to science, an opening wedge (as a critic of her feminism later charged) to the view that social science is nothing more than a vehicle for social reform.[30] Bernard never openly endorsed this latter conclusion; rather, she attempted a balancing act that was easier in theory than in practice, as Project Camelot would soon show.

Unlike Lundberg, Bernard did not assume that one's values were simply a matter of personal preference. But in rooting them finally in the values of the existing social system, she was also in her way more conservative than he. Unanswered were questions of how or even whether one finally could choose among competing values (as projected in the differing strategies of a Hitler and a Gandhi, for example) or evaluate solutions when accepted social standards were unclear (as concerning the position of women in society, for example). In taking people as they actually behave, that is, game theory appeared to rule out genuine change.[31]

For whatever reason, Bernard's excursion into this new area gained few adherents. Although she attempted to give her theorizing a practical twist by applying it to marriage counseling, the counselors themselves showed no interest ("not their dish of tea," she later realized).[32] When she attempted to apply it to her own daughter's troubled marriage, it appeared painfully irrelevant (see chapter 8). She initially liked game theory in part because its practitioners seemed the brightest and most amusing in the social science business. But she also quickly realized that she was in over her head. By the mid-sixties, although still interested in new conceptualizations in the field, she was ready to admit that her original model had few applications in real life. "The theater of the absurd may have its devotees," she wrote, "but scientists cannot bear a theory that leads to absurdities. Certain games did precisely that." By this time, she was ready to see game theory itself as another case study in the sociology of science.[33]

Bernard was never a cold warrior of the George Kennan or the Reinhold Niebuhr variety, the so-called new liberals of the 1950s. Both *American Community Behavior* and *Social Problems at Midcentury*, despite their criticism of Soviet society, drew many parallels between the social problems of the United States and of the Soviet Union, including the tendency of both redbaiters and Communists to use we-they scare tactics. Nor did she accept the fashionable realpolitik, Niebuhrian or otherwise, with its equally fashionable neo-Calvinist view of human nature. "I am excluded by my own ideology from understanding the Dionysian world of evil," she wrote perceptively to a correspondent in the early 1960s, explaining why she had not been even more critical of Communists.[34]

The end result was not that different from the new liberal position. Just as her personal experience with the split of Jews and Gentiles, not to mention her turbulent marriage, initially convinced her of the reality and permanence of conflict, so the cold war deepened her conviction that no amount of scientific analysis could eliminate international conflict or achieve utopia.

B ernard's professional-cum-political activities during the Penn State years demonstrated both the payoffs and limitations of her sociological analysis. Three episodes in particular deserve attention: her involvement from 1951 to 1963 in the Society for the Study of Social Problems (SSSP), a group of sociologists who deplored the increasing tendency of their discipline to ignore social problems; her participation in the government-sponsored Project Camelot during 1964; and a brief and less satisfactory service with the Iron Mountain Project, which came to public attention three years later.

Bernard joined the SSSP soon after Luther's death in 1951. At the time the group included Alfred McClung Lee, who had earlier provided an analysis of Father Charles E. Coughlin's speeches for the Institute for Propaganda Analysis; Arnold Rose, who had worked with Gunnar Myrdal on *An American Dilemma* (1944) and himself published an abridged version as *The Negro in America* (1948); and Ernest Burgess, the aging Chicago sociologist who served as first chairman. At the organization meeting at Roosevelt University in September, Bernard was elected secretary-treasurer, a position she occupied for several years during which the organization had virtually no money in its treasury. In 1953, as chair of the society's new Projects Committee, she contributed a report to their *Bulletin* on the sociological aspects of health, state vital statistics, and the educational uses of recordings. The previous year, the group had already launched the journal *Social Problems,* to which Bernard later contributed a piece called "Social Problems as Problems of Decision." In 1963, she served as the organization's president.[35]

Although Bernard has left little record of her reasons for joining the group, they would appear to have combined a vestigial interest in sociology's reform mission and some narrower professional concerns. In several ways, the SSSP was a direct descendent of L.L.B.s crusade within the AAS in the 1930s. Indeed, in planning their moves, the organizers, Lee later wrote, were "aware of L.L.B.'s inability to keep afloat the rebel periodical *The American Sociologist*." Just as Luther and his followers had opposed such New Deal mandarins as Ogburn, Stuart Rice, and Dorothy and W. I. Thomas (the "T-O-R group," as they called them), so the organizers of the SSSP criticized Samuel Stouffer and other sociologists who, during the 1940s, abandoned sociology's historic concern with social welfare in favor of the management and control of soldiers and civilians. Again the complaint was against a narrowly quantitative sociology that stressed means over ends and, worse, obtained a lock on foundation funds (now, in turn, labeled "scientism" and "elitism"). The question, as Lee later remembered it, was "How could the secure hold of grantspersons and abstract theorists be somewhat offset or relaxed?" That Burgess and Rose were then fighting McCarthyism in their own localities added a further dimension.[36]

"Our gripes were manifold," Bernard summed up these concerns two decades later. "We objected to the elitist direction the ASA was following, its lack of interest in social problems and issues, its antiseptic 'line' on research, its cronyism, and its complacent acceptance of the increasing trend of putting logical research at the service of business and industry." She also shared their concern over the protection of freedom in teaching and research during the McCarthy era. Although she recalled that C. Wright Mills was their "ideological patron saint," she said nothing more about the group's theoretical orientation or political agenda.[37]

Bernard's involvement in the organization, in any case, turned out to be relatively minor, despite the offices she held. One reason was probably logistical, since the most active organizers worked together at Brooklyn College or in the New York area, far from Penn State. A second, perhaps, was that Bernard's politics during the fifties edged subtly to the right, as a comparison of *American Community Behavior* and *Social Problems at Midcentury* alone reveals.

A third may also have been her growing recognition within the profession. In 1953 she was elected president of the Eastern Sociological

Society, and the following year, vice-president of the ASA (1953–1954). Moreover, the SSSP itself soon blurred into the establishment. Lee later called it "too academic," while one of his successors in office, Alvin Gouldner, branded the group "merely the market researchers of the welfare state." Bernard agreed with the thrust if not the specifics of this complaint. "Before too many years had passed we became respectable," she recalled. Members of the ASA elite not only joined the SSSP but became officers, until in the end one could scarcely tell one beard from another.[38]

DESPITE its short, unhappy life, Project Camelot was a better measure of Bernard's politics, at least as they had developed by the early 1960s. The project began in mid-1964 as an offshoot of the United States Army's Space Operations Research Office. Its objectives, as stated in a memo to a group of scholars in December, were threefold: to devise methods for assessing "the potential for internal war" (i.e., revolution) within national societies; to identify actions that governments might take to "relieve" the conditions that provoked such conflict; and "to assess the feasibility of prescribing the characteristics of a system for obtaining and using the essential information needed for doing the above two things"—opaque jargon that boiled down to influencing political and social changes within the designated countries. The project was to last three or four years, at an annual cost of approximately half a million dollars. The focus was to be on Latin America.[39]

As Camelot developed, it meant something different to almost every observer. To the reporter who broke the story, it was another episode in the ongoing battle between the Departments of Defense and State, the latter finally the victor when it was canceled. To the army, it was a way of predicting trouble. To the Chilean politicians who protested vigorously when they learned of it in the spring of 1965, it was an unwarranted intrusion in their country's affairs, or worse, simple spying. To Senator Fulbright of the Foreign Relations Committee it was a symptom of the crisis of values in behavioral sciences that cared more for means than ends.[40]

For sociologists generally, it became an occasion for even more gnashing of teeth and splitting of hairs than this sort of issue usually provokes: would the findings change if the "insurgents" were restorationists? was the data-gathering process to be determined by the needs of social science or of American foreign policy? why was there to be no inquiry into conditions under which revolutions might be successful? why was there no symmetry in the research design, with some attention to the role of the United States in these countries? Faced with criticisms from home and abroad, Secretary of Defense Robert McNamara cut off funding in early July following a directive from President Johnson canceling any projects which, in the opinion of the secretary of state, adversely affected United States foreign relations.[41]

Bernard's reasons for participating must be reconstructed from a few brief comments and one post hoc analysis.[42] An important one, as for many participants, was her belief that researchers would be free to pursue whatever questions interested them and that the information would be made public. A second reason, also shared by other participants, was probably that the project promised to get sociology out of the cloister and into the streets—what's more, into Latin American affairs, a special interest of Bernard's late husband following their stay in Argentina four decades earlier.

A third, as Bernard suggested after the fact, was her growing conviction that violence as a way of resolving conflict not only could be minimized but was quickly becoming anachronistic in social systems characterized by "mechanical" rather than "organic" solidarity. When the latter prevailed, one tribe could annihilate another and emerge a pure winner—a zero-sum game in the lingo of game theory. In the modern world, where victors often had to restore the vanquished (Germany and Japan being the dramatic examples), zero-sum games became "mixed motive" ones, with no clear winner or loser. From the game theory perspective, radical revolutionaries were those who refused to calculate their chances: "The probabilities in their matrix are 1.0 and 0.0. They believe they are bound to win." Their opponents must challenge these "subjective probabilities," she continued, suggesting how game theory might dampen revolutionary ardor. "It is not easy."[43]

For these same reasons, Bernard played down or ignored most criticism of Project Camelot. The Chilean charge that this research was "spying" (as echoed by a columnist in the *Washington Post*) revealed popular ignorance of the difference between fact-gathering for practical and for theoretical ends, she observed, in effect taking refuge in a concept of disinterested social science she had already questioned. Ignoring the many charges that Defense Department sponsorship inevitably tainted methodology and approach (however free and open the inquiry), she viewed Chilean resentment as illustration that research itself was a "conflict process." One reason this was the case was that certain populations were unnecessarily "secretive," either because inexperienced in the ways of social science (and thus unaware that "the data will become undifferentiated in the data hopper"), or because of simple xenophobia. To the charge that the "social systems" approach was inherently biased against instability and change, she noted that such bias had a counterpart in the proinsurgent sentiment inherent in "American populist bias." Against allegations that a managerial orientation, and hence an operations approach, dominated the project, she insisted that it was only one of several methodologies. And, like others, its findings remained unclassified.[44]

Bernard's assumption that Defense Department sponsorship would not bias research was doubtless a product of her own commitment to minimizing domestic violence. Yet this very commitment apparently blinded her to the danger that the project had various built-in premises, whether deriving from the circumstances of its sponsorship; from the fact that research was a one-way street; or from certain lines of inquiry simply not being pursued (so its critics alleged).

To critics then and since, Project Camelot was but one example of the cooptation of liberal elites—the "best and the brightest"—in the service of cold war. From this perspective, Bernard's professed naiveté concerning the aims of the project may appear incredible. Yet, accepting her testimony that she believed she was merely doing her duty as an American, just as revealing was her failure, after a decade of writing about the science-values issue, to take these criticisms seriously once they were voiced. This myopia, in turn, was at least partly due to her earlier waffle on the issue of whether or not values were extrinsic to science. Sharing the general goals of United States foreign policy, she did not see that, to critics who did not share those goals, it was not enough that research be free and unclassified since values (that is, the goals of the military sponsors) informed the project from the start.[45]

This myopia was the more striking given that an unhappy association with the Iron Mountain Project had already offered a lesson of another sort on the value-bias of "objective" government-sponsored studies. Launched in secrecy in August 1963 and shrouded in mystery even after it became public knowledge, this project brought together fifteen social scientists, including Bernard, for monthly meetings of two days each over a period of two and one-half years, the first and last being held in an underground nuclear shelter near Iron Mountain in upstate New York—hence its name. Their aim was to assess the consequences of war and peace on American society and economy. Their report to a shadowy "interagency committee" of the government was to be kept secret. However, the cover was blown in the winter of 1966 when a John Doe gave the report to one Leonard C. Lewin, who published it as *Report from Iron Mountain on the Possibility and Desirability of Peace* (1967). Whether intended or not, the volume was an everything-you-wanted-to-know-about-the-evils-of-social-science. Its message—as the press quickly reported it—was the chilling one that peace could be a national disaster.[46]

Since Bernard did not contribute to the final result, the ensuing debate is unimportant, save to note that commentators divided sharply over whether or not the whole thing was an elaborate spoof. Bernard herself endorsed the spoof theory. As a reductio ad absurdum of the systems approach it was OK; as a sendup of the functionalism of the fifties it was a "good try," she wrote in a post-mortem symposium in *Trans-action*. But it trivialized the serious issue of whether the American economy (with Vietnam escalating daily) could really stand peace. "War and peace are too serious to be left to the satirist," she wrote in this symposium on the Lewin volume. "Especially to a satirist manqué like Doe, who is neither a Swift not a Veblen nor even a Buchwald."[47]

But that was not, as they say, why she came—or rather, why she left. In her contribution to the *Trans-action* symposium, Bernard wished to explain why, as Iron Mountain's one woman participant, she had been obliged to quit early in the proceedings. The group wanted to talk about crime, unemployment, social welfare, and cultural uplift, she explained. "I wanted to talk about the relations of the sexes." At one meeting she explained how wars had usually improved the condition of American women, noting how the post–World War I generation (her own) had achieved the right to smoke, wear short hair, and "demand orgasm." The male participants, apparently still straightfaced, insisted that they were uncertain whether to count such things as costs or benefits to the system as a whole. Believing that all gains for women were losses for men, one psychologist finally took comfort that guns and bombs were one of the few monopolies left to men: hence, war was good for them, too. Bernard replied that modern technology had already broken this monopoly, since women just as easily as men could push buttons in a war room. In the end, the group, in any case, refused to test Bernard's theory on the computer (computer time being a major item). "The very thought of the war system under the control of women was just too much," Bernard recalled sardonically. "The horrors of war began to look as intolerable as the horrors of peace. That did it. My presence was so clearly abrasive that I withdrew."[48]

Did Bernard secretly regret her participation in Project Camelot, thus adding a lesson concerning the perils of positivism to the many she had learned since the late 1930s? Did Iron Mountain add a twist to these lessons by making her sex the issue? In view of Bernard's consistent denials, the answer to the first will probably never be known. Nor was her account of sexism at Iron Moutain totally convincing given the time lapse. But it is significant that she chose to remember and report the latter in these terms five years after the event. Nor was this an isolated instance. For years a number of apparently unrelated questions had nagged just below the surface. Why had so many of her favorite sociological terms—the contributions of which she was most proud—failed to catch on, while the closely related phrases of others entered the sociological lexicon? "Judgmental" and "autonomous" competition, for example, instead of the substantially similar "contest" and "sponsored" competition of another sociologist? Or "community dissociation"? Or "bicultural" as an improvement on Robert Park's "marginality"?[49] Were the reasons the same (as she now suspected) as those behind the Iron Mountain group's steadfast refusal to ask the computer whether war might not be good for women and bad for men?[50] Could it all be simply because she was a woman?

For many years, Bernard either did not see, would not recognize, or had no language to describe a deeper pattern in these experiences. When bias (values) presented itself in terms of world peace or even patriotism (as in Project Camelot), she continued to think that the procedures of science (free access to information and unclassified findings) were sufficient guarantee of objectivity. But where the sexes were concerned she now had second thoughts.

Almost two decades later, an anecdote at the close of *The Female World* provided a clue to experiences she had been storing in her subconscious. The story was "so common that it has become a cliché," she wrote. A woman proposes an idea to a male audience, whose members then ignore it. Minutes later, almost magically, "the same idea is proposed by a male member and . . . enthusiastically embraced." Should the woman be satisfied that her idea had triumphed after all, indifferent, in traditional feminine fashion, to competition for "credit"? Or should she demand recognition in her own right?[51] In the early 1960s, Bernard had barely framed these questions, let alone answers to them. But, as the *Trans-action* report suggested, it wouldn't be long.

7

Academic Woman (1964)

> However convincing individual cases of prejudiced discrimination are, it is difficult to prove its existence on a large or mass scale. The most talented women may be and, indeed, are victimized by it, but apparently not academic women en masse.
>
> —Jessie Bernard, *Academic Women*

Although Bernard enjoyed her years at Penn State, by the early 1960s she had had enough. "I found that grades were becoming all too important," she explained to a group of visiting Venezuelan educators four years after her formal retirement in 1964. Between the selective service and the industrial corporations, "a man's whole life was coming to depend upon them." Bureaucratic rigidities and a maze of prescribed courses prevented good teaching, while the demands of the classroom and endless committee meetings robbed valuable time from her own work. "If I wanted professional recognition," she added with usual candor, "I had to spend more time in research and writing so that the students became my enemies." Academia was becoming too noisy," she repeated many years later. "[It] was no longer a congenial habitat."[1]

Despite a late-1960s tinge to these memories, Bernard's restlessness was apparent for several years before the draft became an issue. "Pretty soon I am going to ask different universities for one-term or one-year appointments just for the fun of visiting different parts of the country," she wrote Lundberg in 1958. Berkeley was at the top of her list, but an offer from Princeton was the first to materialize (1959–1960). By the time she arrived, she had already determined to take early retirement following a sabbatical and two more years at Penn State.[2] In 1961 she moved to Washington, commuting to Penn State for the few hours a week required to teach. There she researched and wrote *Academic Women,* her valedictory to academia and her most important book to that date.

On Bernard's road to feminism, *Academic Women* would prove to be transitional in several respects: from scholarly analysis to more popular writing; from the academic liberalism of the fifties to the more radical world of the 1960s; from the ethos of professionalism to the ethic of sisterhood. In this book, however incompletely, she would raise three issues that continued to occupy her attention for the next two decades: the nature and extent of sexual discrimination in American society, the sociology of "the female world," and the sociology of science, with particular reference to theory in the social sciences. For the moment, however, discrimination was at the top of the list.[3]

━━━━━━━━━━

Although Bernard's professional world had been almost exclusively male, she could not help but be aware of the special needs and problems of women in academia. Even before her appointment at Lindenwood, a woman's college, a letter to Luther from the department head there (concerning a recent flap within Alpha Delta Kappa, a national honor society to which both belonged) revealed a complaint common then and later among women professionals. "I do thank you for your consideration of me as an *individual,* not as a woman," she wrote. "I resent being dealt with in terms of sex, marital status, age, etc." Most men and women seemed to think that a woman must be dealt with "in a delicate manner with special preference, or that she should be ignored and regimented." "Women," she added, "are in large part to blame for this antiquated primary group attitude, I fancy."[4]

Although little of this apparently rubbed off on Bernard during her tenure at Lindenwood (1940–1947), the conservative attitudes of women students in a class on women and society during her first year confirmed the truth of this surmise. Most of the women saw no problem with women receiving unequal pay for the same jobs as men because they planned to marry in a short time and did not want their husbands competing with women, she reported to a friend. "It is surprising, too, how many think women should be discriminated against in hiring. They feel men should be given preference for all jobs." But how did Bernard handle this? "It is hard to make them see that women rarely compete with men for the same jobs," she continued this analysis, apparently invoking the sex segregation of the marketplace as an argument for equal pay in the few areas where the sexes did compete. "We have interesting discussions," she concluded noncommittally, "and perhaps they will be a shade less conservative when they get thru."[5]

Although Penn State's faculty was predominantly male (Bernard's department by 1960 included only one full-time and one part-time woman besides herself), she first developed some of the ideas in *Academic Women* in informal discussion with several female colleagues there. Yet once again, the atmosphere was hardly conducive to feminism as it would later emerge. The two women she best remembered more resembled the person she had been than the one she would become—in turn, self-deprecating, ironic, or depressed as they contemplated their situations in life. One, although a competent professional, sometimes joked that she pursued a career so as to avoid the numerous community projects that might otherwise call on her expertise, an example of what Bernard later described as the "fringe benefit" academic.[6] Another was a brilliant, beautiful, and most unhappy person who looked down upon men, as she did upon almost everyone, as being less than her intellectual equal. By the time *Academic Women* appeared, the first of these two was mired in administrative work at the university, no longer "fringe" but professional; the second was dead, a suicide.[7]

At Princeton (1959–1960) Bernard confronted the male world in its primeval splendor. Billed as the university's "first woman professor," she entered an arena where her discipline was almost as suspect as her sex. Among the major universities, Princeton was slow in adding sociology to its curriculum even by the glacial standards of the Ivy League. When the discipline was being established half a century earlier, a leading Princeton economist publicly ridiculed it in the pages of the *Nation* and elsewhere.[8] Although the first doctorate in the field was granted in 1939, the university was not seriously in the business of training graduate students in sociology until the late 1950s. When

Bernard arrived, sociology remained "officially" yoked to economics in a single department.[9]

After two months, Bernard was nonetheless pleased with the situation, or so she reported to her colleagues at Penn State (although omitting the "personalities," she noted in sending Lundberg a copy of the report). Part of the appeal was simply the change of scene: no committees, small classes, and "high caliber" graduate students. But she was also pleased with her reception personally. "The demeanor of the faculty has been impeccable here. One would never guess that female professors on this campus were anything new or anything to be noted." Local shopkeepers sometimes expressed surprise, especially in situations when she had to divulge her financial resources. Otherwise, recognitions of difference on campus were mostly charming: a welcome to "lady and gentlemen" at the opening faculty meeting, or students calling her by name instead of "Sir," the customary professional address.[10]

Three months later, however, hints of trouble surfaced as she described the graduate students to Lundberg in preparation for a visiting lecture. As a group, they had "more than the usual amount of hostility toward the generation ahead of them," she began. Although they had been "appreciative" of a nonserious talk she had given on her experiences abroad, they had been disappointed in every guest speaker save one. Among the disappointments was Talcott Parsons, even though he "spoke deprecatingly of empiricists and especially of what he called 'dust-bowl empiricists,' the worst kind of all"—a position many of the students shared. "I am sure they will react positively to you even though they may not agree with your general point of view," she assured Lundberg. Their problem, she added, was that they had "no teaching jobs, no apprentice research jobs, and hence no way to define themselves or to evaluate themselves. As a result they feel they must be very critical to show how good they are." All this "off the cuff," she concluded, since she still liked them all and found them "extremely able." Omitted was the fact (which the alumni magazine later noted with a curious mixture of contrition and pride) that Princeton was the only American university besides Catholic University that did not admit women to its graduate programs.[11]

In the end, however, it was the undergraduates who precipitated a hail and farewell for which Bernard would best be remembered, if at all, by Princetonians. The occasion was a final meeting of her class on social problems. The topic: how readings in the course could be applied to understanding "the frustration, anger, and hostility" some members of the class had displayed throughout the term. When, at the first meeting, she was greeted with a mixture of applause and hissing, she initially interpreted the latter as a purely ritualistic response. "Certainly not personal. Certainly not hostile." But as the term went on, she changed her mind. Now she was ready to do some "sociological stocktaking," analyzing the gradations of hostility from the perspective of functionalism, MacIver's theory of social causation, the Allport J-curve (her perennial favorite), Freud, Durkheim, and even Robert Merton.[12]

The responses, as Bernard classified them, were of three kinds: the view that "a fraud-has-been-perpetrated," most prevalent among seniors; the "there's-something-wrong-here" reaction," one common in introductory sociology courses; and an outright "hostility reaction" among a small but belligerent hard core. The subject matter and even her teaching were arguably at issue in the first two. Bernard conceded that she had tried to cover too much, that she had lectured when she should have had students read original sources, even that she had graded too hard. But the simple "hostility reaction" had a simpler explanation: "the fact that I am a woman."

Was Princeton thus her Wittenberg? Had she finally nailed her feminist thesis (one if not ninety-five) to the classroom door? To the editors of the *Princeton Alumni Quarterly* it apparently seemed so, as they headlined a published version of her remarks " 'Breaking the Sex Barrier': Our First Woman Professor Finds It Rough Going in This Fortress of Anti-Feminism." Yet, a careful reading of the published lecture suggests how different was Bernard's response in 1960 than it would have been a decade later. For one thing, she effectively admitted that much of the hostility (perhaps the bulk of it) was rooted in issues other than her sex, not surprising given Princeton's sociological nontradition and the attitude Bernard herself discerned among the graduate students. More importantly, where sex was the issue, Bernard did not see the problem in terms of the larger discrimination within academia, let alone the distribution of power and wealth in society. Rather, she concluded, the hostility was rooted in the fact that she projected a "mother image." "A woman in the role of professor is probably more tainted with family symbolism than a man," she observed. "At this time [in the life of the average Princeton senior, mother is] the enemy."

From the feminist perspective (that of Betty Friedan's *Feminist Mystique,* to mention a book that would soon reorient Bernard's thinking), this analysis unfortunately fell into the trap of justifying something in the process of explaining it, much as she had seemed to justify anti-Semitism in her earlier writings—but now with a Freudian twist. If, in breaking the maternal tie, adolescent males reject the "mother image," is this rejection not part of "normal" psychological development? Moreover, if "momism" was at the heart of the problem (as misogynists had been insisting since the 1942 publication of Philip Wylie's *Generation of Vipers*), were women not somehow to blame?

This is not to say that Bernard was not angry and hurt. Despite her insistence that she bore no ill will (a sociologist might as well be angry at the snow or rain, she observed in an opening display of strained objectivity), the experience clearly upset her. Whatever the cause of the students' behavior, a veil had fallen to reveal an ugly underside to the "impeccable" behavior of the previous fall. Yet Bernard's attempt to interpret the issue within the context of adolescent rebellion (a rebellion, as will appear, she was beginning to experience in her own family), also underlined her lack of vocabulary appropriate to the situation, and the corollary that one cannot really think something if one cannot say it. The problem was not exactly "discrimination" in the legal or even economic sense, the focus of traditional liberal analysis. But in its way it was something almost worse so far as women were concerned. If the Princeton experience did not provide the answers, it at least raised the question.

B ernard began *Academic Women* by surveying women in academia since the mid-nineteenth century. This history, as she saw it, divided into four overlapping periods: the age of the pioneers, beginning in the 1840s and cresting in the 1890s; the age of the academic reformers, as earlier gains were consolidated between 1900 and 1920; a "surging flood of disillusion" during the 1920s, as women took academic careers more in stride, but the earlier rate of increase slowed; and a great withdrawal from 1930 through the 1950s, a period that saw a more substantial decline, if not in absolute numbers, in the proportion of women academics as compared to men.

Bernard's main concern was the decline of women in academia since 1930, not coincidentally the period of her own entry into academic life. Weighing possible explanations, she rejected two arguments on the "demand" side: that female participation had declined because of a reorganization of higher education or because of a shift in curriculum toward more traditionally "male" disciplines. The first was wrong because the greatest increase was in teachers' and junior colleges, both with a relatively large proportion of women on their faculties; the second, because such "feminine" disciplines as the foreign languages had also increased in number.

Still on the demand side, she also discounted the charge that discrimination against women had increased. Rather, she acknowledged only that it may have affected an elite of women professors, but not the rank and file. In support, she marshaled an array of facts: that the proportion of women faculty had also declined at such women's colleges as Wellesley and Vassar, known for their historic commitment to hiring women; that National Science Foundation grants and other such awards were apparently given proportionately to women in the qualified group; and that the percentage of women in academic life as of 1962 (21.9) was roughly the same as those in the labor force with five or more years of college education, the minimal qualification.[13]

The explanation thus lay on the supply side: in female attrition between high school and college; in the decline in numbers of women seeking advanced degrees; in competition from government and other nonacademic institutions for these declining numbers of highly trained women; and in an increasing interest among women in marriage and the family. Although mentioned almost as an afterthought in an early chapter, this last factor—now labeled the "feminine mystique"—assumed greater importance in a final one titled "Wives and Mothers," apparently added after Bernard read Friedan's *Feminine Mystique*, which appeared as her own book was already in press. "There was a reevaluation of the family," she wrote in a statement that certainly described herself in the mid-1930s. "After rejecting maternity . . . for several decades, women seemed suddenly not able to get enough of it." Nor did she regret the result as applied to academic women. Most studies, blindly adopting the standard of the professions, took a "pity-the-poor-woman-professor" attitude toward academic women with children. But not the women themselves. "They are willing to pay the price career-wise for the satisfactions derived from children."[14]

The facts in her own case again confirmed these conclusions. Throughout her career, she was fond of saying, she had not experienced (or at least did not believe she had experienced) significant discrimination. Rather, she had been protected and supported by male colleagues from day one. "Doors were opened to me, job negotiations were carried on for me. Promotions and salary increases came without asking, as a matter of course." When her children arrived, university authorities made concessions that seemed appropriate at the time, even if inadequate by later standards. "[If] there was discrimination along the road," she concluded, conveniently putting the Princeton year behind her, "I had no way of knowing or I was too naive to detect it."[15]

Criticism came quickly. In one of two introductions to the study, Bernard's dean at Penn State faulted her timidity. "[Certain] departments will hire no women," he insisted; "others will not promote women to the higher academic posts; and most departments have a strong prejudice against female administrators." Although less blunt, David Riesman coupled comments on her "cautious" interpretation with reports of discrimination within his own experience.[16]

Reviewers seconded these sentiments. One hoped that Bernard's account of differences between men and women academics would "irritate enough feminists . . . to provoke further research." Interestingly, however, only one suggested that what was needed was a new conception of "discrimination"—and this only obliquely. "The 'discrimination,'" wrote the Barnard sociologist Mirra Komarovsky, paraphrasing Bernard, "stems rather from the existence of certain role definitions and the absence of certain institutional devices."[17]

As debate concerning the nature and extent of discrimination continued, later scholars challenged *Academic Women* on two further grounds. One concerned the dating of the numerical decline, a relatively technical but significant issue. Even using Bernard's figures, one historian argued, women's share of academic employment continued to grow until 1940, a decade after Bernard dated the start of the great withdrawal. Indeed, if one takes into account that female employment declined from 21.4 percent to 13.2 percent during the 1930s in women's colleges and normal schools, women actually showed a gain during the decade in other colleges and universities. Moreover, if the figures are refined by looking at annual rather than decennial statistics, the actual decline did not begin until 1947. Similar corrections applied to Bernard's figures on the number of women taking Ph.Ds.[18]

Other critics meanwhile shifted attention from the supply to the demand side of the equation. One survey of women in all professions suggested that the employment of women academics varied as a reflection of shifts of interest within the professions, not the motivations or attitudes of women themselves, the further assumption being that women were concentrated in certain "feminine" fields. Expanding the argument, another historian related the decline to changes within higher education and of the role of women in society generally. Although the institutional mix and changing demands for women's subjects played a part, the decline was a function of ordinary market forces (level of salaries) combined with occupational segregation in the economy as a whole. Having a choice of the most prestigious professions, men turn away from academia when salaries are relatively low, and return when they are high (as in the 1950s). Ironically, as the historian Margaret Rossiter has recently noted, newly prosperous women's colleges contributed to these developments in hiring male faculty to boost their prestige.[19] In emphasizing the "feminine mystique" Bernard, in sum, effectively blamed the victims for market forces beyond their control.

———————————

W hy, then, had Bernard argued as she had in *Academic Women?* The simplest answer concerns methodology: she had used decennial figures compiled by the U.S. Department of Education in the mid-1950s instead of computing more complete figures from the Department of Education's annual reports. To supplement these incomplete data, she included a number of personal testimonials, usually anonymous, that added flavor but not precision. Hence, she attributed to the distant past a decline in the employment of women in academia that was relatively recent.

The more interesting question remains: Why did she so readily accept this evidence and proceed untroubled to her conclusions? To this question, there are three sorts of answers: one relating to her personality and personal life; a second to her intellectual development, in particular to her newfound enthusiasm for functional analysis; and a third to fundamental ambivalence concerning her own professionalism.

On the personal side, Bernard, by her own admission, was generally naive and basically indifferent to financial matters. For this reason alone, the role of market forces would simply not have occurred to her—a blind spot that would persist in her later feminism. Throughout *Academic Women* generally she showed a tendency to impose her own experience upon the profession as a whole. Since she had trouble getting her career going in the 1930s, indeed was torn between profession and motherhood, it made sense that other women had the same experience. Like her earlier work, this study was thus a more personal testament than at first appeared.

More importantly, Bernard choose to ignore, or had simply forgotten, substantial evidences of discrimination as she attempted to launch her own career in the late 1930s. Despite Luther's help, her road into academia was bumpier than she later described it. Once the decision was made to remain in Washington in the late thirties, she sought various positions with mixed results. In government, these attempts included unsuccessful applications for a position under the sociologist Stuart Rice at the Central Statistical Board in 1937[20] and for a transfer to the Women's Bureau in 1938. In academia, she pursued leads at Tulane, Sweet Briar, Reed, Stanford, Bennington, and in schools and colleges in the St. Louis area, also to no avail despite her impressive credentials.

"I hope I am not paranoic but I have a feeling I am being discriminated against for one reason or another," she wrote Luther after several unsuccessful attempts to find something in government to replace the hated job at WPA. Since government agencies were filled with women, she was not yet ready to suspect gender as the cause. "Perhaps in Rice's case it is revenge on you," she noted, recalling her husband's bitter fights with what the Bernard rebels had called the "T-O-R [Thomas-Ogburn-Rice] group" in the ASS several years earlier.[21]

In academia, however, the issue was almost impossible to ignore. At Sweet Briar, she was told flatly that they wanted a man, a fact she apparently forgot when talking about Wellesley and other women's colleges. At Stanford, the department head confessed openly that there was "a certain prejudice against having women on the staff," although he hoped it might be overcome in this instance. At colleges in the St. Louis area, there was not even this bit of hope. "Outside of women's courses, and even there," she wrote Luther, "women are discriminated against for everything except social work courses." The St. Louis school system was even worse. "The Board of Education," its spokesman wrote, "has enforced rigidly its rule against the employment of married women in the Department of Instruction for many years." From Bennington she learned after the fact (and without explanation) that the position had been filled by a husband/wife team. At Reed, the dean insisted that they *wanted* a woman, but added that Bernard's separation from her husband made her unacceptable. "[Although] he liked me a lot I think he will hesitate to hire me," she reported to Luther; "said so frankly, because I am married to you and not living with you."[22]

The Bernards responded to this mosaic of discrimination in characteristic his/her fashion. Although Luther supported Jessie's job search wholeheartedly, using his influence and connections wherever possible, he seized upon antifeminist sentiment as a reason why she *must* return to him. "In the second [place] they suspect you because you are separated from your husband," he lectured her after the 1937 professional meetings produced no results. "Even when I do my best to allay those suspicions, the administrators will be afraid to trust you in the long run. Almost all of them are married. They know a lot about the mentality and irrationality of women and they fear it like poison."[23] Preparing for the convention the following year, he repeated the refrain: "You should try by all means to see the Illinois people (Hiller, Albig, and others) personally and be seen in company with me there, if you want to have any chances of a job. Almost *no one* would take you if they thought you were estranged from me."[24]

Jessie, understandably, was less willing to swallow her resentment. "I have not heard from LaPiere and imagine that there will be prejudice against women," she wrote of the Stanford position in early 1938.[25] As we have seen, she was right. Concerning Reed, she was visibly annoyed. "It seems unfortunate that this should be such a handicap," she wrote six months later, "especially when people consider me better qualified than other people."[26] Spurred by the prospect of a transfer to the Women's Bureau of the Department of Labor in the fall of the 1938, she showed new interest in the situation of women. "I think interpreting the position of women in our society is a worthwhile sociological job and I think I shall want to do it all my life," she wrote Luther, adding that if she got the appointment she would approach the *Nation* and the *New Republic* to review books on women. "In time I should like to write a column about women in our society for some newspaper syndicate, interpreting their problems sociologically. . . . I should like to teach a course on women at one of the local universities."[27]

But just as quickly, she found herself caught in the middle of a feud between two women at the Women's Bureau that apparently doomed the transfer. Meanwhile, a similar disagreement among women in her own office blocked her appointment to work on a new labor study. The result was an end of her talk of writing about women and a new round of scolding from Luther. "IT IS PERFECTLY CLEAR THAT YOUR JUDGEMENT IS ABSOLUTELY WORTHLESS IN THESE MATTERS AT THE PRESENT TIME," he wrote in caps, as she struggled to find work. "THE ONLY THING FOR YOU TO DO NOW IS TO QUIT TRYING TO MAKE ANY DECISIONS FOR YOURSELF."[28]

In the end, Bernard accomodated to the realities, less to please Luther than to realize her own ends. Her desire for a permanent position, not simply for its own sake but as a way to having children, outweighed any inclination to fight the system: first, as she accepted a job beneath her talents at Lindenwood College in 1940; then, as she went to Penn State rather than seek a more prestigious university. If discrimination was a reality, she would at least make the most of it. After the Sweet Briar interview, she suggested that she would have

been willing to lower her salary demands in the hope they might settle
for a woman if the interviewer had made the overture. By this standard, being a woman was almost an advantage. "They could get me
cheaper than anyone of equal qualifications, say $5500," she wrote
Luther of the possibility of the chairmanship at Penn State. "Being a
woman, I would not raise competitive hostilities in other members of
the department. I would make a point of running the department
democratically."[29]

INTELLECTUALLY, Bernard's growing emphasis on role and status and
the functionalist assumptions underlying them, rather than the
organization-disorganization models of her earlier work, also shaped
her conclusions. To Betty Friedan, indeed, functionalism was at the
heart of the problem. " 'The function is' was often translated 'the
function should be,' " she wrote in *The Feminine Mystique*. "By giving
absolute meaning and a sanctimonious value to the generic term
'women's role,' functionalism put American women into a kind of
deep freeze." Classroom textbooks were most flagrant, for example
Henry A. Bowman's *Marriage for Moderns* (1942). But even leading
social scientists were guilty, among them Talcott Parsons, Margaret
Mead, and Mirra Komarovsky, whose *Women in the Modern World*
(1953) Bernard had praised lavishly. "Functionalism was an easy way
out for American sociologists," Friedan continued. "There can be no
doubt that they were describing things 'as they were,' but in so doing,
they were relieved of the responsibility of building theory from facts,
of probing for deeper truth."[30]

Academic Women, although not mentioned by Friedan, was proof of
the pudding. Throughout the book, Bernard took the self-perceived
role and assigned status of women as givens, rather than as the source
of the problem. Concerning attrition between school and college, the
greater willingness of families to invest resources in a son than in a
daughter and the preference of many young women for marriage
were not evidence that discrimination was more complex than one
imagined, but reasons why discrimination was not a factor. Faced with
a situation where sexual stereotypes figured in the "functional" qualifi-

cations for a position (for example, the dean who refused to hire a woman to teach tax economics because she would have to deal with tax assessors and collectors who did not think the role an appropriate one for a woman), Bernard equivocated. The "determined protagonist" might argue that this was just prejudice by another name; but the dean "could probably vindicate his policy." The nature of the feminine "role" likewise explained why women *chose* certain disciplines and certain types of institutions that just happened to lack power and prestige.[31]

To be sure, Bernard never explicitly translated "function is" into "function should be." But she sometimes came close. "Women tend to serve in institutions which emphasize different functions, and they themselves are attracted to different kinds of functions," she noted at one point. Elsewhere she added: "It takes a great many people in many roles to insure that all these services are performed."[32] In the long run, Bernard's adoption of the role-status perspective, like her embrace of motherhood and family, would prove crucial in her formulation of her later feminism in that it focused attention on gender as a category to be taken seriously. But for the time being, it was one reason why *Academic Women* soon came under feminist fire.

———

A *cademic Women*, finally, revealed Bernard's unwillingness or inability to transcend the canons of professionalism and to see the full implications for women as a whole of the organization and specialization of scholarship during her lifetime. Although denying that the restructuring of higher education produced a decline in the proportion of women professors, she conceded that women found certain aspects of university life less congenial than did men: the shift from "local" to "cosmopolitan" orientation; declining emphasis on teaching and the collapse of "the old intimacy of a closed social system" as students led their own lives; and the growing demand for administrative ability as universities increased in size and complexity. At one point she even suggested that the structure of university learning worked against women. "A latent function of discrimination against women," she wrote of the combative ritual of the "defense" of thesis, "is, in fact, to keep learning tough." This statement, if reversed, potentially contradicted her assertion that changes within higher education were not a factor in the decline since 1930. But this reverse connection she could or would not yet make. The rise of modern university training did not add up to a picture of "women seeking positions and being denied," but rather of their "finding alternative investments of time and emotion more rewarding." In short, women wanted it that way.[33]

Contrast this with the view of a recent revisionist—a subtler and richer explanation that not only revises Bernard but in the process helps explain why she saw things as she did. The modernizing of American higher education, Patricia Graham has argued, involved far more than the restructuring of a few elite institutions. Rather, it saw the emergence of a new monolithic standard for all colleges and universities, based not on the classics (as before 1875), but on the generation of new knowledge, the ideal of graduate research. Although American education contained "a strikingly heterogeneous array of acceptable and praiseworthy institutions" from approximately 1875 to 1925, the new standard spelled an end to this diversity, as the normal schools and community colleges, no less than the private colleges and universities, knuckled under. Just as the period of diversity was one of advance for women, so the "loss of variety" was a more serious loss for women than for men.[34]

The reason Bernard could not see the full implications of this transformation was that she had been and remained thoroughly immersed in processes that worked against women generally. One was the rise of the professional ideal, with its shift of emphasis from institution to discipline, from community to professional association, from a toleration of eccentricity and idiosyncrasy to a stoical objectivity. If this ideal violated the essence of traditional assumptions about home, family, and femininity, it was precisely because they rejected these values that both Bernards—Luther and Jessie, the latter sometimes kicking and screaming—lived so completely in a world of scholarly meetings, publications, and professional intrigue. Nor did Jessie personally prefer teaching to scholarship, despite her initial enthusiasm over her students' published efforts. All professors see students as potential thieves, she once wrote: stealing time and energy that might better go to scholarly work. So, likewise, during the fifties, she easily accommodated herself to the image of "man of affairs"—advising government in public policy—apparently unaware that this change diminished the influence of women collectively.

Bernard's own education was part of a process that left a mixed legacy. The vast expansion of undergraduate education through the 1920s brought increased opportunity to young women. But it resulted finally in a proportionate decline of women faculty as nonelite institutions (including some of the women's colleges upon which Bernard based her case), unable to afford the luxury of limiting their undergraduate students to males, sought prestige by hiring more men faculty and administrators. The expansion that benefited Bernard as an undergraduate, that is, contributed to exclusion in the long run.

Finally, Bernard's youthful attempt to combine sexy and brainy mirrored a more general change during the 1920s whereby all American women were increasingly expected to conform to a single standard of looks and behavior—a development not unlike the standardization of speech and even of names among ethnics (one she also knew first-hand). Although piety and purity were no longer central to this feminine ideal, they were replaced by an unstable mix of youth, beauty, and availability, on the one hand, and domesticity, on the other. Unlike its Victorian forerunner, this ideal was quite compatible with college attendance. ("Co-eds Make Good Wives Say Experts," the *Minnesota Daily* reported in Jessie's senior year, quoting the head of Cornell's School of Home Economics: "A college girl can spend her husband's money more intelligently than one who is not college bred.")[35] Graduate school was another matter, since eroticism and sensuality seemed the antithesis of rigorous, rational analysis—a point L.L.B. would not let her forget. One way out of the dilemma was to marry and have children, a choice that Bernard and an increasing number of women Ph.D.s made from the 1940s onward.

WITHIN A DECADE, Bernard would come full circle on most of these issues. Discrimination not only was widespread, she wrote in *Women and the Public Interest,* but posed a threat to the public interest.[36] When

Academic Women was reissued in the early seventies, she publicly re-canted: "I had not pushed my analyses far enough; I had not exam-ined all the forces operating to keep the qualified pool of academic women low."[37]

What underlay this change? Despite Betty Friedan's attack on functionalism and Bernard's own tendency in *Academic Women* to translate function *is* to function *should be,* her changing perspective in one sense was an extension of functionalism. So long as she viewed society through the Parkian competition-cooperation, organization-disorganization model, women *as* women played little part in her analysis.[38] In *American Community Behavior,* neither *women* nor related terms warranted an index entry, but rather appeared only in the context of family disorganization and juvenile delinquency (including the problem of "promiscuous women"). Society depends on families to raise children rather than setting up "common homes" staffed by professionals, she wrote, apparently endorsing the decision. When "the family does the job well, it is a very satisfactory arrangement." When not, the result is juvenile delinquency. And what of women in all this? "Mothers are willing to devote seemingly endless amounts of time and attention to their children if they love them." If not, the result is again social disorganization. "Even if parents have money and are willing to pay [for child care], this is no guarantee that they will be able to find someone else who will do it for them." The commu-nity in its own interest must thus "do everything it can to keep the ideal of family stability alive in all sections of the social structure."[39]

Social Problems at Midcentury, in contrast, revealed how attention to "roles" shifted the focus to women *as* women and to the problems they faced, as now she examined "status anomalies" and "role conflicts" in modern society. "The first lesson to be drawn from the above analysis is the complete futility of blaming women or preaching to them," she wrote, as if at last answering Luther's tirades against the "new woman." "There is no reason to suppose that women are willfully shirking their obligations and duties. . . . It is just that the kind of role performance which was possible a hundred years ago, is not possible at the present time." Much of her analysis, she added in a footnote, was indebted to Mirra Komarovsky's "perceptive" study of *Women in the Modern World.*[40]

Bernard herself noted the new uses to which functionalism could be put. The functionalist paradigm, she wrote to her graduate student biographer, "became one of the major weapons of the young radicals when they attacked the status quo, even tho young sociologists snickered when the very word was used at the meeting of the ESS [Eastern Sociological Society] in 1970."[41] So viewed, even *Academic Women* may have been more subversive than it appeared on the surface. Such was the testimony of a woman sociologist who wrote Bernard that the book had helped her at the time to "formulate my own situation and to talk to others," wondering more generally if it "did not provide part of the background build-up that preceded and made possible the women's movement."[42]

This indirect debt did not keep Bernard from jumping on the antifunctionalist bandwagon in the early 1970s, as criticism of the Parsonian paradigm mounted. "How come a man who got his degree at Columbia is such a devoted Parsonian?" she wrote Terry Clark of the University of Chicago.[43] To a doctoral student preparing a thesis on her work, she wrote "that the whole concentration on functionalism in the 1950s cast a terrible blight on sociology." In a sense, of course, "all sociology is functionalism," she continued. She herself had adopted some Parsonian terms simply because they had become "coin of the realm." But she had not accepted what she called his *systemism*. "And, oh boy, how wrong much of his applications of his theories proved to be! And how really ridiculous some of his theorizing about family and women look today."[44]

The debt was real nonetheless. Although the notion that assigned roles are a necessary part of a well-integrated social system could in theory lead to acceptance of the status quo, Bernard's awareness of role-playing in practice sensitized her to the forces that contribute to female subordination. At the same time it alerted her to the dysfunctional nature of a too exclusive division of roles (for example, father-the-provider, mother-the-domestic-specialist) and conflict among functions (for example, reproductive and child-care functions interfering with labor-force participation). Feminist critics of Parsons "point out that it is one thing to analyze the way social structures operate," she noted looking back on her own development, "but quite another to accept the sexual allocation of functions in any given system as intrinsic to social systems." Such was the result of the departure begun in her prefeminist *Social Problems at Midcentury,* and developed in *Women and the Public Interest* and her later feminist writings.[45]

Whether or not Bernard misread her debt to functionalist analysis, the result was a new sensitivity to the realities of discrimination, and a personal crusade to do something about it. Her education in this regard began with the reception to *Academic Women,* as scholars ignored its conservative implications to focus on the fact of discrimination.[46] Others wrote directly to Bernard, chronicling discrimination in their own cases. "As it turns out, there is a giant split in the department between the quantitative people and the qualitative people, a split I didn't take too seriously until recently," one soon-to-be-prominent young sociologist wrote Bernard of her department at a major university. "With the growing recession and no FTEs [full-time teaching equivalents] for sociology next year, the split has widened and that has contributed to the negative notes ('We have to get her out to make room for our bright young quantitative man')." Although they might accept a woman, she continued, a woman, a feminist, and a qualitative sociologist was too much. When the department considered her case, she was introduced as thirty-four years old, married, and the mother of a three-year-old, whereas no male candidates were similarly described. When this same person was looking for a job two years later, Bernard in support wrote puckishly: "Please do not be put off by the fact that she is young and beautiful."[47]

At the same time, Bernard moved beyond a narrowly civil rights approach to women's issues—the focus of older "liberal" feminism. "The term *sexism* was brilliant," she wrote in *Women and the Public Interest,* describing the importance of this concept in her transformation on this point. "More than prejudice alone had been responsible for discrimination in the past and its continuance into the present." Young women now saw that discrimination ("oppression" as they now termed it) was "built into all our institutions. The term [sexism] became essential in the study of sex relations as it had in race relations, because adverse discrimination was surviving legal banning."[48]

Replying to an article in the May 1970 issue of *Playboy,* she expanded the point: "There are two separate, though related issues in the modern woman's movement, one discrimination and one sexism."

Indeed, if one sets up things correctly, "one does not need discrimination; the same result is achieved automatically." Rather than a deliberate act, sexism was "the unconscious, taken-for-granted, assumed, unquestioned, unexamined, unchallenged acceptance of the belief that the world as it looks to men is the only world, that the way of dealing with it which men have created is the only way."[49]

This discovery of sexism did not end the debate, nor did Bernard go as far as most younger "radical," socialist, and other more extreme feminists were demanding by the early 1970s. On the spectrum of feminism, the emphasis on female roles and consciousness-raising would ultimately seem little more than an attenuation of liberal individualism.[50] Yet, for this very reason, some in the early years judged her an especially effective champion of the cause. "Bernard is an old pro, as a writer as well as a sociologist," wrote one editor, evaluating the manuscript of *Women and the Public Interest*. "And while she writes in basic sympathy with the new feminists, she is never shrill—as they so often are, and she maintains a complexity of perspective that opens up directions of thoughtful consideration rather than closing them off."[51] Shrill or no, she had in any case come a long way since she stood before her class at Princeton a decade before. If Friedan and functionalism were part of the reason, there was also considerably more to it.

8
Single Parent (1951–1968)

> There is no way a woman can come through a day-by-day account of her relations with her children as a heroine.
> —Jessie Bernard, *Self-Portrait of a Family*

When Bernard decided to leave Penn State in 1964, she considered various locations ("cased the joint," as she put it, with a growing fondness for colloquialisms). The options, as she saw them, would not have surprised most academics: Berkeley-San Francisco, Cambridge-Boston, New York, or Washington. "There was scarcely any contest," she recalled: "It had to be Washington." There she had had her first taste of freedom in the late 1930s. There she had done much of the research for *Origins of American Sociology*. There she had just finished *Academic Women*. "I never regretted that choice," she wrote more than two decades later.[1]

In several ways, the 1960s brought new opportunities and a new sense of freedom. For one thing, she could now indulge her instinctive eclecticism and interdisciplinary interests. Although none of her works had been "bona fide textbooks,"[2] she was never entirely able to ignore the academic penchant for dividing human knowledge into ever-smaller chunks. For another, her audience changed, if not in the type of persons she addressed, at least in the settings in which she addressed them. Conferences became surrogates for university collegiality; the informality of the college circuit replaced the classroom. Finally, and perhaps most importantly, Washington turned out to be *the* prima city of talented, brilliant women, a fact that Bernard had never so clearly appreciated before. For all these reasons, the books she wrote in her retirement years were not the same ones she most likely would have written had she stayed at Penn State.

Bernard's new works also owed a general debt to the social ferment of the decade. Just as her earlier publications bore the imprint of one or another of her mentors—Ogburn, L.L.B., and Chapin, editor of the series in which *American Family Behavior* appeared—so now different editors and new times shaped her interests. In the case of *Remarriage* (1956), it was Stanley Burnshaw, founder of Dryden Press; in that of *Marriage and Family among Negroes* (1966), it was a request to work on a Children's Bureau study of unwed black mothers. *Women and the Public Interest* began as a position paper for the Democratic campaign of 1968. By this time Bernard also took the initiative, for the first time writing books on subjects that she chose rather than someone else. Each of these, as it happened, showed evidence of her deepening commitment to feminism: obliquely in *The Sex Game*, more forcefully in *The Future of Marriage*, and finally, most personally in *Self-Portrait of a Family*.

In another way the 1960s were also a time of trial, as Bernard's three children brought home some less happy aspects of the decade. Her oldest child and only daughter, Dorothy Lee (b. 1941), taught the most, as she moved through elite boarding schools and universities, and finally into a star-crossed marriage. One lesson was the precarious position of young American women caught between pressures to succeed academically and an ideal of femininity that undercut these values. Another was the great thirst of the young for a cause. During a junior year abroad in London (1961–1962) Bernard's daughter first embraced the Coalition for Nuclear Disarmament, and with it a young man of working-class background and vaguely socialist views, then a Harvard stop-out whom she met in Morocco the following summer and later married. For the rest of the decade, mother and daughter watched this love die as "Brick" (as Bernard called him in *Self-Portrait of a Family*) systematically snuffed out his promise with drugs and alcohol.[3]

Bernard's two sons meanwhile taught lessons somewhat less painful but no less important. From Claude, the oldest son (b. 1945), it was the trauma of the Vietnam escalation, as war transformed his plan to be a foreign service officer into two years of alternate service as a conscientious objector, followed by a career in school teaching. From David (b. 1950, shortly before L.L.B. died), it was the chilling realization that a single mother could never quite replace a father. As mother and son grew apart physically and emotionally, this son talked privately of suicide, experimented with marijuana, and finally jettisoned a planned career in sociology for one in environmental medicine, a move that seemed to his mother to be a deliberate rebuke.[4]

Together, these experiences formed the background to Bernard's "conversion" to feminism in the late 1960s. At least two elements in this conversion were common to other academic women who joined the movement: a growing discontent with professionalism and bureaucracy within academia, which, when not openly biased, seemed to couple opportunity for women with a denial of feminine values; and the development of a communications network, created in part by the sixties college circuit, in part by the greater availability of mimeographing and finally of photoduplication (Bernard's feminist writing, as one critic later noted, relied heavily on "fugitive literature").[5] But a third factor—the "precipitating crisis," in the language of sociological analysis—was more intensely personal, as Bernard struggled with single parenthood and her children's coming of age against a background of the 1960s revolution in manners and morals.[6]

════════════════════

Although Luther's death in 1951 left Jessie with three young children, the full impact of single motherhood was delayed for several years. Within a short time, if not already, she was involved in a serious though finally unsatisfactory relationship with a Penn State colleague, the chairman of the department that hired her and later a dean of the university. Like Luther in better days, "Ezra" (as she later called him in *Self-Portrait of a Family*) was a model of WASP manhood, although softer and more sympathetic. Born and educated in Pennsylvania, a year younger than she, he had served as a Protestant minister for several years before seeking his doctorate in sociology. Called to service as navy chaplain during World War II, he participated in a dozen South Pacific campaigns, for which he received numerous campaign stars. "How did I love Ezra?" Bernard told her son David a quarter-century later; "I couldn't count the ways. And he was handsome. The very prototype of every 'tall, dark, and handsome' hero in romantic literature."[7]

For his part, Ezra admired Jessie from the start. When most other chairmen were saying they would "love to hire Jessie, but didn't think they could cope with LLB," Ezra alone was "supremely confident that he could handle the situation," Bernard recalled years later. Even before the Bernards arrived, Luther was "Dr. Bernard," and she "Dr. Jessie," a potentially patronizing reference softened by an assurance that Penn State had never in his knowledge discriminated against women. Eventually their relationship was more than collegial. "He shot me up the academic ladder to the top in record time," Bernard later wrote with characteristic candor. "Even before we became lovers." During the final months of Luther's illness, Ezra came almost daily to offer help and support, and for the next two and a half years was lover to Jessie and surrogate father to the children, the only one the younger Bernard boy ever knew. In spirit, at least, family was intact.[8]

Unfortunately, Ezra was also married and soon over his head in alcohol. Although Penn State officials asked only that he not embarrass the university publicly, town authorities were less tolerant. When a public incident sparked a crisis neither could ignore, Jessie extricated herself by taking a sabbatical in Europe, planning and hoping that Ezra would join her family there. Her plan was to study sociological research in postwar Europe—"wholly legitimate," she later noted somewhat defensively, but promising a "psychological" rather than a scholarly payoff.[9]

During the academic year 1953–1954, she thus ventured abroad for the first time since the mid-1930s, this time not to Paris alone, but to Graz, with three young children. Practicality dictated the location, since Austria was then one of the cheapest countries in Europe. Unfortunately, Graz had also been a cradle of nazism, a legacy that lingered (so Bernard concluded) in prejudice against her youngest son if not herself, the local assumption being that anyone named David must be a Jew. Just as Ezra had blunted the full impact of single parenthood, so the United States cultural attaché in Graz now assumed a similar role, providing numerous contacts and even looking after the boys during her absences. Meanwhile, Bernard waited for word from Ezra. But when the letter finally arrived, the answer was no: he would not be joining them. What was to have been a new start at family became overnight an apprenticeship for "solo motherhood."[10]

Adjusting to this "stark fact" was not easy, Bernard later wrote, in an account that described the surface of these events but only hinted at their effect on her. Her first response was a trip through Spain with a woman friend. Eventually, her trips took her also to the Balkans and much of northern Europe. By the following May, she had stopped going to Graz's Amerika Haus to check the *New York Times* for the weather in the city to which Ezra had moved.[11]

Despite his desertion, Ezra remained emotionally a part of her life. A decade later, as Dorothy Lee stood on the threshold of an ill-fated marriage, Ezra paid her a call, their first meeting since his departure. "He was smaller than I remembered and has white hair but very attractive," she wrote her mother of the meeting, adding that he seemed to have sympathy for her fiancé Brick, an understanding rooted in his own earlier experiences with alcoholism. When in the late 1960s Bernard's youngest son was struggling with personal and emotional problems, she appealed to Ezra again to intervene as the only father the boy had ever known. When Ezra remarried a few years later, she wrote to him and his new wife to explain "why I love him so dearly and always will." While drafting an account of their affair for *Self-Portrait of a Family,* she wrote lightheartedly to offer to change his name for publication, but supposed no one would any longer care about this bit of ancient history. When he made it clear that he indeed *did* care, Bernard decided to seal this chapter of her life from further scrutiny.[12]

Although one must thus guess at the full impact of the episode on her development, Bernard's hopes in these years appeared between the lines in *Remarriage,* a textbook-cum-monograph published two years after her return from Graz but written during the Ezra years—a book that owed so much to his collaboration, Bernard claimed, that his name would have been on the title page save for his "modesty." Stripped of its many charts and tables (e.g., "The Frequency of Attitudinal and Nonattitudinal Variables Associated with Success in Remarriage"), this pioneering inquiry challenged conventional wisdom on several points: remarriage *was* marriage (not some inferior copy); it was not necessarily harmful to children (although younger children fared better than teenagers); and it enjoyed a higher success rate than most people believed. Already on the increase, remarriage would most likely continue to grow, especially as divorce came to be seen as an acceptable way out of a bad union. A brief "*apologia* for love in the middle and later years" (as she later characterized one section) captured some of the feeling she had experienced with Ezra. But a hint of pathos also crept in, in a remark that modern life had "attenuated the concept of duty as related to family life," leaving "little but the slender support of love and satisfaction" to sustain it. Still looking to "science" for salvation, Bernard in conclusion suggested ways that sociologists might predict success or failure in remarriage.[13]

Although reviewed less widely than many of her other works, *Remarriage* received a favorable if somewhat mixed reception. The notices in the two major sociological journals applauded Bernard for tackling a subject too often ignored, but regretted her attempt to layer her conclusions with charts and statistics. The textbook/monograph hybrid was "neither fish nor fowl," complained Meyer Nimkoff, a sociologist who had earlier collaborated with William Ogburn on an extremely successful text. The second reviewer wondered whether sociology really had the "frame of reference and the research tools" to cope effectively with such a complex subject. Citing Bernard's use of one well-known study of "adjustment" in remarriage, he asked: "Really, now, what 'facts' do we have here for widely disseminated conclusions?"[14]

Whether because or in spite of her statistics, Bernard could nonetheless claim that she had the best of the argument by the time *Remarriage* was reissued fifteen years later: remarriages among divorced men and women had increased markedly and were lasting longer; indeed, for the women involved, just as long as first marriages. The need and possibility of love and sex throughout life was increasingly recognized. Concepts like "limited commitment," "two-step marriage," and serial monogamy could mean that "the very institutions of marriage and remarriage may become attenuated with time," she now speculated. But for now her original findings still seemed valid.[15]

By this time, however, the stakes were different than in the early

1950s. In theory at least, Bernard in her own case left open the possibility of remarriage for a decade or more, while continuing to enjoy the attentions of men. "Yesterday a young man tried to pick me up on the streets of NY," she reported to her youngest son in her sixty-sixth year. "I am grateful—not proud, not conceited—that, even at my advanced age, I still appeal to men." But, as the preface to the new edition of *Remarriage* suggested, her interest in the subject had subtly shifted. Then it was defense of remarriage as a necessary adjustment if the companionate family were to survive; now, the implications of the increase in remarriage for the emancipation of women.[16]

In the fall of 1954 Bernard returned to Penn State, to the house she and Luther had purchased seven years before. A sizable living room, five bedrooms, and a study proved ample space for the four Bernards and the housekeeper who lived in during the weekdays. A large picture window, added soon after the return from Austria, provided an arresting view of the nearby mountains, while others looked out on a lush garden. "The view from our back windows is heavenly with all the flowers and blooming trees," Jessie wrote to Dorothy Lee several years later. "We really are lucky to live in such a lovely spot."[17]

But households, as Bernard already knew, also take care, and on this score, her earlier experiences cannot have been cheering. Throughout their married life, Luther had assumed many of the chores, including buying and cooking the food. But his behavior suggested that the househusband may not always be the answer to a woman's prayer. "He constantly nags me," Jessie wrote on one occasion, chronicling his many complaints about the way she conducted her portion of the household duties. One day it was the soap she had bought; the next, that she did so poor a job tucking in the covers of his bed that "they didn't even cover him." He would give up bathing, he threatened, because he always had to let out the water she had left in the tub.[18]

Jessie meanwhile had her own grounds for complaint. During the thirties she became increasingly critical of the clutter of their apartments and an unorthodox living style wherein Luther often worked nonstop all day and retired to bed immediately after supper. "It goes back to your childhood when you didn't have enough of anything," she wrote of his pack-rat compulsions. "And now you have lots of everything. So that wherever you live tends to become a warehouse." She also wanted more power over household affairs. "If I had had it in my power to determine our style of living and the power to make decisions and spend money we should have lived much more normally, it seems to me," she began one diatribe. "I should probably have spent more for housing and household maintenance, but in the long run it would have been worth while because of increased efficiency and also greater happiness and contentment on my part." Since she knew how he felt about money, she was not anxious to spend for spending's sake. "But I should like to have enough money to have an orderly and clean home and someone to help me keep [it] orderly."[19]

The need for child care during the Lindenwood years compounded the problem when the arrival of help in the form of her sister-in-law, Helen Bernard, brought new tension. A decade earlier, Helen had already complained to Luther that their mother could not live in his home "on account of the disorder and confusion [there]." After fourteen months with the Bernards in St. Louis she told her brother that their "greatest cause of trouble with neighbors" was their neglect of their property and garbage. To this she added complaints about Jessie's permissive treatment of the children ("D.L. runs around naked at 6. Claude went up to the street last summer in Laramie naked") at the same time that she (Jessie) boasted "that she was an authority on family and childrearing—& on marriage." Helen also chided her brother for doing the housework: "You waste such a great deal of energy on small household duties—even cooking, planning use of food, supervising the family. Things which certainly, in our social culture, belong to women not professional men."[20]

Luther closed this circle of complaint in his diary. Not only did he do most of the cooking, but Jessie by the late 1940s refused even to take meals with the family because she liked different foods. "So tonight," he continued this particular entry, "I tried to get some understanding by asking J. what proposals she had to restore some community to the meals." Nor did her level of child care meet his ever-crankier standard.

"J. attributed [the baby's] crying to her being in another room, not to the [word illegible] he ate—some more brushing off," he wrote of their two-year-old son. "She can always rationalize any situation with a justification of her own behavior."[21]

In the years immediately after Luther's death, Ezra assumed many of the chores, again shielding Jessie from the full burdens of single parenthood. His departure accordingly left a conspicuous gap. "Handymen were always hard to find," Bernard recalled, especially "for the almost daily nagging little maintenance and upkeep chores which are the bane of every household." Fortunately, her oldest son, Claude, soon stepped into the breach—changing fuses, fixing screens, building shelves, repairing furniture. After leaving for boarding school at age fourteen, Claude continued to offer advice by mail, concerning a malfunctioning TV, for example, or a window pane broken by police when Jessie locked herself out of her house. From handyman, Claude soon graduated to assistant, even surrogate spouse, as his mother increasingly put him in charge of his younger brother.[22]

For Bernard's part, "the banalities of homemaking" (as she called them) were from the start an annoyance at best, a curse at worst. "You wrote me that you hoped I wouldn't settle into complacency as a housewife," a former student wrote her during the Lindenwood years, adding that she unfortunately had "done absolutely nothing constructive" as a result of the demands homemaking had placed upon her.[23] By the late 1960s, the mounting frustrations of caring for her own home helped cure her of the last of her earlier fantasies concerning "normal" home life. In *The Future of Marriage* she accordingly saved some of her sharpest barbs for housework and housewifery. " 'The housewife is a nobody,' " she wrote, quoting the psychologist Philip Slater, "and almost everyone agrees." However important a part of the infrastructure of production, housework is a "dead-end job; there is no chance of promotion." As with marriage generally, the destructive effect of "housewives' syndrome" was a matter of fact, not conjecture, since working married women were "overwhelmingly better off" than nonworking wives with respect to eleven of twelve symptoms of mental distress. "In terms of the number of people involved," she concluded, "the housewife syndrome might well be viewed as Public Health Problem Number One."[24]

When it came to the children, Bernard fortunately had money, a commodity often in short supply among single mothers. After many difficult years financially—particularly following a disastrous stock market loss in 1931—she finally profited from Luther's parsimony and some shrewd investments of her own. At the time of his death, the value of the estate in stocks alone amounted to more than twenty thousand dollars, a not insubstantial sum. But, after observing IBM's "Think" motto posted in the more obscure corners of Europe during her year abroad, she parlayed this portfolio into sky-rocketing IBM shares, whose dividends eventually replaced her academic salary.[25]

On the surface, Bernard's single parenthood was thus partly a story of the things money makes possible: an endless succession of baby sitters, a live-in housekeeper, summer camps, and private schools. The summer after Luther's death, Claude at age seven was packed off to camp, a decision his mother later openly regretted. Arriving in Ostende in the fall of 1953, she left twelve-year old Dorothy Lee in sole charge of her brothers, an act that later "dumfounded" friends and colleagues and even gave Bernard second thoughts.[26] For Dorothy Lee, the remainder of youth was a series of the best private schools: the International School in Geneva (1953–1954), the George School near Philadelphia (1954–1959), and finally Sarah Lawrence. For her brothers a similar path led to George School and Sidwell Friends and then college at Johns Hopkins and Haverford respectively. For the family it meant occasional exotic trips (for example, to Panama and Central America in the summer of 1957), alternating with frequent separations as their mother's professional career took off. Since Bernard did not drive (the result, she claimed, of being traumatized by an accident in her youth when her father had almost killed a young boy with their new Nash), she was spared the "mother-chauffeur trap" even when at home. "True I had qualms," Bernard later confessed of the self-reliance this regimen forced on her children. "But, as I so often reminded them . . . I could not afford to have children who could not look after themselves."[27]

Money also affected family relationships more directly. Professional mothers of the fifties and sixties dealt with conflicting pressures in various ways, Bernard concluded after attending the Twelve Professional Women conference years later. One restricted herself to a single conference per school year, and took the children along after they were five. Another preached the value of sacrifice to the children, while a third extolled the virtues of having a working mother. In contrast, Bernard now admitted, she bought them off. In family letters, talk of money abounded: from her son's early IOUs for a loan granted for some purchase or other to mundane banking matters later. "I was always wracked by the temptation to buy the children off," she conceded. But, she added, "it was a solution not without its own peculiar psychological hazards."[28]

Despite her resources and her toughmindedness, a chief hazard for Bernard herself was a guilt that was palpable, not only in retrospect, but throughout her years as single parent. "I sometimes think this was not a good thing," she wrote to thirteen-year-old Dorothy concerning the year in Geneva. Later she viewed the first term at the George School as one of the "worst times" in her daughter's life. When, in later years, Dorothy Lee expressed fears of losing her mother, either through death or as a result of her own domestic crisis, Bernard's guilt flooded back. Was this "a residue from the times I used to leave you with babysitters?" she asked. "Or from having only one parent?"[29] In the case of the boys, and especially the younger, a succession of memories further tugged at her conscience: of a three year old waiting each day at the door for her homecoming; of complaints of being "banished," first to camp, then to the far corners of Europe; of being forced to attend kindergarten; of sleeping in his mother's bed "frequently" during the Graz year. "I used to laugh at myself," she wrote years later, "saying that I deserted my own family to talk to other people about families."[30]

Although this guilt sometimes surfaced directly (in countless apologies for not attending this or that function, for example, or in a tendency to overpraise their every effort),[31] it also showed indirectly in an insistence that the children's difficulties stemmed from the absence of a father, a lingering testament of Bernard's earlier belief in the "ideal" family. As related to Dorothy in the late fifties, the story went as follows: "You were born to parents who were pretty old to have children, but who adored you. . . . Your father read to you almost before you could understand words. He took you on long walks, he made you feel important. It was a great shock when you lost him."[32] Part of Bernard must have known there was more to it. Until the arrival of Claude—or so her sister-in-law, Helen, alleged at the time—Bernard had allowed Dorothy Lee to "monopolize her" and become "extremely dependent" upon her. "Now suddenly she is shut out completely," Helen continued, urging Luther to provide the necessary emotional security. Moreover, even as Luther played this role, Jessie herself had seen that father and daughter were on a "collision course" before his death. "At nine, she was only beginning to resent the iron hand in the velvet glove," she wrote in a passage apparently intended for (but not included in) *Self Portrait of a Family* "—less and less velvety as death crept up on him in the last year."[33]

By the late fifties the story assumed the proportions of family myth, designed at once to glorify Luther in his daughter's memory and to provide a father figure for the boys. To Jessie, a comment from Dorothy Lee in the mid-1950s that it seemed "forever" since her father had died was proof of the story, although the remark could as easily have been read as a sign of fading memory. In time, the absent father also explained most family problems, whether Dorothy Lee's marriage ("She lost her father when she was 9 and has no model since then of a normal husband-wife relationship," Bernard wrote to a psychiatrist they were consulting); her older son's lack of confidence (the result of being raised in a house with two strong-minded women and no father figure); or her younger son's emotional difficulties ("We have often spoken of the deprivation you felt in not having a father").[34]

While conventional assumptions concerning fathers and family nourished guilt, "scientific" opinion lent it authority. Among Dorothy Lee's early difficulties, few troubled Bernard as much as her apparent inability to spell: "recomended" for "recommended"; "elimanated" for "eliminated." Not that serious in the scheme of things, but at the time occasion for constant admonition, even a list of misspelled words along with corrections. By age fifteen Dorothy had had enough. "Nothing makes me happier," she wrote sarcastically, "than to receive your letters, especially when you fill them with my spelling mistakes."

As in the mid-1930s with her own marriage, Bernard turned to psychology for help, only again to be told that her failure to play a proper womanly role was the problem. Her daughter's refusal to spell correctly marked a "symbolic rejection" of her mother's career, a psychologist at the clinic insisted, a retaliation for perceived maternal rejection. Only several years later did Bernard see the absurdity of this "ridiculous" analysis when Dorothy was diagnosed as having a mild form of dyslexia. At the time, it "laid a heavy load of guilt on me."[35]

A final manifestation of guilt, as the spelling exchange suggests, was an endless analysis of the children's problems ("overmanaging," one reviewer of *Self-Portrait of a Family* charitably termed it), coupled with the suggestion that their separation from their mother was responsible.[36] At one level it was simple nagging: about spending too much money on clothes; about grades; about smoking, overeating, and overweight ("when I see a boy of 18 permitting a certain grossness to creep up on him I think it is time to pay attention").[37]

At another level it was analysis, often overanalysis, the worse for being probably true most of the time. "I believe it is beginning to dawn on you that growing up into adult responsibilities isn't much fun," she lectured sixteen-year-old Dorothy Lee at another painful time in her junior year at the George school. "You have been able to meet most life tests so far just on the basis of being a lovely attractive girl. But that isn't going to be enough." Perhaps also in her "unconscious" was a fear of forming adult relationships with boys, but "I am not sure." Maybe it would be better after all if she returned to Penn State for college. "A mother ought to be with a girl when she goes through these growing pains, don't you think?" As preface to all this Bernard noted: "You will reject this analysis because you don't like it, but here it is anyway." Years later, when Dorothy's marriage was falling apart, the message was different but the prelude the same: "I know you hate to have me sociologize, but. . . ."[38]

Bernard's sons also received the benefit of her expertise. Although Claude was in the top 10 percent on quantitative tests and top 13 percent verbally, she wrote to him at one point, he appeared to lack self-confidence. "If it is true we must find out why." "Perhaps [your sister and I] have undermined your self-confidence. Having an older sister may have made you too passive." A few years later the problem was "defensiveness." "When you have studied enough psychology you will understand why the personality has to have defense mechanisms," she wrote, offering to send a copy of Anna Freud's *Ego and Its Defenses*. But in his case it had gone too far. "Does it ever occur to you that maybe, just maybe, I might be right once in awhile?" she continued with a frustration all too familiar to parents of adolescents. "That 60 is bigger than 18?"[39]

In the wake of the youngest son's problems in the late 1960s, Bernard again could not resist blaming herself. "I have often felt that I didn't give any of my children the close body contact children need," she wrote to him years later. "Not enough hugging and kissing." Perhaps it was best to face the pain, maybe even to let it out in tears. Yet in the very act of giving this advice she was in a "catch-22 spot," since her role of analyst made it more difficult for him to follow the advice given. "On the one side I am suggesting that you reexperience the pain of the deprivation and, on the other, I am trying to help you control it. So you are, in effect, damned if you do and damned if you don't."[40]

Applied to her own years of serving as mother and analyst, this insight poignantly expressed the central tension of Bernard's career: between emotion and control, feeling and intellect, feminine and masculine. As she attempted to play mother and father in the single-parent years, she steered an uneven course between emotional support and harsh criticism, permissiveness and convention. The result, as she later put it, was "a Hamlet-like ambivalence . . . with a powerful superego overseeing the whole process."[41]

Would things have been different had Luther lived longer? if Bernard had married Ezra? if the children had not been raised in a single-parent household? These questions, although easy to debate in the abstract, are more difficult to answer definitively in any single case. What can be said is that, in the absence of any alternative models of family or even of single motherhood, Bernard fell back on assumptions concerning "normal" family life that she first nurtured during her four-year crusade to have children and later developed in her earlier sociological writings. At times she was mother; at other times father. Meanwhile, talk of the absent male made up for any shortcomings.

GIVING ADVICE concerning dating and mating, Bernard mingled convention and sympathy with a growing concern with the "feminine mystique," most especially in her relations with Dorothy Lee. Convention and sympathy came first. Although mother and daughter early sparred over the amount of freedom a young girl should have (concerning a proposed trip to Florida in the company of some boys, for example), the greater problem was Dorothy's apparent disinterest in the opposite sex. Although attractive to boys, she confessed at age seventeen that she found their advances unappealing. "Am I normal?" she wondered. Bernard in reply outlined the essentialist view of sexual difference that in one form or other informed her thinking throughout life. After assuring her daughter that her feelings were quite "normal" since girls matured at different rates, she cautioned her not to make men feel that "you disapprove of them . . . or feel superior to them because of their stronger sex drives, which, after all, were built into them and were not of their own doing." Women, she added, "would not want it any other way." For the same reason, she hoped that Dorothy did not envy men their freedom or feel competitive with them, but rather enjoyed "being a woman."[42]

When a troubled Dorothy returned from her year abroad, a year of sexual experimentation, Bernard walked a tightrope between permissiveness and convention. "As you well know, I have never been one to believe that a few years of virginity before marriage were worth fifty years of inhibition after marriage," she wrote in response to a "senior year depression" her daughter was experiencing back at Sarah Lawrence. But she had to point out that this normal state of affairs was "complicated . . . by the fact that it coincides with a certain phase of your sexual development." "I am not being critical," she added, "just explanatory." Seeking help, she wrote a psychiatrist early the next year (1963) that one possible cause was the absence in the home of a "conventional feminine model."[43]

To Claude, Bernard's advice was similar, although the flip side of the same conventions. "Girls like masculine men but not brutes," she wrote as he was about to leave for college in the summer of 1963. "And being masculine means you don't have to put on a blustering act." She continued: "Women like to feel like women and masculine men do it for them. Don't act as though girls were just like boys. They are different and the difference should be enjoyed. Not by running down the feminine approach but by playing it up in an appreciative way." A few weeks later she added: "During the next few years you will have to make the two most important decisions of your life—mate and career." As to the first, he should look for "a mate who will encourage you socially, make the programs and contacts for a good social life. . . . A wife who will make an attractive home to which you can invite your friends and who will make friends for you will round out your life."[44]

In Dorothy's case, however, there could be too much of a good thing—a fact that worried Bernard increasingly after her reading of Betty Friedan's *Feminine Mystique* as she was finishing *Academic Women* that same year. For some time, Dorothy Lee had been sending out disturbing signals on this score. "It's funny," she wrote early in her first year at college, "but just from the few months I've been here I am convinced that at a certain age boys take over from girls intellectually because the really creative thinking seems to come from them." When the following year she received only an average grade on a law aptitude test, she again retreated into femininity. "I have no desire to be treated as an equal in a man's world," she wrote her mother. "I'd just as soon be a woman and be treated as one."[45] Initially, Bernard let such statements pass without comment. But when it appeared that Dorothy Lee was ready to sacrifice herself to this ideal by marrying a drug-crippled college dropout without ambition or prospects, the issue of the "feminine mystique" assumed new urgency.

⸻

As the United States came apart in the mid-1960s, Bernard saw her hopes for her children's futures also unravel one by one. One set of problems, the less serious as it turned out, concerned Claude. By his final years at boarding school, the signs were already visible in his reluctance to come home for holidays or weekends and his failure to phone or send a card for Mother's Day. In their form and frequency, she decided, his letters from Johns Hopkins told much of the story: increasingly illegible handwriting ("a form . . . of self-hiding"); an impersonal tone (a "third person newspaper format"); and fewer and fewer letters as the years went by. Like his father half a century before (already probably unknown to him), Claude poured his confusion and bitterness into poems and colloquies ("You talk of hope. . . . But for me there is no hope"). Although mother and son had planned a career for him in the foreign service, he now experimented with various occupations from stockbroker to theater technician. During 1967, he shared the antiwar passion then sweeping American campuses, finally accepting alternative service as a conscientious objector during the next two years.[46]

By this time, however, Claude's problems took a back seat to those stemming from Dorothy's courtship and marriage, a situation that reached crisis proportions by the summer of 1967. The relationship, as Bernard later told it, was doomed from the start. "Brilliant, beautiful, talented, Brick came out of the Southwest, more as troubadour than as Lochnivar," she wrote in *Self-Portrait of a Family*, the literary reference masking her true feelings. After three "miserable years" at Harvard, he left for Europe with his guitar, playing first for the armed forces, then for anyone who would listen in Paris and finally Tangiers. There Dorothy met him in a communal household, "sick and demoralized." Although each month brought new and more disturbing evidence of irresponsibility, alcohol and drug addiction, and even mental illness, Bernard presented a cordial front to her future son-in-law while privately urging Dorothy not to sacrifice herself to an apparently hopeless cause. When the wedding finally occurred (December 1963), Bernard bowed to the inevitable. Perhaps an "authentic miracle" was in the making, she wrote in congratulations, suggesting that each had had a positive influence on the other. But, as it turned out, her initial fears were better founded. As a result, the next four years were in many respects the worst in a life not noted for its tranquillity.[47]

For all its candor, Bernard's account in *Self-Portrait of a Family* skirted these darkest days, only hinting at the emotional toll they took. From the time Dorothy returned from Tangiers, mother and daughter rode an emotional roller coaster. Should Dorothy marry Brick between terms in her senior year at Sarah Lawrence? Should she join him in Mexico, where he decided to find himself as a writer (a replay, in fact, of a similar debate Jessie had had with Luther in the darkest days of their marriage in 1938)? When the Mexican quest came to nothing, the couple moved in with Bernard until Brick resumed his studies at Harvard in the fall of 1965. After his graduation the following June, things continued their downward spiral: alcoholic binges, brief success with an insurance firm, then hospitalization after total collapse during an insurance indoctrination session in Hartford.

By the spring of 1967, this worsening situation drove Bernard to near desperation. As throughout her career, she had mobilized all the resources of intellect and learning she could muster, filling pages of analysis to psychiatrists, to herself, and above all to her daughter. Initially, she assumed that the fault lay in a failure in the socialization of "proper" sex roles, a revealing analysis given her advice to her children in the years immediately before. Why was their relation so "tender, gentle, and playful rather than passionate"? she wondered. Had Dorothy Lee, despite having a "very feminine psychology" in wishing to be loved and approved, rejected femininity in a quest for an intellectual standard her father had set for her? Was Brick latently homosexual ("His novella, he reported, had homosexual overtones," Bernard noted)? After three years of frustration, however, she was simply puzzled. "I do not know how sensible it is to view such a relationship as "sick" or "neurotic," she confided to yet another psychiatrist, frankly asking for guidance. "The rewards must make the costs seem worthwhile."[48]

In letters to Dorothy, Bernard's appeals veered from scholarly interpretation to sympathy to old-fashioned anger. Perhaps "game theory" would help in projecting the future, she suggested at one point. Whatever happened, it was Dorothy above all that she cared about. Then, anger born of frustration: "I have before me a whole file of letters and notes I have written to you in the last ten days when I have been able to think of little else than you," she prefaced some harsh words in early August. "All of them are sympathetic, designed to build you up and help you cope. Today my mood is different."[49]

By this time Bernard feared for her own mental health. In late July she drew up anguished lists of "Points to Discuss with DLB." "[Brick's] message: I want out. I want you to take care of me, protect me, but I want to be free and irresponsible," she noted, preparing for their confrontation. "He will always desert her in crisis. She will never be able to count on him." Behind this indictment were vivid memories of the many times her son-in-law had let her daughter down, perhaps even of Ezra's effective desertion of her: the failure to show up as promised the Thanksgiving after their return from Tangiers, for example, or most recently, an apparently deliberate affront when Brick took off to New York on Dorothy's birthday. "I take it as a personal assault," Bernard wrote in early August, in a *cri de coeur* addressed "To Whom it May Concern (mainly my own Superego)." "And I am offended that she is willing to take it lieing [*sic*] down."[50]

By this time Bernard had reached the end of her rope. "I find I can't take the situation anymore," she wrote in an apparent postscript to a letter intended for Dorothy. "I want out. I'm too old. I have to protect myself. Otherwise I'll need a psychiatrist . . . to deal with it."[51] In practical terms, opting out meant withdrawing the financial support she had been providing for her son-in-law's treatment and hospitalization over previous two years. Emotionally, it meant a rift with her daughter that took several years and many tears to overcome.

By the following February (1968), the strategy appeared to have worked, at least so far as Bernard's personal equilibrium was concerned. "I am completely reconciled to the situation," she wrote. "I hardly think about it at all." Designed partly to diminish Dorothy's guilt over causing her mother to suffer, these brave words unfortunately were not the last ones on the subject. Nor, with her younger son's problems still in the wings, was this the end of maternal tribulations.[52] But for the time being, they expressed at least a partial truth. "I'm absorbed in work I love," Bernard continued; "I do lots of interesting things; I have friends, etc." Among the "interesting things" was the writing of what she described as "a sort of hush hush position paper . . . on talented women," a piece intended for Lyndon Johnson's noncampaign that year but finally published as *Women and the Public Interest*. Among her friends, then or soon after, were a growing number of young feminists, whose meetings she first attended sometime that spring.[53]

After her daughter's marriage finally ended in divorce almost a decade later, Bernard attempted to put the best face on things. They had had a "good marriage," at least in the sense that Dorothy Lee had known "total love in the Pauline sense"—more than many people can say, she added. But the more important lessons for Bernard had been even deeper. One was a reminder of the barrier that separates the sexes. In Dorothy's words, written in the summer of 1963 shortly after Brick's return, "Men are much different than women and it is small wonder that communication is difficult"—the central theme of *The Sex Game* five years later. A second was the limits of rational analysis. "So beautiful. . . . So brilliant," Bernard wrote of the young man whose tragic fate she had attempted to understand for more than a decade. "I have long since given up trying to explain."[54]

━━━━━━━━━

While coping with her children's problems, Bernard remained extraordinarily prolific, publishing several dozen articles and four books, among them *The Sex Game, Women and the Public Interest,* and *The Future of Marriage.* Together these three studies provide a record, not only of her own development, but that of a number of younger women in these years: from the sexual permissiveness of the mid-1960s to political activism and finally to social criticism. A comparison of the first and third, in particular, suggests how far she had come.

On the road to feminism, *The Sex Game* seemed almost a detour. Bernard's "sixties book," as it were, it provided a survival guide to sexual strategies in the new age, a how-to book for swinging times. It was also evidence again of the conflict and confusion between sexual permissiveness and women's emancipation in her thinking. Starting her story with Adam and Eve, Bernard traced the changes whereby sex among humans ceased being seasonal—silencing "Nature's bell," as she put it—and the relations between the sexes became "cultural" rather than simply "biological." As words replaced acts (Bernard had always said she was as much turned on by talk as by action), the "sex game" became a complex mosaic of social and verbal cues, not to mention of fumbling and missed opportunities. If one result was "unparalleled intimacy between individuals," another was the fact that collectively, "men in a fundamental way are strangers to women and women to men."[55]

The result was a readable tour de force, more amusing to some readers than to others. "I found it delightful," wrote Vance Packard, who knew pop sociology if anyone did.[56] But to others it seemed cynical, even sexist, in offering women advice on how to negotiate the status quo rather than how to change it. One reviewer found it "rambling and disappointingly ambivalent about feminism." Another young woman, in the course of writing a doctoral thesis on Bernard's career, could not resist editorializing: "My question is, does the communication between the sexes have to be looked upon as a 'game'? And, what about altruism?"[57] Reacting to a passage in which Bernard approvingly described newly fashionable "touch-and-go" lunchtime assignations, an anonymous reader penciled in the margin, deliciously unaware of the irony: "Has anyone in your family had an affair? How did you feel?"[58]

In *The Future of Marriage,* woman's world, if still not a happy place, was at least her own. All marriages are "really two marriages," Bernard began, and the two "do not always coincide." More than subjective impressions, these perspectives were rooted in "objective" structural realties (law, convention, etiquette). Men and women profited from marriage accordingly: for him it was good; for her, an almost unmitigated disaster. Nor was this conclusion a matter of opinion. Although Bernard had once argued that one index of female superiority was less susceptibility to mental and emotional breakdown,[59] she now presented detailed evidence that married women have a higher incidence of mental and physical ailments than either married men or single women. Marriage, in short, was hazardous to female health.

To illustrate these points, Bernard dusted off the "shock theory" of marriage she had developed three decades before, and in the process revealed how much of her own experience had gone into this new book. The "shocks," as she described them, were virtually a rerun of her own marriage, and with slight change of detail, of her daughter's: the conflict between attachment to parents and to husband; "the end of romantic idealization that terminates the honeymoon"; the sobering realization that the husband is not "really so strong, so protective, so superior." Despite these shocks, many women, some out of love for their husbands, pay dearly, "clinging to marriage regardless of the cost."[60]

Looking to the future, Bernard surveyed various alternative arrangements. "Household," read the index entry: "see communes; cooperative households; life style; ménage à trois." Concerning the latter, she predicted an increase in the kind of marriage "which tolerates, if it is not actually sympathetic with extra-marital relations." Another change she particularly favored was one of "shared roles" within the family. True to her earlier defenses of marriage and the family, Bernard did not envisage an end to the institution. Since marriage was not likely to disappear, an improvement of marriage for women was at the top of the agenda. But she foresaw no ideal solution. Marriage was "intrinsically tragic," she concluded, using a word rare in her vocabulary, perhaps remembering what sexual affairs and shared roles had meant in her own case, and most certainly what mother and daughter had been through for almost a decade.[61]

As revealing as these conclusions were the methods and assumptions that underlay them. Of the various ways of predicting the future, Bernard now distinguished three: the historical, the statistical, and the prophetic, the latter based on "human wishes and desires." Although she continued to employ the first two, it was the third that now fascinated her, in particular the role of the "random event" that defies all previous statistical predictions. Her source was an article by fellow sociologist Robert Nisbet in *Commentary* several years earlier. But her more personal inspiration was the sudden appearance of the "feminine mystique" in the 1950s, and with it an increase in early marriages, birthrates, and related trappings of domesticity. Together, these developments defied the best statistical predictions she and other family sociologists had been making for more than two decades, just as in her life they underlay (so she saw it) her daughter's difficulties. Once again it appeared that "science," at least as she had once defined it, did not have all the answers.[62]

"Just as my sister [Clara] had brought the new world of the 1920s home to my parents," Bernard concluded of the tumultuous years of her single parenthood, "so my children were bringing the new world of the 1960s home to me."[63] As the foregoing suggests, however, the lessons were significantly different. Then it had been a promise of social freedoms to be enjoyed by young women as equals with men. Now it was the apparently impassable barrier that separated mothers and sons, women and men, and the unexpected revival of a "feminine mystique" within a context of social freedom. Then it had been the siren call of "profession," physically embodied in the professors who graced the Ravitch home. Now it was a realization that professionalism for women threatened "defeminization" and alienation from the "female culture" of home and family. Then it was the allure of science as statistics; now an appreciation of the way random events upset the best of predictions. By the early 1970s, Bernard was already incorporating these lessons in her feminist writings.

9
Feminist (1968–present)

I speak from the women's liberation point of view, much to the surprise of many people, and I believe that hearing it from a dumpy little old lady like me has a tendency to make it more respectable; at least not frightening.
— Jessie Bernard to Gwendolyn Safier, October 23, 1972

For Bernard the female world was reality before it was theory. By the spring of 1968, when she attended her first feminist meeting, she was beginning to enjoy the friendship of women for perhaps the first time in her life after decades of depending in one way or another on men. Her immediate circle consisted of women in the local area, some associated with nearby American University. Among them was Raphaela Best, a teacher whose work on the sex role socialization of children Bernard later incorporated in *The Female World*. Close associates within the social sciences included Elise Boulding, a recent Ph.D. in sociology (Michigan 1969) whose husband was the economist Kenneth Boulding; Catherine Chilman, a psychologist and social worker who worked with the Children's Bureau and the Department of Health, Education, and Welfare (HEW) until becoming dean at Hood College in 1969; Muriel G. Cantor, a young sociologist whom she first met at American University in 1969, and with whom she later taught a course in the Women's Studies program at George Washington University; and Jean Lipman-Blumen, a recent Harvard Ph.D. (1970) who also worked with HEW in the mid-1970s before accepting a position at the Claremont Graduate Schools.[1]

Two other friends of these years were even more frankly radical, at least by the standards of the times: Dana Densmore and Roxanne Dunbar, contributors to the *Journal of Female Liberation* who together voiced the disgust of many young women at the misogynous underside of male radicalism and at the confining demands of traditional family life, themes not unfamiliar to Bernard in her own life. "Mr. Smug Liberal, I've tried your delicious masochistic sex and it nauseates me," wrote Densmore in one of several statements that Bernard quoted in *The Future of Marriage.* "I'm a person and not a delectable little screwing machine." "All the love between 'man and woman' in the world," added Dunbar, "will not make that tiny unit any less lonely, any less perverted to the child who is raised within it." Since Bernard's generation generally did not talk this way no matter how they felt, this was heady stuff. "I was pressed into service by the young liberated women and it was sheer fun," she wrote an old friend in 1970. "They are a joy, literally."[2]

During the early seventies, Bernard's female world gradually expanded. By this time she had joined an informal feminist group that met more or less regularly, eventually in the bare-bones Washington office of *Quest,* a feminist quarterly founded in 1974 under the editorship of Charlotte Bunch. "*Quest* recognizes total change as a necessity for survival for the majority of people—not as an individual choice for securing personal comfort," wrote one contributor in the first issue, setting a radical tone that would characterize the journal for the rest of the decade. Attempting to unite theory and action in a feminist institution based on cooperation and sharing, the editors of *Quest* also spearheaded debates over lesbian alternatives and the role of heterosexuality in setting women against one another. Without entirely agreeing, Bernard again listened intently.[3]

In these years she also discovered Twin Oaks, an experimental community in Louisa, Virginia, about one hundred miles south of Washington. She retreated to Twin Oaks periodically, initially to study their arrangements for child care, eventually for relaxation. A legacy of the counterculture, the community was founded in 1968 on the neobehaviorist principles of B. F. Skinner's *Walden Two* (a work whose central character, "a queerduck . . . named Frazier," bore an eerie if remote resemblance to L.L.B). By the time Bernard discovered Twin Oaks, the community, like herself in these years, had shed many of its positivist principles in order to explore various forms of alternative living. "*Walden Two* and behaviorism are no longer an issue at Twin Oaks," one observer later reported, "although somewhat to the embarrassment of Twin Oakers many visitors still associate B. F. Skinner and his novel with the community." Although Bernard had been somewhat cool to "utopian households" in *The Future of Marriage*, she now characterized Twin Oaks as a "model of communitarian zeal," describing their experiments in childrearing sympathetically, if realistically, in *The Future of Motherhood*.[4]

Meanwhile, she devoted countless hours to helping younger women scholars with words of encouragement and letters of recommendation. Among the beneficiaries were a number who would soon make important contributions in their respective fields, among them Arlie Hochschild in sociology, and the historians Kathyrn Kish Sklar and Carroll Smith-Rosenberg. Taking as well as giving, Bernard profited from these contacts. "At the San F meetings [of the American Studies Association], I learned about the female networks that supported women in the 19th century," she reported to a correspondent in the fall of 1973. "This was a new and fascinating area for me as a sociologist." In *The Female World* she attempted, in effect, to describe the sociological reality of the "separate sphere" these and other historians had delineated.[5]

At a time when her relations with Dorothy Lee remained on edge, these contacts provided personal no less than professional satisfaction. "Dear Jessie" the letters usually began, although the correspondents were typically decades younger. Even when the business was serious, affection shone through. "Hi. It's been a long time since we talked, too long," began one request for help against apparent discrimination. Often the tone was simply playful. "I would like to have knitted you some long underwear, or something equally female networkish," wrote Kathryn Sklar, sending a copy of her biography of Catherine Beecher. Younger women, Bernard commented at the time, viewed her almost as "mother."[6]

When a doctoral student at the Unmiversity of Kansas in the fall of 1970 asked permission to write a thesis on Bernard's career, she could scarcely contain her enthusiasm. "My typewriter ribbon almost burst into flames under the speed of my reply," she recalled. Next to having some "scientific achievement" named after her, "this was the highest accolade." When a proposed visit to Kansas for an honorary degree did not pan out, she offered to buy the young woman a plane ticket to Washington ("for a Christmas present"). When finally they met for "four exhausting and gruelling days" of interviews, she discovered a "strange . . . phenomenon." Although the student had mustered all sorts of good reasons for doing the thesis to satisfy her doctoral committee, her "real reasons were far subtler." Like Bernard, she had struggled with problems of ethnic identity stemming from a Jewish background. Like Bernard, she had a son named David. "I was only the last person in her own long search for an ethnic identity." For Bernard, the shock of recognition seemed more than coincidence—"if I were not a scientist I would call it occult."[7]

In Bernard's personal life, the early feminist years were also a time of healing. When the two first met, a friend later recalled of the late 1960s, Bernard's scars were still plainly visible in half-suppressed resentments toward her late husband; in guilt over her role as a mother in the temporary alienation from her daughter; in lingering ambivalence toward Judaism; perhaps even in her failure to receive the recognition in sociology she felt she deserved. For the successful professional, pounding a typewriter was as much a way to release aggression as to communicate—a point Bernard herself seemed to endorse in resolutely refusing to trade in her balky manual for an electric model.[8]

One by one she now came to terms with these legacies of her past. In her writing, as already noted, the result was the analysis of his/her marriage in *The Future of Marriage* and her frank confrontation of her guilt in *Self-Portrait of a Family*. By the fall of 1970 the gulf that separated mother and daughter was already beginning to disappear as the two traveled together across Asia on the Trans-Siberian railroad, on a trip designed to take Dorothy's mind off her disintegrating marriage. At the urging of her close friend Raphaela Best, she also attended several meetings of a local synagogue, in the process gaining new appreciation of her Jewish past. Although the doctoral study of her career remained unpublished, her growing prominence among feminist sociologists removed any doubt as to her position within her discipline and any worries as to why this or that concept had not "caught on." To her younger women colleagues, as one of them put it, she would always be "Ms. Sociology."[9]

Although Bernard's energy often appeared boundless, a heart attack in January 1974 sidelined her for several months, and left a legacy in diminished reserves for several years. Ostensibly, she remained as active as before, serving successively as Visiting Fellow at the National Institute of Education (1974–1975) and Scholar in Residence at the United States Commission on Civil Rights (1975–1976). In memos and letters she waged open battle against forms of discrimination whose existence she once appeared to deny. "In the female network, your university along with several others, has acquired the reputation of going through the motions each year of looking for women candidates as a sort of charade to impress HEW," read one form letter she prepared for the Commission on Civil Rights to be sent with lists of available women applicants. "Think about it."[10]

Meanwhile, in letters far and wide, she continued a decade-long campaign against sexism generally, the list of offenders finally including *Playboy;* the sociobiologist Richard Herrnstein; and the television characters Mary Richards ("Mary Tyler Moore"), Edith Bunker ("All In the Family"), and the title character of "Mary Hartmann, Mary Hartman." ("Your program . . . will never go," she wrote Norman Lear, the producer of this immensely popular show in the mid-1970s. "The characters, especially the women, are so excruciatingly silly that adults won't want to watch. . . . I watched the first night but never again.")[11]

But age and health finally took its toll, at least temporarily. At the Civil Rights Commission, a close friend recalls, she moved in a cot to allow for periodic rests—understandable enough for many seventy-three-year-olds, but not for Jessie Bernard. By the end of 1976, a combination of fatigue and disillusion with office politics led to her resignation. Due to her "myocardial infarction," she wrote one correspondent at that time, she was forced to curtail her activities more generally.[12]

For a while it appeared that Bernard's public appearances might henceforth be largely ceremonial. Honorary doctorates became almost an annual event: Washington University (1976), Northwestern (1977), Hood College (1977), Radcliffe (1978).[13] Awards likewise were as regular as the seasons: from the American Association of University Women (1976), from the Society for the Psychological Study of Social Issues (1976), from the Association of Women in Science (1977), and from the Association for Women in Psychology (1979).

By the late 1970s, however, her energy returned. In rapid succession she accepted successive appointments as visiting professor at

Mills College in Oakland (1980), at UCLA (1981), and at the University of Delaware (1982). If any doubts remained, she dispelled them with a six-hundred-page study of *The Female World*—a world that had been hers for more than a decade. In this book, and her other feminist writings of these years, Bernard completed her transition from positivism to feminism. As several critics were quick to point out, however, the transition was less complete than at first appeared.

Professionally, Bernard poured much of her energy during the 1970s into the Sociologists for Women in Society (SWS), an organization rooted in an informal women's caucus first organized at the ASA meetings in San Francisco in 1968. By the time she joined the group (she was in London at the International Population Conference during its first meeting in 1969), the organizers of the caucus had already succeeded in getting the ASA council to grant a room for their exclusive use at the 1970 convention, time and space for a general business meeting, and child-care facilities provided by the organization ("but avoiding any model of a ladies auxiliary of local woman"). In preparation, a round-robin letter was sent to about twenty women who had previously expressed interest—Bernard being one of them. The following February she joined a group at Yale who founded the SWS as a formal organization, independent of the ASA.[14]

Although Bernard played no active role at the 1970 caucus meeting in Washington, she listened as others described possible organizational models: an ASA-sanctioned Commission on the Status of Women in Sociology; a frankly political caucus with a wider range of interests; or a hybrid of these two models.[15] As things turned out, a proposal endorsing the first passed unanimously at the general business meeting, along with a resolution condemning sex-based discrimination within academia. Among other caucus business was the establishment of a steering committee of twenty-five, again including Bernard, and the appointment of four regional coordinators, among them Alice Rossi, then of Goucher, and Arlie Hochschild of Berkeley, both of whom had taken a lead in organizing the original caucus.[16]

At this same 1970 meeting, Bernard also had occasion to observe some of the problems the movement faced, some amusing, some more serious. Although the promised child care was provided, mild embarrassment ensued when determination to avoid an "auxiliary" of local

women baby sitters translated into high-priced professional care used
initially by only one child, while in a nearby room two volunteer men
struggled to accommodate fifty children of the radical caucus—a situation Rossi moved immediately to remedy.

More serious was radical dissent within the caucus, when one
young member stormed out of a final meeting after denouncing the
group as "elitist" and "career opportunist." "Our experience since the
first Sociology Liberation Movement in Boston is clear," she fumed,
summoning an analogy then popular in radical circles: "If you sleep
with dogs you'll pick up fleas." Almost as threatening was the nervous
generosity of the ASA general meeting as it passed the two caucus-
sponsored resolutions virtually without debate, a victory whose ease
disturbed caucus members who wanted a fuller discussion.[17]

When, the following February, Bernard met at Yale with a group of
twenty from the Washington meetings, "liberals" and "radicals" (as
she termed them) again squared off. But this time she consciously
played the role of mediator. Both groups got something, she reported
in a newsletter account of the meeting: the "liberals" in obtaining a
constitution and some semblance of order in the assignment of organizational responsibilities; the "radicals" in establishing a Committee on
Social Issues to supplement the work of two other committees on jobs
and discrimination. The organization's new name was "terrible, she
conceded, "for where else does one find women but in society?" Yet,
after choosing the name SWS, the group itself had dissolved in laugh-
ter, proving to Bernard that sisterhood and a cooperative spirit had
prevailed over differences.[18]

In an account of her "four revolutions" published in the *American
Journal of Sociology* in 1973, she reflected further on the splits within
the SWS and her own position among the contending forces. The
movement now seemed to be split four ways: those concerned mostly
with discrimination within sociology versus those who wanted to fight
discrimination within society at large; those who wished to make sociology "an instrument for total revolution" versus those concerned with
sexist bias in sociological theory. Again the peacemaker, Bernard repu-
diated none of these. Indeed, she was sorry that feminist sociology
would no longer benefit from the criticism of the radical secessionist at
the 1970 meeting. For the moment, however, she was most concerned

with how sexist assumptions had skewed sociological theory—the thrust of much of her writing in the mid-1970s and one of the two main themes of *The Female World.*[19]

DESPITE her conciliatory efforts, Bernard soon learned that controversy was not so easy to avoid. One especially sensitive subject was maternity and female biology. At an SWS panel in late 1972, Bernard found herself bracketed with Alice Rossi in maintaining (so their critics said) that "motherhood remains the manifest destiny and highest goal of all women"—a controversy that anticipated the furor that followed the publication of Rossi's "Biosocial Perspective on Parenting" in *Daedalus* five years later. At the time, Rossi explained that she and Bernard meant to suggest only that feminists be a bit more cautious when talking on the subject: "Housework is not all shit-work; having a baby is NOT the same as giving birth to a calf." Although Bernard took no part in this exchange, she apparently shared the feeling that Rossi was treading on dangerous ground. For the moment, however, the issue rested.[20]

An even more divisive issue was homosexuality, one increasingly difficult to ignore thanks in part to the efforts of Bernard's friends at *Quest.* In her earlier years she almost never mentioned the subject, but when she did, it was more as cause for mild amusement than for overt censure. "The relationship is . . . homosexual, I think, tho not grossly physical" she wrote to Luther of a longtime woman friend and her companion in the late 1930s. "But [one] acts just exactly as a wife and [the other] as a husband. It is rather amusing."[21] Throughout the 1950s, her silence on the issue bespoke the attitude of liberals who defend the right of consenting adults to do as they please in private, so long as they personally don't have to know what that is.

In her own life, Bernard remained resolutely heterosexual, differing in this regard (as in others) with Margaret Mead, who believed that, in an ideal world, everyone would be heterosexual in the middle years and homosexual in youth and age.[22] When one of Bernard's associates in the early 1970s pushed for a closer, perhaps physical relationship, she declined lovingly but firmly. "Why do I withhold the commitment that would mean so much to you?" she asked in a poignant attempt to explain her refusal. "Why did I deprive you of something that would, actually, cost me nothing?" When the subject was first broached, Bernard had said it would simply be "phony" for her to act otherwise. Now she had a more complex answer, one that revealed a great deal about her developing self-image. "For some unexplained reason, I represent some sort of model or ideal, a reassuring—perhaps mother—image to a lot of young women," she began. She had first glimpsed this when discussing with some young women why she would never remarry. "Any commitment, to a man or a woman, would deprive them in some strange way of me." Perhaps an analogy was the insistence of the Catholic church on celibacy, she continued, admitting just as quickly that the idea was a bit "preposterous." In any case, friendship and professional cooperation would have to be enough.[23]

Personal preferences aside, Bernard nonetheless developed new sympathy for the lesbians within the women's movement, and by extension, for gay men within sociology. When at the 1974 meeting of the ASA homophobic sentiment seemed rampant, she arose at the business meeting to denounce these attitudes, later accepting a position as SWS liaison to the Sociological Gay Caucus. In the height of enthusiasm, she claimed publicly that she was indeed a "certified" lesbian. In early 1976 she accepted an invitation to attend a conference of gay men at Penn State the next summer (a conference unthinkable in her time there, but one that was nonetheless moved without explanation to an off-campus Holiday Inn after the invitations were issued).[24]

Although Bernard meant by "certified" only that she understood and sympathized with the cause, she had, by the time of the Penn State conference, already learned that she had probably gone too far. "I know you made that statement to show your solidarity with the lesbians, to keep the movement from splitting on this issue and with the best of intentions and lovingness," one lesbian activist wrote. True, some in the movement welcomed the support of a "straight," this correspondent conceded. But others were distinctly uneasy. "One said that it made light of being a lesbian. Another that you got the credit for being liberal but did not have to pay the price." Responding immediately, Bernard was appropriately contrite. By her public self-designation, she meant only to indicate her support, much as had the Danes during World War

II by wearing the Star of David on their sleeves the day Jews were ordered to do so. "But if it looks like a putdown I will cease and desist at once."[25]

Whether for this reason or others, the mid-1970s proved to be the high point of her public statements and support on this issue. In reporting the Penn State conference, she reiterated her approval, but noted parenthetically that a "celebration" the second evening (which she was unable to attend) "was too gay-oriented for some of those present." In *The Female World,* she treated lesbianism briefly as one of several "issue-related" faultlines, hence less fundamental than class, race, or ethnicity. The issue had seriously divided the movement during the mid-1970s, she reported. But happily (so she now viewed it), it was resolved when the delegates to the first National Women's Conference in Houston passed a prolesbian plank that not only demanded protection of gay rights, but noted that fear of the label "lesbian" oppressed all women. Where did Bernard herself stand? "There were a few who were impressed by the lesbian analysis," she wrote in a brief aside that probably came closest to expressing her own feelings, "though not converted to it."[26]

While Bernard wrestled with these and other potentially divisive issues, her association with the SWS remained a source of strength and comfort over the years. In 1976 her friends in the ASA succeeded in establishing an annual Jessie Bernard Award. In 1988 the SWS dedicated an entire issue of their recently established journal *Gender and Society* to her, with celebrations of her career by her longtime friends Muriel Cantor and Jean Lipman-Blumen. "Hers is a gentle rebellion that . . . enhances our sensitivity to issues—intellectual, social and emotional," Lipman-Blumen concluded. "More than that, she mothers us with humane understanding, affection, and wisdom—not to mention more than occasional reprimands to attend to our scholarship."[27]

G roup structure came first. Although Bernard had addressed this issue tangentially in *Academic Women,* she there resisted several conclusions that her evidence appeared to suggest. Sociologically, women faculty came from a higher social class, had higher

IQs, and were older than their male counterparts. They also taught in less well paid disciplines and at lower prestige institutions, and remained closer to their place of birth throughout their careers. Culturally, they tended to hold different educational values as a group then their male colleagues, to prefer people over money, and to be politically more liberal and unconventional. Yet, having said these things, Bernard quickly retreated from the suggestion that this world constituted a sociological entity. Sex-based differences might be "only" statistical, and outweighed by others, she noted. Moreover, gender was often less important than other divisions, such as between college and university, "fringe" and "professional," home economics and liberal arts. Not to mention the difference between academic and nonacademic women.

Concerning the "female world" among blacks and whites, *Marriage and Family among Negroes* also equivocated, revealing as much for what it omitted as what it said. Black women would appear to have constituted a model of a female world: objectively, in having higher education and income than black men, closer contact with the white world, and even better access to its social agencies; subjectively, in being more likely to be among the "acculturated." "Negro men and Negro women have . . . tended to live in somewhat different worlds," Bernard conceded, anticipating her later conclusion. But, though she praised black women to the point of caricature (for such an "antistereotypic" book, another reviewer noted, such comments were difficult to explain), she did not expand the analysis to make them part of a unified "female world."[28] In fact, the same factors that produced this division among blacks worked against any sense of solidarity between black women and their white sisters. Quoting Frazier's *Black Bourgeoisie* (a book, one reviewer remarked snidely, that Bernard alone mistook "for a serious scientific work"), she described the particular resentment that middle-class black women felt toward whites who married black men.[29] Again, women separate, but not a female world.

IN THE EARLY 1980s, Bernard was ready to state positively what had appeared piecemeal and mostly negatively in these earlier works. The "female world" was analogous to "sporting world," "music world," or "business world"—terms "well enough understood" in everyday speech, even if lacking in sociological precision. Past observers had conceptualized it in terms of biology ("the easiest and most naive way"), of place, of occupation, and of culture. Of these, Bernard preferred the last, so long as culture was defined in terms of an "encompassing system of institutions" (occupation, marriage) and the rules and norms that governed them.[30]

Following a historical survey of women's sphere, *The Female World* provided a sweeping, sometimes incisive, sometimes rambling synthesis of the literature dealing with the social and group structure of this world (parts 3–4) and its characteristic culture (part 4)—Bernard at her best and her worst, or so the reviewers decided. Structurally, the female world displays distinctive patterns: the unstructured and relatively free "prime-time" of unmarried young women, for example, or the relative absence of class distinctions as compared to the world of men.[31] Its group structure reveals a predominance of associations based on kinship and community, the forms of Gemeinschaft rather than Gesellschaft. Its culture consists of distinctive language, technologies, literary and artistic production, and its own "ethos" of love (eros), duty, and caring (agape).[32]

Was the balance between the male and female worlds changing? Here Bernard was cautiously optimistic. Adopting a framework similar to the "cultural lag" thesis of W. F. Ogburn, she argued that women, even though left out of the process of modernization (the world of Gesellschaft), had performed a salvage function even during the era of industrialization—in philanthropy, social work, and "friendly visiting." "The self-interested ethos had not been permitted to operate in pristine form. It had to be restricted." By the 1920s, "people-oriented" styles of management suggested that the "ethos of *Gesellschaft* [was] becoming more congruent with the ethos of the female world." As the United States entered its postindustrial phase, "the female style may prove to be just what a lot of doctors . . . have been ordering for some time."[33]

Reviewers again were not entirely convinced. Several felt that she had overstressed differences at the expense of similarities. The latter, one critic noted, included common voting patterns, preference for the same type of occupations once opportunities are equalized, and more general values such as democracy and consumerism. Making a related point, Ruth Shonle Cavan, a Chicago Ph.D. (1926) and the closest in age to Bernard (b. 1896), added that she failed "to discuss the vast area of behavior that lies between the extremes of male and female ethos as she describes them."[34]

Other critics faulted her methodology, and overall conclusions. In many (most?) cases, factors other than gender explain a given response; for example, age and level of education as related to support of or opposition to forced busing or abortion. Indeed, it was not clear if Bernard was describing a distinctive female perspective (psychological or cultural) or only the structural characteristics of their world (sociological). If the former, then she was open to the criticism that men often expressed so-called feminine values. If the latter, then the question was whether similar conditions produced a permanently distinct "culture." Another sociologist, employing the analogy of abortive attempts to identify a black "culture," questioned whether alleged female traits—as with those ascribed to blacks—were anything more than situational, to disappear once the situation was changed.[35]

Possibly the most serious challenge, however, came not in the reviews but in a paper written in response to Bernard's initial statement in "My Four Revolutions" a decade before. "Is Gender Dichotomy Real?" asked Sarah Matthews, a sociologist at Case Western Reserve. Answering her own question, she first argued that there exists an important difference between establishing gender identity and internalizing a gender role—between knowing that one is male or female and acting in "masculine" or "feminine" fashion. The first is stable and immutable: a condition of participating in western society. The second is contingent upon specific situations; that is, individuals display "masculine" and "feminine" traits according to circumstances. Precisely because gender is a category that sorts people neatly into two groups, it is not very useful to social actors, who may be more or less masculine or feminine in different settings. Gender thus does not have a "universal meaning" but rather "indexes different things depending on the context in which it is used." In this, it is no different than indices such as age, race, and class. But compared to them, it is, for the sociologist, a "poor index."[36]

Cases in point. Although single parents are more likely to be women than men, relevant variables for analyzing their situations are availability of child care, income level, and the like. To identify their gender is to add little or nothing. Likewise, lack of education, vocational guidance, or role models equally characterizes the failure of lower-class adolescent boys to achieve in the marketplace—a point illustrated by a string of quotations that seemed to describe women but in reality concerned adolescents.

Although Bernard responded, the argument was never fully joined. One reason was her failure (whether intentional or inadvertent) to deal with the distinction between "gender" and "sex roles." This failure, in turn, reflected the ambiguity in her work between describing structural attributes of the female world (sociological) and the different ways women view things (psychological). After stating that she had little use for the category masculinity/femininity (sex role) because it was psychological not sociological, she continued as if she had been criticized for treating sex roles as reliable indices of the social world; that is, for arguing that a female perspective (psychology) rather than structural characteristics (sociology) distinguish the worlds of men and women. In fact, the target of this particular attack was her sociology, as the example of the adolescent boys indicated. Anticipating reviewers of *The Female World,* this critic concluded that the significance of gender was assumed rather than demonstrated.

A more basic reason for this disagreement (articulated by another participant in this same exchange over the Matthews article) concerned the uses of social science, an issue Bernard had been wrestling with since the 1940s. Feminism "is explicit about its bias," this sociologist argued, crediting Thomas Kuhn among others for unmasking the value-free ideal. In supporting this ideal, Bernard's critic from Case Western Reserve was herself an unreconstructed positivist. At bottom, the issue was the purpose of studying sociology. If one wished merely to describe the structural factors affecting a group (single parents, for example), crucial variables were income, accessibility to child care, and perhaps age and social class. But if one wished to improve the situation of women, the fact that more women than men are single parents is of primary significance. In response, the author of the initial critique granted that gender could profitably be used "cautiously"; she insisted that social scientists should not deliberately impose explanations a priori that may blind them to alternatives.

———

The faultlines of race, ethnicity, and class also posed a problem. *Acdemic Women,* as the sociologist David Riesman noted at the time, was conspicuously silent on the issue.[37] Concerning race, *Marriage and Family among Negroes* seemed to its critics to mark a step backward. Race, for Bernard as for most educated whites of her generation, was something you mostly read about in books. Except for a picturesque ex-slave, and a few couples of mixed race, she had had little or no contact with blacks during her youth or, the record suggests, during her professional career. For *Marriage and Family among Negroes,* she relied largely on the published work of earlier sociologists (particularly E. Franklin Frazier), on travelers' accounts and slave narratives collected by B. A. Botkin (for whom she worked briefly in the late 1930s), and on historical work, including Stanley Elkins's controversial *Slavery* (1959). Although she spiced her text with comments from casual interviews conducted by others, she apparently made no attempt to interview blacks herself.

Until this time, her views on the subject were those of an openminded, well-meaning, 1950s academic liberal. By this standard, open prejudice and discrimination were routinely disapproved, although even here Bernard generally limited her public comments to passing references in other contexts.[38] Otherwise, as she demonstrated in *American Community Behavior,* "Negroes" were "they," however charitably described. Unthinking caricatures also sprouted unexpectedly among the liberal sentiments (for example, in reference to the "isolated rural Southern type which is retarded almost to the point of feeblemindedness").[39]

In tune with the changing times, *Social Problems at Midcentury* devoted some fifteen pages to black America and the desegregation victories of the Eisenhower years. But Bernard's treatment was again essentially vintage civil rights liberalism—in focusing on legal barriers, in stressing recent economic gains, and in assuming that remaining problems were mostly in the South. Nor did the events of the early

sixties fundamentally alter this view. "Too awful about the unregener-
ated Southerners," she wrote to her daughter following the Freedom
Summer of 1964. "I sometimes wonder what we are going to do about
Mississippi."[40]

Although well-intentioned, *Marriage and Family among Negroes,* like
the more explosive Moynihan report of the previous year, showed
how difficult it was for anyone to tackle this subject in the climate of
the mid-1960s.[41] Bernard, like Moynihan, was concerned with the
increase in out-of-wedlock births and female-headed households in
the black community. But her purpose was sociological analysis, not
policy making. Since the demand that children be born in wedlock was
part of white America's norm of monogamic marriage, a change in
the proportion of out-of-wedlock births among blacks could serve as
an index for the institutionalization of monogamy. Charting a "marriage trajectory," she included among reasons for change over time
the existence of two "cultures" within black America—the "externally
adapted" and the "acculturated," the former being far more ready
than the latter to abandon national norms.

Did not this formulation effectively establish the white standard as
the norm, with blacks deviating in varying degree? Despite the reference to "culture," did it not deny the relativism inherent in the use of
the term? Thus reentered Bernard's lifelong ambivalence concerning
culture and cultural relativism. On the one hand, she knew that some
social scientists maintained that apparent evidences of deviance/
disorganization might be seen from *inside* a culture as solutions rather
than problems. Anxious to avoid offense, she chose the terms "acculturated" and "externally adapted" over "respectable" and "non-
respectable" or even more demeaning pejoratives. In a preface, she
stated explicitly that she had excluded control data from the white
population because she did not wish to present blacks simply as deviating from the white norm.[42]

On the other hand, the belief in a common standard died hard. The
danger of cultural relativism, she now argued, was that it freed the
observer "from any responsibility or guilt" concerning the subject under study, and hence could easily breed indifference. Although she
used the term "culture," she would not accept the "ethical implications"
of relativism. The rejection of cultural relativism was, so to speak, her

way of caring. In effect, however, she had it both ways: overtly treating childbearing and marriage patterns among blacks in nonjudgmental fashion, while covertly holding blacks to white monogamic standards.

The reviewers, in any case, would have little of it. Her alleged sins ranged from uncritical use of biased sources to "frailty in reasoning" and crude stereotypes of the two black cultures. The recent upsurge of interest in blacks had produced three kinds of works, the historian August Meier wrote: sound but narrow, mediocre, and incompetent. "The book under review here belongs in the last category." The result, he concluded, was a double caricature: of black subculture and of "all that is worst in recent sociological writing about Negroes in the United States."[43]

The rise of militant black protest by this time further strained Bernard's attempt to balance her devotion to common standards and her desire to treat black culture on its own terms. In her personal dealings, an abiding guilt struggled against a disapproval that would not quit. "In my own case, I am sure my anxiety stems from guilt feelings," she wrote a colleague in 1967 concerning a study of predictors of minority success. As a result, she had always "leaned over backwards," giving passing grades to "Negro summer-school teachers" because it meant so much to their promotions; overpaying cleaning women, even tolerating one who spent "a good part of the day drunk in the basement"; being cheated by young blacks who fraudulently "collected" as newsboys. "But why go on with it?" she concluded this agonizing self-appraisal. "I still feel guilty, as though it is somehow or other my fault that I am better off than they."[44]

She also disapproved of the tactics of the new generation of black leaders. Distinguishing between violence as a spontaneous outburst of human emotion and violence as strategy, she told a group of South American educators the following year (1968) that she feared the second more than the first. In charging that violence was "as American as cherry pie," the black activist H. Rap Brown was simply wrong. It was only "better reported" in this country. Included among those leaders who proposed violence as strategy, she claimed, was the recently murdered Martin Luther King, Jr. "He and his followers," she told this same audience, "did things which they knew would provoke a violent reaction among racist Southerners."[45]

Nor did things get better as the sixties gave way to the seventies. Returning to the issue in *Women and the Public Interest,* Bernard briefly decried the "underutilization" of black women and even attempted a diplomatic retreat from some earlier comments she had made concerning their fears of emasculating black men through their success. But in *The Future of Marriage,* she wrote as if whites were the only ones who married. "To me," one angry black college student wrote after reading the work, "your book is just another way of telling Black people that they don't count."[46]

By this time, Bernard seemed almost willing to give up. "I sympathize with the black militants who tell us they are tired of having white people diagnose their disabilities and prescribe white-biased remedies," she wrote in an unpublished piece sometime in the early or mid-seventies, perhaps the angriest she ever penned. "I long since, therefore, ceased and desisted from writing in the area of race relations." Her angry comments were thus "For White Readers Only." Frustrations and mea culpas out of the way, she proceeded to attack the false notion that modern society is white society. "Western culture today is not 'white,' " she insisted. "It belongs to any race that wants to take it over"—the Japanese, in her view, being a case in point. "There may be a black culture, but that does not mean that black people cannot achieve western culture." The black power movement of Stokely Carmichael was a welcome attempt of blacks to take responsibility "for their own weaker and handicapped fellows, as other ethnic groups have done." But whether it would be used constructively or abused remained to be seen.[47]

Although Bernard did not give up, her treatment of the "race faultline" in *The Female World* was restrained, even pessimistic when compared with the upbeat tone of the work as a whole. Evidence of the hostility that black women felt toward their white sisters seemed stronger now than when she reported it fifteen years before. Indeed, the issue had recently made the pages of *Ms.* and the *Washington Post.*[48] Grasping at straws after watching a segment of "Bill Moyer's Journal" concerning an ugly neighborhood clash following the arrival of a black family, Bernard imagined that the white ethnic women did not feel hatred toward the blacks personally (as did the white men), but simply did not want "their cosy, intimate relationship [with their white community] disturbed." In the end, however, she conceded that the tension between black and white women, particularly when it involved competition for men, was "not an inspiring one."[49]

As TO CLASS and ethnicity, Bernard was more optimistic, but not much more successful. Concerning class, a critic for the *World Marxist Review* put the matter bluntly: "Professor Bernard cannot even define social class. One hundred pages of quotations, charts and anecdotes avoid facing the fact that social class, equally for women as for men, is determined by one's ownership or non-ownership of the means of production." Although less didactic, other reviewers agreed that her treatment of these faultlines, taken together, was one of the weaker sections of the book. "Those waiting for a scheme that incorporates women's unpaid domestic labor into the class structure of capitalist societies will not find it here," wrote one critic. In picturing a middle-class, egalitarian female world, Bernard likewise ignored the feminization of poverty during the past two decades. Still another reviewer noted that she cited but did not "adequately deal with the antagonism existing between working-class women, particularly black women, and feminists."[50]

Behind these complaints lay some important policy issues, among them compensation for housework, equal pay for comparable work, and affirmative action. As in her discussion of discrimination/sexism, Bernard was more concerned with basic concepts than with specific policies. Just as fundamental was a series of questions that underlay many of the specific criticisms of *The Female World* as of her earlier works. Can one reconcile the recognition of difference (whether based on gender or race) with a common standard? Does the recognition of gender add anything significant to sociological analysis? Can one have a sociology that is at once "feminist" and "scientific"?

Addressing this last question, Bernard moved finally to a feminist critique of science. In the early seventies, she first realized that a rethinking of social science was to be the next order of business. "It occurred to me that women should not only ask for equal status in their profession but also that they should contribute to the major paradigms of their disciplines," she wrote on New Year's Day 1973 to several feminist scholars. "I am now, therefore, saying: Ask not what your discipline can do for you but what you can do for your discipline."[51]

The occasion was the appearance that same month of an autobiographical account of her "four revolutions" within sociology, the last being feminism. Moving beyond the issue of discrimination, Bernard observed that feminist scholars were already revising their disciplines in several ways. At the most basic level, this revision involved awareness of the gender bias of most (male) sociologists. At a second, still the level of "normal science," scholars were modifying, correcting, or refining traditional sociology, as she herself had done for Parsonian functionalism, and as others were attempting for symbolic interactionism.[52] Revision here involved recognizing that certain conceptualizations did not apply equally to the worlds of men and of women, studies of upward mobility being a case in point. Even the classic distinction between status and contract (as stages in the development of modern societies) has a gender bias since women by and large continue to inhabit a world of status, while males alone occupy that of contract and the cash nexus. Meanwhile, some feminists were challenging certain "methodological and technical predilections" of their disciplines, now termed the "*machismo* factor in research."[53]

Bernard reached these conclusions by weaving together various strands in recent scholarship. One source, as the references to "paradigm" and "normal science" indicated, was Thomas Kuhn's *Structure of Scientific Revolutions* (1962). When she abandoned her debate with Lundberg in the early fifties, the issue of science and values was essentially unresolved. Were values inherent in science or external to it? If the latter, were values rooted in social convention, individual conscience, or elsewhere?

Kuhn, as she read him, provided a framework for answering these questions.[54] For a start, science was a communal, not an individual enterprise. Communities of scientists organized around paradigms, defined as "universally recognized scientific achievements that for a time provide model problems and solutions.[55] These paradigms, in turn, determine the selection of problems, methodologies, and conceptualizations. Scientific revolutions occur when some members of a scientific community can or will no longer tolerate anomalies within an existing paradigm. A new paradigm triumphs, not because it is necessarily superior or is proved against nature, but because it has succeeded in a competition.

So much is familiar. What made it significant in Bernard's case was the lessons she drew. Although she was unsure whether social science contained paradigms in any strict sense, Kuhn's formulation seemed to settle the value issue. No group of scientists could function "without some set of received beliefs," he wrote. And these beliefs, as Bernard now saw them, were entirely external to science. A basic one was "that science should (or need not) be socially useful"—the choice apparently being up to the investigator. A second sort of belief derived from values dominant in the culture. No American sociologist, for example, "would be likely to offer a racial [racist] explanation of any community phenomenon." Belief in social egalitarianism likewise shaped studies of class, mobility, stratification, and poverty. A third source was "arbitrary" factors ("personal and historical accident"), whereby one group chooses to study rural and another urban problems, for example, or one sponsoring institution bestows greater prestige on a project than does another.[56]

Bernard initially embraced Kuhn's theory in the early 1970s in connection with a study of community, a work in which women (and feminism) were virtually absent. But the lesson did not stop there. One "arbitrary" element in science, she observed in passing, "has been the sex of the scientist offering the paradigm." Thanks to Kuhn, she could now place sociology squarely at the service of her new cause without worrying that to do so was unscientific. The result, as one reviewer commented of the opening chapter of *The Female World*, was an approach that was not only not "value free," but was "value explicit."[57]

A second source of this new orientation was assorted scholarship in history and the social sciences, most importantly several works by three women scholars to whom Bernard addressed her New Year's call to arms: an analysis of "The Political Economy of Women's Liberation" by Margaret Benston, a Marxist feminist; a survey of the absence of women in historical writing by Gerda Lerner, then at Sarah Lawrence; and two pieces by the psychologist Rae Carlson of the Educational

Testing Service.[58] From Carlson, in particular, she adopted a distinction between agentic and communal research. "Agency has to do with separation, repression, conquest, and contract," Bernard explained; "communion with fusion, expression, acceptance, noncontractual cooperation." Agentic science seeks manipulation, mastery, and control, as with controlled laboratory observations of monkeys. Communal science, disavowing controls, seeks understanding, as with one recent study of primates in their natural habitat.

In her enthusiasm, Bernard on this last point inadvertently improved on the original, as Carlson gently pointed out several months later. She had not compared the work of men and women psychologists, as Bernard stated, but only of undergraduate psychology majors. "While I think one *could* establish the point, given a well-aimed design, I haven't done it." Moreover, Carlson lectured, "it's all too easy to find exemplars of agentic styles among women psychologists."[59] Although Bernard apparently did not reply, she muted this theme, for this reason or some other, in her later work.

Meanwhile, sociologists and other social scientists were busy expanding Bernard's indictment, producing a literature of which she was only partially aware. From Lester Ward to Talcott Parsons the leaders in American sociology were "Sexists to a Man," as two radical sociologists wrote.[60] Others identified gender bias in theoretical orientations and research procedures.[61] Although no social scientists explicitly developed the agentic-communal distinction, it appeared in various works in the history and philosophy of natural science.[62]

In *The Female World,* Bernard returned to these same themes, although less systematically than one might have hoped. One observation concerned male bias in earlier conceptualizations: status-contract, Gemeinschaft-Gesellschaft, and Appolonian-Dionysian. Although earlier sociologists sometimes recognized the gender dimension to these dichotomies (notably Ruth Benedict, who was responsible for the last of the three), Bernard would now bring them to the fore: women being identified with the first of each pair, men with the second. A second contribution concerned the poor fit between male-generated concepts and the female world; for example, in studies of socioeconomic status (SES). SES is "scalar" and hence quantifiable, Bernard noted. Education, income, and occupation may be measured and scaled, unlike evaluative statements of status in terms of high and low. SES was thus more "objective" and "cool." When applied to women, however, where high education may be combined with low or no income, for example, it can be misleading or meaningless. Although Bernard dropped her earlier references to agentic and communal social science, she implied that the pursuit of hard data was not the best way to understand the female world.[63]

As with her account of the structure of the female world, reviewers were divided on the merits of this argument. From one side came the charge that Bernard had not been radical enough, had indeed been "restrained . . . by the traditional male-created" sociology she ostensibly rejected, specifically in her analysis of demographic, social class, and other structural characteristics of American women. "All in all," wrote this reviewer, "I am not convinced that the application of the traditional ('male created') concepts *deepen* our understanding of the female world." Do women, for example, see each other in terms of social class at all? And if stratification of some form exists, whose interests does it serve?[64]

In a conference paper presented soon after *The Female World* appeared, another sociologist, also on the Left, expanded the list of Bernard's failings. In emphasizing the positive features of the world of women, this critic charged, Bernard "advertently or inadvertently glorified its present status." Hence, she softpedaled the male violence that bounded the female worlds, distorted the "heterosexual strangulation of love and loving," and ignored the ways that patriarchy subordinates the "will and meaning of women." Worse, she omitted all reference to "women's oppression of women" through ostracism and by identification with male values, a faultline as deep as race or class. Although recognizing the "hostile nature of the language we speak," Bernard effectively buried the topic in one of her later chapters.[65]

Others, in contrast, felt she had gone too far. Soon after the appearance of her 1973 statement in "My Four Revolutions," an irate male reader blasted her "dedication to the conception that science cannot transcend culture," since this position made sociology "no more than a vehicle of reform or revolution." Reviewing *The Female World,* Bernard's Chicago contemporary Ruth Cavan seconded the point. Bernard should have tested her assumptions with original research: "Selecting sources to support an assumption while neglecting negative data is always dangerous."[66]

Although Bernard had tacitly allied herself with the opponents of positivism and even of value-neutral sociology, she remained ambivalent and often ambiguous concerning the shape of a feminist sociology, torn once again between the values of her youth and those she had imbibed during the previous decade. Such was evident when she returned to the issue in *The Female World from a Global Perspective*, in a discussion of the "Feminist Enlightenment." Like their spiritual ancestors in the eighteenth century, the feminists of the late 1960s attacked the status quo in the name of reason and science. Like the philosophes, they viewed scholarship as a major weapon. Just as French was the universal language of the original Enlightenment, now a Pidgin English served the same role. Initially, these feminists, mostly American and northern European, were faulted for being white and middle class—a charge against which Bernard now defended them. But since the mid-1970s, in the Third World context, their scholarship appeared "American" or "western"; their feminism another form of colonialism.

The Enlightenment analogy was more apt than Bernard realized, for it was precisely the universalist assumptions of western science and rationality that were at issue. The solution, she argued, was the development of a social science that would serve Third World aims, avoiding the patron-client relation built into western social science. But would such scholarship be scientific in any recognizable sense? Would it be a continuation of the Enlightenment values that in one form or other had been the bedrock of Bernard's career? Or would it be a new form of romanticism—particularistic, emotional, and ideological? Unfortunately, Bernard never quite answered these questions.

DESPITE these unresolved issues, the contours of Bernard's feminism were reasonably clear by the mid-1980s. Stressing socialization and social roles, she looked for solutions through their redefinition (shared roles, elimination of occupational stereotypes) rather than in economic reforms (tax credits for housework or equal pay for comparable work), let alone more revolutionary changes. Although she was sympathetic to "radical" insistence on the integrity of the female realm and of feminine values, she could or would not blame men personally for women's problems. References to male "oppression" and "domination" rarely spiced her writings. In one of her later articles she wondered whether "patriarchs" may not have had a "bad press."[67] True to her lifelong distrust of class and Marxism, she showed neither interest in nor sympathy for socialist versions of feminism. Instead, she emphasized the permanence of difference, exploring strategies whereby the two "worlds" could coexist.[68] Although she led the call for a feminist critique of traditional social science, her suggestions were more in the way of revisions than a drastic restructuring of her discipline.

In seeking a middle ground, Bernard courted opposition from all sides, although, interestingly, more criticisms came from liberals than their opponents. Thus, she was faulted for stressing gender difference at the expense of similarities, for confusing structure (sociological) with outlook (psychological), and even for abandoning sociology's longstanding commitment to objectivity and universal truth. These criticisms highlighted pervasive tensions in her thought concerning equality and difference, environment and culture, science and values.

Yet, if Bernard failed to resolve key issues, she might plead in defense that they involved precisely the dilemmas many women of her generation chose to ignore.[69] Does the attainment of equality and individual freedom require a female solidarity that these same values in turn undermine? Are gender differences objective or subjective, permanent or conditioned? Does scientific objectivity preclude advocacy; are truth and conviction incompatible? In rediscovering the female world and at least raising these questions, Bernard returned, as it were, to the point where her generation came in.

Epilogue

By the time *The Female World* appeared, many feminists were seeking new direction. The meeting of the first National Women's Conference in Houston in November 1977 forged new understanding and alliances, much energy now focusing on the passage of the Equal Rights Amendment. In hindsight, however, the meeting was probably the high point of seventies activism. An anti-feminist backlash, already in the making, took shape in the anti-ERA campaign led by Phyllis Schlafly; in an antiabortion crusade that by the end of the decade had attracted eleven million members to the National Right to Life Committee; and in profamily organizations closely allied with a variety of conservative political groups. Despite several attempts further to extend the deadline for ratification, the ERA finally failed.[1]

Bernard and her associates in the SWS watched these developments with dismay. Even before the Houston conference, Alice Rossi wrote to her that "factionalism among the women's rights people" in some areas had had the "sad effect" of giving victories to "the anti-ERA Schaffley [*sic*] and pro-lifer people." Bernard was also "disconcerted . . . by the strength of their backlash," but, as usual, looked on the bright side. In a strange way, the reaction itself was a victory for feminism, she wrote, since it had stimulated the anti-ERA "housewives" to "learn how to use the suffrage, how to lobby, how to run a meeting." "They may fight us on some issues," she opined, "but they will support us on others."[2]

Ironically, the publication of Rossi's "Biosocial Perspective on Parenting" was at this time sparking debate within Bernard's own circle, one anticipated by the exchange within the SWS five years earlier. Again Rossi seemed to some to suggest that traditional sex roles were biologically determined, a position until then associated with the antifeminist writings of Midge Decter and others. "[Biological] explanations of behavior characterize conservative eras," one of Bernard's allies stated flatly—a charge echoed in one form or other by several contributors to a symposium on Rossi's work published in *Signs* in the summer of 1979.[3]

When Bernard wrote to register her own concerns, Rossi assured her that she did not believe "that biology determines anything." Rather the "mammalian heritage bit," as she characterized it, had only to do with "parameters that facilitate or restrict learning." "Beyond that, and indeed, affecting the expression of any innate factors, are the powerful set of economic and cultural factors that can crowd out expression of any biological predisposition."[4] Whether or not she was convinced, Bernard had both an intellectual and practical stake in the debate. However much she had questioned some aspects of her late husband's radical environmentalist creed, a distrust of biological explanations remained an unshakable legacy of L.L.B.'s attack on instincts.[5] This tradition she honored indirectly in skirmishes with sociobiology during the early 1970s, and now again in resisting Rossi's biosocial analysis, even though it departed dramatically from the crude biologizing of an earlier age. More practically, public identification with a new cult of maternity could discredit Bernard's forthcoming attempt to delineate a female world in purely structural (or sociological) terms, although whether she saw it this way remains uncertain.

At the same time, Rossi was an esteemed ally whose work she had known even before her feminist days. When, in the mid-1960s, Bernard had called for increased communication between the sexes as a solution to perennial division and tension, it was Rossi who wrote that she had not carried her analysis far enough. The problem of "social apartheid between the sexes" was not simply a matter of "technique" or "skills in conversation," Rossi insisted, but was the result of "the sterile and confining role of women to traditional wife-mother roles during the peak of their adult lives." Were women integrated into the world of work, the situation might be different. "Just as a woman can't take her husband for granted if she has opportunities to see him perform in his occupational role," she conjectured, "and sees the responses of other women and men to him in that world, and may

experience a private sexual pleasure to think that this figure is her
lover in marriage, so too, a husband could have a similar experience if
his wife were in the outside world, and he had an opportunity to see
her as a competent sophisticated women, and not just the bath-sweet
homebody who greets him warmly at the door of their apartment or
home."[6] During the next decade, it was also Rossi who mobilized
feminists within the ASA.

Whether from inherited conviction, practical considerations, or
some combination of both, Bernard in her contribution to the *Signs*
symposium thus equivocated. She regretted the loss of the supportive
female world of the nineteenth century; indeed, believed further
study was needed to provide knowledge of "how to rehabilitate it"—
an advance pitch for *The Female World* and, in itself, a revealing statement given that many women, dwelling in a female world throughout
their lives, would not think "rehabilitation" the proper term. However, Bernard did not believe "that the maternal role is adequate as a
core for a modern female world." But had Rossi argued this position?
Without answering this question, Bernard noncommittally applauded
Rossi's "contribution" to the debate. In *The Female World*, she cited
Rossi several times on the history of feminism, but consigned the
controversial article to the bibliography.[7]

From the Right, as some viewed it, "neofeminists" soon joined the
call for greater emphasis on family and a softpedaling of abortion,
lesbianism, and other Houston "hot-button" issues. Notable among
these new works were Betty Friedan's *Second Stage* (1981) and Jean B.
Elshstain's *Public Man, Private Woman* (1981), both published the same
year as *The Female World*. Writing as a liberal aware of the failures of
the liberal demand for gender-blind equality, Friedan criticized earlier
feminism (including *The Feminist Mystique*) for ignoring the family,
while warning against polarization over lesbianism and abortion.
Elshstain, more directly, proposed a "social feminism" that would
make children a central concern, reestablish clear boundaries between
public and private, and even support gender differentiation when
necessary.[8]

As with lesbianism, Bernard was personally sympathetic to the pro-
choice position. Faced with the birth of a third child three decades
before, as her husband lay dying of cancer, she had sought an abor-

tion for herself, even traveling to New York in her second trimester, where she and her sister Clara searched for an accommodating doctor. "To no avail," she reported, finally coming to terms with this episode in *Self-Portrait of a Family*. "We did not know the ropes." During the sixties, she found herself playing weekend host to some of Dorothy's classmates, only later realizing that they were in town seeking abortions. On one occasion, she even paid for an abortion for one of these friends.[9]

Yet, Bernard also had her own reasons for caution, reasons that restrained her from taking a lead on the issue, just as she had agreed to cease and desist in her public identification with lesbians. In her early writings she avoided the abortion issue, perhaps partly because of pressures not to discuss the matter in print, partly because of her continued devotion to scholarly detachment, and partly also because her own near-abortion was finally another source of guilt in dealing with her youngest son. In the early 1970s she asked her graduate student biographer to omit mention of the episode. In *The Future of Motherhood*, she appeared to applaud the Supreme Court's action in *Roe* v. *Wade*, although with characteristic detachment she noted that "for a considerable segment of the population, especially older people, it is not yet a settled issue"—a prescient statement considering developments by the late 1980s.[10] In *The Female World*, three brief references mentioned abortion as an issue dividing Catholic and non-Catholic women (hence, a faultline), as a problem for the indigent in the absence of government funds, and, above all, as a volatile social issue. Although the technology of abortion made the procedure less dangerous to the mother than full-term delivery, she noted, again the observer, "the emotional and political issues surrounding this particular area of technology are so searing that further progress may be braked. At least temporarily."[11]

Events meanwhile raised questions concerning Bernard's faith in changing the "restraining myths" of femininity, whether through "shared roles," experiments with one or another form of "open marriage," or the elimination of occupational stereotypes. In the family, in the workplace, and in society, the attack on gender stereotypes doubtless brought gains for many American women during the seventies. But the media—to mention only the most powerful voice—proved infinitely resourceful in this as in most other ways, whether perpetuating older stereotypes for comic purpose (witness Bernard's critique of "Mary Hartman, Mary Hartman") or creating seductively new ones in its celebration of what one historian has termed the "liberated, dress-for-success-superwoman."[12] With the change in sexual mores in response to the peril of AIDS, and the growing emphasis on family and children even among career women, Bernard's earlier call for open marriages and more sexual permissiveness seemed at best a monument to a more innocent, if not foolish, age. By the mid-1980s, Americans were also becoming familiar with a sobering new litany of problems affecting women, most of which Bernard addressed briefly or not at all: poverty and homelessness among single mothers (the "feminization of poverty"), structural sex-segregation in the marketplace, domestic violence, and child abuse.

Feminist theory was also outrunning Bernard's ability to keep up. Despite an impressive bibliography of some thirty-five pages, *The Female World* ignored a number of important books that had appeared in the previous decade.[13] When included, some were mentioned only superficially, as for example, Nancy Chodorow's *Reproduction of Mothering* (1978). During the 1980s, a new wave of scholarship raised questions that Bernard had not even asked, let alone answered. Among these were significant extensions of earlier analyses, as well as newer ones grounded in poststructuralist and postmodernist criticism.[14] In deconstructing the very notion of "woman," representatives of the latter, in particular, challenged the essentialism that sustained Bernard's analysis of a female world no less than of the "radical" feminists upon which she drew.[15] Whether these departures heralded a renewal of feminist activism, or were merely the owls of Minerva flying once again in the dusk, only the future would tell. By the late 1980s, Bernard's work in any case looked less like a bridge to the 1990s than a monument to the 1970s.

RATHER than attempt to assess her contributions in light of recent developments or to predict the future, this study has focused on the forces that shaped Bernard's vision through the early 1980s. In microcosm, these forces were similar to those that affected the lives of many middle-class professionals of her generation. The starting point was the scientistic ethos of the interwar years, an ethos shared alike by men and women, WASPS and the children of immigrants. In the Minneapolis of Bernard's youth, Yankee values joined the vestiges of the Jewish enlightenment to create an ideal contained in the three words "modern," "scientific," and "American." At college, she found in her future husband, Luther Bernard—a behaviorist, a scientist, and a virtual caricature of WASP values—an embodiment of these ideals. "Contrary to what you think," she once wrote him, "I react very strongly against the Jewish prejudices of my family and cling to you partly as a protection against being a Jew."[16] One result eventually was a professional career of her own. But the price on the way included a struggle with negative self-perceptions in the form of antifeminine and anti-Semitic stereotypes that might have crippled someone less determined and resilient. Personal traumas and professional style, moreover, were not unrelated. A way of dealing with "disorderly data," the rigorous, scientistic sociology she adopted during the 1930s in effect denied those dimensions of experience rooted in ethnicity and gender: the first, in taking a behaviorist approach to social behavior, thus denigrating culture, custom, and tradition, her family's included; the second, in championing emotional detachment and rigorous methodology.

Although rooted in western history, these ethnic and gender stereotypes expressed tensions that beset many Americans as they entered the modern era. Luther Bernard was doubtless an eccentric, but he was also a product of his times. What distinguished her husband was not the inner conflicts that tore him apart, Jessie once wrote, but his ability to bring them out into the open. If seemingly unrelated, his attacks on women and on Jews, combining denial of and yearning for the sensual and material pleasures of modern life, were but one evidence of a split between the public and private selves that manifested itself at every level of his thought and activity. Publicly the austere, censorious, workaholic, "objective" professional, he was, in private, an emotional disaster zone, seeking through his work the denial of feeling and seeking in the domination of others a surrogate for an inner certainty that had long since vanished, if it ever existed. Although

Jessie shared some of his cruder prejudices willy-nilly, the roles each played in this drama during their early years together were mirror opposites: he, the controller; she, the controlled.

To understand their relationship is to see in personal terms how the social and economic changes of the interwar years worked to fulfill one goal of prewar feminism, while weakening or destroying the female network that sustained it emotionally and organizationally. For young women in the 1920s (Jessie Bernard among them), the intoxicating mix of new ideas, new freedom, and new fashions was easy to mistake for more meaningful emancipation—especially so for the bright and ambitious daughter of Jewish immigrants, anxious to prove her "Americanness" in a region still dominated by Yankee values. Through most of her early life—to state the matter abstractly—ethnicity proved to be at least as important as gender, while the flapper ethos bred subtle new forms of competition among women for the favors of men. In achieving professional success, Bernard also looked to men rather than any female network for encouragement and support. Professional success, once achieved, obscured the way that success was won: overcoming (if not hiding) the fact that one was a woman.

Only as Bernard moved beyond these self-perceptions and a coldly quantitative sociology, was feminism an emotional and intellectual possibility. On the negative side, a series of experiences from the mid-1930s onward led her gradually to see the less happy sides of her husband's scientism: the immoral behavior of French positivist Edger as she encountered it in Paris; the "expert" advice of the psychiatrist who urged that she take an "objective" view and return to her husband; the elitist, apparently unfeeling, and even arrogant behavior of her longtime friend George Lundberg in the face of the monstrosity of world war, coupled with her growing recognition of the Nazi abuse of science in the Holocaust.

While these experiences subconsciously chipped away her faith in the professional/scientific ethos, she gradually came to terms with her ethnicity and her sex. A first step was a decision to join the Society of Friends in the late 1930s, at the same time refusing any longer to indulge her husband's tirades against Jews and her family, a process of healing that eventually took several decades. A second, paradoxically, was her crusade for motherhood, as well as the emotional experience of having children. A third was a shift in sociological orientation from the conflict and problems approach she early absorbed from Robert Park and others to an emphasis on role and status. Wedded to a rigorously quantitative sociology in the 1930s, and then the organization/disorganization model in the 1940s, Bernard initially failed to explore the implications of cultural lag for women. Her adoption of a role and status approach in the 1950s, although it did not initially lead to feminism, focused her attention on the socialization of sex roles, on the dysfunctional aspects of current conceptions, and, ultimately, on gender as a category of analysis.

During the early 1960s, Bernard's struggles as single parent (and her relations with her daughter in particular) brought these issues closer to home. Although relative affluence shielded her from the material burdens of child care and household management, it did not free her from traditional assumptions concerning "normal" family life. Thus, she attempted to play both father and mother, analyzing and hectoring in one breath, and consoling and comforting in the next. To her daughter and sons alike, she dispensed advice on how men and women should behave, while blaming any difficulties on the absence of a male. If one result was a nagging guilt, another was a gradual realization of the negative effects of the "feminine mystique" on her own daughter, first in casual self-denigration, then in a tempestuous courtship and unhappy marriage.

Although scarcely feminist by later standards, *Academic Women* marked an important step along this road, a book whose covert message, for some readers at least, outweighed its conclusion that discrimination was not the major problem. Bernard's attempt in the mid-1960s to come to terms with the cultural patterns of African Americans (in *Marriage and Family among Negroes*) and the separatist demands of black power advocates forced her to face, however unsatisfactorily, the realities of cultural difference; while Thomas Kuhn's theory of scientific revolutions convinced her that even science could not transcend culture. By the early 1970s, she was persuaded that, just as blacks faced a racism more pervasive and insidious than discrimination, so sexism permeated American society and culture. While battling discrimination, she thus explored gender bias within social science and the contours of women's world. However much intrigued by the analyses of younger radicals of the early 1970s, she could never quite accept the separatist or subjectivist implications of their work. The job of feminism, as she finally pictured it in *The Female World*, was not to restructure the existing order or to withdraw from male society, but "to rethink, reconceptualize, revamp the female world to adapt it to 'modern times.' "[7]

An underlying theme in this intellectual odyssey was an ongoing tension between reason and emotion, objectivity and value, professionalism and activism. In her early years Bernard experienced these tensions as a Jew and a woman attracted by the promise of science and professionalism. In her public debate with George Lundberg in the late 1940s, in her embrace of game theory in the late 1950s, and, finally, in her call for a feminist sociology, the question was whether values are extrinsic or intrinsic to science. In her excursion into conflict theory, it was whether the reality of permanent conflict can be effectively eliminated with the help of scientific analysis. In still another form, it was the relative power of culture and environment or, finally, whether cultures (of American blacks, Third World peoples, or even women) can and should be studied and judged by universal standards.

IF BERNARD'S intellectual development both resembled and differed from that of male professionals of her generation, the question remains whether in moving from positivism to feminism she was not simply adopting the latest sociological fashion. A superficial reading might suggest this conclusion. At every stage she was, if not at the cutting edge, rarely more than a conference or two behind. But in the context of her life and career, the case was more complicated. As a Jew and a woman in a world predominantly Gentile and male, she was acutely aware of her marginality, or biculturality. Yet its implications for her thought were even greater than she supposed. In the effort to escape her ethnicity and sex, she sought to be American, to be scientific, and finally to have a "normal" family. In her quest for professional recognition, she likewise adopted the latest sociological theories ("coins of the realm") almost without thinking. At the same time, the realities of ethnicity and sex provided a critical distance, and resulting doubts on each point. Was she American? objective? even normal? Echoing women writers of a century before, she toiled relentlessly at her profession while denying she was "running a career."[18]

A similar dialectic persisted in her feminist writings. Although her emphasis on gender bias and the integrity of Third World cultures pointed to relativism and subjectivism, her belief in a universal reason and common standards (a faith preserved in her continuing work on a "Female Enlightenment") was too indelibly part of her acculturation to be easily abandoned. Despite the charge from one of her critics, she never quite said that there "can be no science of sociology" apart from its ideological uses—again being unwilling and/or unable to reject the canons of professionalization that guided her throughout her career.[19]

An understanding of this career also explains why Bernard altered her position on key issues. Having denied the existence of "feminine" instincts, she now posited separate male and female spheres. Having insisted on the priority of environment over culture, she now appeared to suggest that cultural stereotypes could be altered apart from structural changes in the environment. Having once practiced agentic sociology with a passion, she now called for a communal (and hence feminist) social science.

These changes, in effect, were a chronicle of her life. Just as her stormy marriage found echo in her interest in conflict and game theory, so it produced a nagging sense that some differences between men and women are irreconcilable. Hers was not simply a "bad" marriage, but rather a relationship held together by the determined search for strategies for mutual survival. Just as she finally did not leave Luther, so feminism must improve on marriage, not repudiate it. Although society will improve if "males" adopt "female" values, "his" and "her" remain immutable categories.

Bernard also learned the power of cultural stereotypes the hard way. Whereas some individuals in every society have the good fortune to rise effortlessly above current stereotypes, whether of themselves or others, she felt their power with peculiar intensity—negatively as the "unpolished" Jew or "hysterical" female; more positively as the "new woman" of the 1920s or the wife and mother of the 1940s "feminine mystique." Feeling this power—indeed, at one point suggesting that stereotypes play an important role in social relations—she as easily assumed that their demise would usher in the millennium.

Bernard's critique of science and the professions also registered the price she paid in her personal dealings with her husband, in her experiences during the difficult years of single parenthood, perhaps even in the inner turmoil that so long characterized her emotional life. Although her speculations concerning agentic science have found some confirmation in a growing literature documenting male bias in science and social science (including Sandra Harding's 1986 *Science Question in Feminism,* a winner of the ASA's Jessie Bernard award), much of Bernard's critique will surprise only those who once believed that social science somehow exists totally apart from the culture in which it develops. Just as this objectivist credo was a caricature of the scientific enterprise—and as such arguably followed a WASP male agenda—so also Bernard's attack on agentic science ignored the emergence within these same social sciences of some of the best feminist writing, also observing traditional scholarly canons. The universalistic standards she now questions have served as a vehicle for the entry of non-WASPS and women into the professions, once overt discrimination has been eliminated.

"I am as undisciplined a feminist as I am an undisciplined sociologist," Bernard reminisced as she approached her eighty-fifth birthday, taking pride in the ambiguities and even contradictions in her thought. "I mind being restricted to any one ideological position." As a result, some feminists called her a Marxist (as a compliment), while others leveled the same charge in criticism (both quite wrong, as this study suggests). "If either charge is true, it is coincidental," she continued. "My preferred stance is non- or omni-ideological." Then, more critically: "I find myself unable to catch the delicate nuances that require one to reject all of any particular canon in order to accept any part of another—even opposite—canon."[20]

Whether one judges such eclecticism a strength or a weakness (and here opinion again will differ) this self-analysis captures the basis of much of Bernard's appeal: an openness to new ideas, an ability to articulate issues before others have done so, and an engaging frankness concerning her own shortcomings. A liberal sensitive to radical perspectives, a professional woman aware of the limits of professionalism, she has been a feminist for all seasons. To many of her colleagues, her scholarly accomplishments provide reason enough to applaud her career. To others, she deserves celebration as a rebel, albeit a reasonable one.

Although it is probably too early to assign Jessie Bernard a permanent place in the history of feminism, let alone of sociology, the absence of her name from several recent surveys of feminist thought suggests that she may be better remembered as mentor and role model than as feminist theorist. Whatever the future, this study has attempted to show that the past is more interesting and complex than either her critics or admirers may have assumed.

Notes

ABBREVIATIONS

The following abbreviations are used in the notes to identify manuscript sources:

GAL George A. Lundberg Papers, University of Washington Library

HWO Howard W. Odum Papers, University of North Carolina, Chapel Hill

JB   Jessie Bernard Papers, Labor Archives, Pennsylvania State University Libraries

LLB Luther Lee Bernard Papers, Labor Archives, Pennsylvania State University Libraries

PPB Provided by Professor Bernard

RB   Read Bain Papers, Michigan Historical Collections, University of Michigan

TP   Talcott Parsons Papers, Harvard University

WFO William F. Ogburn Papers, University of Chicago

INTRODUCTION

1. Adopting the usual conventions, I refer to Bernard as "Jessie" as a youth, and "Bernard" or "Jessie Bernard" as an adult. I sometimes also use "Jessie" when other individuals on stage would have thought of her as such, or to distinguish her from her husband, Luther Bernard. In the notes, Bernard refers to Jessie Bernard unless otherwise identified.

2. Bernard, "My Four Revolutions," 775; Safier, "Jessie Bernard," 298–302; Sociologists for Women in Society, *Newsletter* 1 (March 1971): 1.

3. Bernard, *Future of Marriage*, 327–328.

4. "Major ASA Awards Given in San Francisco," *Footnotes* 17 (October 1989): 1.
5. Bernard, *Female World,* ix.
6. Bernard, "My Four Revolutions." Her source for this distinction was Carlson, "Sex Differences in Ego Functioning," and "Understanding Women."
7. Bernard, *Female World,* 23.
8. Jessie to Dorothy Lee Bernard, March 25, 1959, excerpt, JB.
9. Bernard, "Letters Department," 5–7.
10. For a recent taxonomy of feminist thought employing these categories see Tong, *Feminist Thought.* To those listed, Tong adds a discussion of postmodern feminism, mostly work written since the early 1980s of which Bernard was unaware. Variations of this taxonomy may be found in Scott, "Gender." For an earlier summary of feminist thought (including "liberal" feminism) from the "socialist feminist" position see Jaggar, *Feminist Politics and Human Nature.* A less complete and hence less satisfactory taxonomy of feminist thought may be found in Ferree and Hess, *Controversy and Coalition,* chapter 7, who distinguish four positions within contemporary feminism: "career" (highest priority on parity in labor force); "liberal" (equality under law); "socialist" (fundamental change in social order); and "radical" (altered consciousness tending toward separatism). Wandersee, *On the Move,* xiii–xvii, labels the first two "liberal" (or "reform") feminism and the latter two "radical," noting a split in the radical camp between "New Left feminists" ("politicos") and "cultural feminists." See also Donovan, *Feminist Theory.* For useful theoretical discussions of the issue see Harding, "Instability"; and Offen, "Defining Feminism." Since all categories serve both polemical and practical purposes, and in any case are rarely airtight, they should be treated accordingly.
11. Tong, *Feminist Thought,* 26–29.
12. Bernard, *Female World,* 494–495, 19–20, 132.
13. Bernard, "Age, Sexism, and Feminism," 137.
14. Bernard, *Female World,* 553.
15. For use of this term see O'Neill, *Everyone Was Brave.*
16. For example, Bernard is mentioned in none of the surveys cited in note 10 above.
17. Of the sociologists mentioned, only two to my knowledge have published autobiographical accounts of their careers. See Hughes, "Maid of All Work," and her "Wasp/Woman/Sociologist"; and Cavan, "Chicago School of Sociology." This study of Bernard's career is preliminary to a larger study of American women social scientists of this generation, including several of the figures mentioned.
18. Bernard, *American Family Behavior,* 458. For this criticism see Safier, "Jessie Bernard," 173.

19. See chapter 7.

20. Bernard to Gwendolyn Safier, September 12, 1971, JB.

21. Explaining this concept, Robert H. Lowie wrote: "This means that [the anthropologist] will account for a given cultural fact by demonstrating some other cultural fact, by merging it into a group of cultural facts or by demonstrating some other cultural fact out of which it has developed" (Robert H. Lowie, *Culture and Ethnology* [New York: D.C. Murtie, 1917], 66, quoted in Cravens, *Triumph of Evolution*, 89).

22. For example, see Bernard, *Female World*, 372: "Culture is dealt with here as coeval with social structure, not independent of it, but enough different from it to warrant separate discussion."

23. For examples of this debate see O'Neill, *Everyone Was Brave*, vii; Lemons, *Woman Citizen*, vii; and Ware, *Beyond the New Deal*, 130–131.

24. Cott, *Grounding of Modern Feminism*, chapter 1.

25. Kraditor, *Ideas of the Woman Suffrage Movement*.

26. See Lemons, *Woman Citizen*, chapter 9; Sharf, *To Work and Wed*.

27. At first glance the figures seem to belie this assessment since the percentage of employed women classified as professional rose from 8.2 percent in 1900 to 14.2 percent in 1930. The group of "professional and kindred" workers was 40 percent female when the total work force was only 20 percent female. But these figures are misleading. Three-fourths of the increase in female professionals before 1920 was the result of the expansion of teaching and nursing. As Cott has summed up the case, "[The] high point in woman's share of professional employment (and attainment of advanced degrees) overall occurred by the late 1920s, and was followed by stasis and/or decline not reversed to any extent until the 1960s and 1970s" (*Grounding of Modern Feminism*, 218, 220). For a survey of this literature see Brumberg and Tomes, "Women in the Professions."

28. Cott, *Grounding of Modern Feminism*, 233, 237, 239. An apparent exception was the support professional women gave to the ERA—apparent because this support was out of self-interest and bred a split within the women's movement that persisted for decades. See Lemons, *Woman Citizen*, 41, 199–205.

29. Cott, *Grounding of Modern Feminism*, 216.

30. For useful discussion of the relevant literature see Anderson, *Wartime Women*, 8–11; Honey, *Creating Rosie the Riveter*.

31. Rupp and Taylor, *Survival in the Doldrums*.

32. She eventually became more than aware of this underside. See Bernard, *Future of Marriage*, 244–257; chapter 8; and Evans, *Personal Politics*.

33. Telephone interviews with Professors Frank Clemente at Penn State and Marvin Bressler at Princeton.

34. Bernard, "Academia 1947–1964," 6, MS PPB. This manuscript was for her projected autobiography.

35. For example, Safier, "Jessie Bernard."

36. Ralph Turner (UCLA), quoted in "Major ASA Awards," 1.

37. Bernard herself has stressed its suddenness, using the term "epiphany" on at least one occasion (Bernard, "Academia 1947–1964," 12, MS PPB).

CHAPTER ONE: THIRD CHILD

1. Bernard, "A Nineteenth-Century Childhood," ca. 1980s, MS PPB. Much of the material in this chapter is taken from this autobiographical sketch. See also Bernard, *Self-Portrait of a Family,* xvii–xix. Barney Kantar [cousin] to Jessie Bernard, February 2, 1982, JB, provides an expanded account of family genealogy based on his own research. Kantar found that Jessie's grandmother made three trips to the United States and lived for a time with a second husband in Florida prior to bringing her daughter to New York. The date of the original immigration is thus in doubt. Although this same source gives the family name as "Kantar," I use "Kanter" as given in the 1900 United States census for Minneapolis (cited by Bernard, *Self-Portrait of a Family,* xviii).

2. Kramer and Leventman, *Children of the Gilded Ghetto,* 39; United States Census 1890, *Population,* vol 1, cl. For background see also Plaut, *Jews in Minnesota.*

3. Kramer and Leventman, *Children of the Gilded Ghetto,* 42–43.

4. Ibid., 37–38, 56. See also Bernard, "Nineteenth-Century Childhood," MS PPB.

5. Salisbury, "Victorian City in the Midwest," 49–75; Federal Writers' Project, *Minnesota: A State Guide,* 80.

6. Bernard, "The Twentieth Century Seen through the Life of an American Woman," 3, ca. 1980s, MS PPB.

7. Bernard, "Sarah Gordon," 44, ca. 1928, MS JB.

8. Ibid., 44–45.

9. For example, see Walker, *American City.*

10. Bernard, "Biculturality," 286; "One Alumna's Story," 55; Safier, "Jessie Bernard," 29, 44.

11. Bernard, "Biculturality," 267.

12. Bernard, "Nineteenth-Century Childhood," 6, MS PPB.

13. Bernard, "Biculturality," 284.

14. Bernard, "Some Disadvantages of Being a Happily Married Woman," ca. 1927–1935, MS JB.

15. Bernard, "Biculturality," 271.
16. Bernard, *Self-Portrait of a Family*, 326.
17. Bernard, "Nineteenth-Century Childhood," 11, MS PPB.
18. Bernard, "Sarah Gordon," 22, 37, MS JB.
19. Quotes in this and the previous paragraph are from Bernard, "Biculturality," 277. On Jenks see Fine and Severance, "Great Men and Hard Times."
20. Bernard, "Biculturality," 277. Cf. Ehrenreich and English, *For Her Own Good*, chapter 5.
21. Bernard, "Little Sister," ca. 1928–1935, MS JB.
22. Decades later, Bernard described her sister as "a strong, courageous, vastly creative child. The world was her oyster" (*Self-Portrait of a Family*, 326).
23. Clara Lambert to Jessie Bernard, April 28, 1929, LLB. Clara Rose Lambert (1898–1953) served as Director of Teacher Education at the Play Schools Association during the late 1930s and 1940s. Her many publications include *Manhattan: Now and Long Ago* [with Lucy Sprague Mitchell] (New York, 1934); *I Sing America* (New York, 1941); and *Understand Your Child–From Six to Twelve* (New York, 1948). See her obituary in the *New York Times*, August 12, 1953, 31.
24. Bernard, "Lucy Page," MS JB.
25. Bernard, "Biculturality," 284, 277.
26. Ibid., 268–269, 270.
27. Bernard, untitled essay, ca. 1928–1937, MS JB; "Sarah Gordon," 31, MS JB.
28. Bernard, "Sarah Gordon," x, 35, MS JB.
29. Safier, "Jessie Bernard," 31.
30. Bernard, MS fragment, 288a, ca. 1937, JB. This fragment was preserved only because Bernard used the paper for another letter. The remainder was apparently destroyed, although it may have been a reworking of the novel "Sarah Gordon."
31. Bernard, "Sarah Gordon," 6–8 MS JB.
32. Gordon, *Jews in Transition*, 46.
33. Kramer and Leventman, *Children of the Gilded Ghetto*, 43.
34. Bernard, "Biculturality," 283.
35. Ibid., 285.
36. See especially "Biculturality," 279–280.
37. Gordon, *Jews in Transition*, 162–163. For a more detailed account see Plaut, *Jews in Minnesota*, chapters 16–30.
38. Bernard, "Biculturality," 281.
39. Bernard, untitled autobiographical fragment, 11–12, ca. 1980s, MS PPB. The book was Paul Cowan, *An Orphan in History* (Garden City, N.Y.: Doubleday, 1982).

40. Bernard, "Biculturality," 281.
41. Bernard, *Self-Portrait of a Family,* 41–47.
42. Bernard, untitled autobiographical fragment, 8, MS PPB.
43. The study was Young-Bruehl, *Hannah Arendt.*
44. Bernard, untitled autobiographical fragment, 11, MS PPB. This fragment provides the basis for the analysis in the following two paragraphs.
45. Young-Bruehl, *Hannah Arendt,* 233, quoted in Bernard, untitled autobiographical fragment, 14, MS PPB.
46. Bernard, "Nineteenth-Century Childhood," 5a, MS PPB.
47. Luther to Jessie Bernard, March 27, 1938, LLB.
48. See the following works by Bernard: "Culture as Environment"; "Neighborhood Behavior of School Children"; "Biculturality"; with Meahl and Smith, *Dating, Mating, and Marriage;* "Where is the Modern Sociology of Conflict?"

CHAPTER TWO: HÉLOÏSE

1. *Minnesota Daily,* May 22, 1924, advertising a series in *Photoplay Magazine* for June 1924.
2. Bernard, "A Twentieth-Century Girlhood," ca. 1980s, MS PPB.
3. Gordon, *Jews in Transition,* 313.
4. Bernard, "Twentieth-Century Girlhood," 9 MS PPB; "One Alumna's Story." For background see Gray, *University of Minnesota.*
5. Bernard, *Academic Women,* 6–8.
6. Bernard, "Twentieth-Century Girlhood, 7, MS PPB.
7. "Kindergarten Skirts," and "The Lyre," *Minnesota Daily,* November 4, 1920; "Masculine Femininity vs. Feminine Masculinity," ibid., December 2, 1920.
8. "Men Wash Dishes While Fair Sex Seeks 'Position,' " ibid., October 13, 1920; "Women Plead for Chance at Tyrant Profs," ibid., February 2, 1922; "Girls Set Date for Tribute to Maria Sanford," ibid., November 20, 1923.
9. "Kappa Rho Society Girls Meet Friday," ibid., December 1, 1921.
10. Bernard, "Biculturality, 274–275. Although Bernard called the subject of this analysis Milltown, the descriptions were taken from Minneapolis.
11. Jessie to Luther Bernard, August 12, 1922, LLB.
12. Ibid., August 15, 1922, LLB.
13. Safier, "Jessie Bernard," 43.
14. Jessie to Luther Bernard, August 19, 1922, LLB.
15. On Minnesota sociology see Martindale, *Romance of a Profession;* Fine and Severance, "Great Men and Hard Times"; and Bannister, *Sociology and Scientism,* chapters 9 and 10.

16. Florence A. Johnson to Luther Bernard, August 2, 1927, LLB.

17. Jessie Bernard to Gwen Safier, July 12, 1971, JB.

18. Lila Kline to Luther Bernard, July 26, 1920 [?], LLB; Martha Shubert to Luther Bernard, ca. 1920, LLB.

19. Elizabeth Hayes to Luther Bernard, August 28, 1920, LLB.

20. Bernard, *Self-Portrait of a Family*, xix.

21. The material in the following three paragraphs is adapted from Bannister, *Sociology and Scientism*, chapters 8–9. It is fully documented there.

22. Helen to Luther Bernard, ca. 1947, LLB.

23. For full discussion of this issue see Bannister, *Sociology and Scientism*, chapter 8.

24. Luther Bernard, Diary, June 14, 1925, LLB. The Bernards sporadically kept diaries in notebooks and datebooks of various sizes and lengths. All are here called "Diary."

25. Luther to Jessie Bernard, December 25, 1937, LLB.

26. "Heather," Diary, December 1921, box 18, packet 29, LLB.

27. Luther Bernard, Diary, April 22, 1917, LLB.

28. Jessie Bernard, Diary, January 10, 1925, LLB.

29. Luther Bernard to Ernest Reuter, January 3, 1926, LLB.

30. I refer to this young woman as "Heather" throughout the text and notes.

31. Heather to Luther Bernard, May 18, 1922, LLB.

32. Luther to Jessie Bernard, May 4, 1936, LLB.

33. Luther Bernard to Heather, August 20, 1921, LLB. The above two paragraphs are based on Bannister, *Sociology and Scientism*, 132–133.

34. Jessie to Luther Bernard, June 19, 1923, LLB.

35. Martha Shubert to Luther Bernard, June 18, 1924, LLB.

36. Luther to Frances Bernard, ca. fall 1921, LLB. He reported this remark to his first wife.

37. [Name withheld] to Luther Bernard, November 24, 1922, and April 22, 1924, LLB.

38. Elizabeth Hayes to Luther Bernard, June 30 [1920]; Martha Shubert to Luther Bernard, June 18, 1924, LLB.

39. Luther Bernard, "Statement of Motives," September 12, 1933, LLB.

40. Jessie to Luther Bernard, August 4, 24, 1922, LLB.

41. Ibid., August 27, 31, 1922.

42. Bernard, "Twentieth-Century Girlhood," MS PPB.

43. William McDougall, *An Introduction to Social Psychology*, 8th ed. (Boston: Luce, 1914), 390–391, quoted ibid., 3.

44. On Theda Bara see Banner, *Women in Modern America*, 164–165.

45. "Twentieth-Century Girlhood," MS PPB.

46. Jessie to Luther Bernard, August 25, 19, 1922, LLB.

47. Ibid., August 19, 1922.

48. Ibid.

49. Ibid., August 12, 1922.

50. Ibid., August 24, 1922.

51. Ibid., August 12, 1922.

52. Ibid., August 15, 1922.

53. Ibid., "Wednesday Night," April 1923?, July 3, 1923.

54. Ibid., ca. September 1923.

55. Ibid., June 26, 1923.

56. Bernard, *Female World*, 543. The evolution of this anecdote in Bernard's memory is revealing. In one autobiographical sketch, the antifeminist is a "gentlewoman" ("Twentieth-Century Girlhood," 7, MS PPB) but in later versions, a male. The teachers likewise evolve from "suffragists, their version of feminists" (7) to "staunch feminists."

57. Jessie to Luther Bernard, August 25, 31, 1922, LLB.

58. Ibid., ca. 1923.

59. Ibid., July 7, 1922.

60. Ibid., n.d. [but filed with letters dated September 1923].

61. Ibid., January 6, 1925.

62. Ibid., January 1, 1926.

63. Ibid., January 21, 1924.

64. Ibid., January 1, 1926.

65. Ibid., August 27, 1922.

66. This book was probably Phyllis M. Blanchard's *Adolescent Girls from a Psychoanalytic Viewpoint* (New York, 1920).

67. Jessie to Luther Bernard, August 27, 1922, LLB.

68. Ibid., August 24, 1922.

69. Luther Bernard, Diary, June 8, 1925, LLB. For a more detailed account of this incident see Bannister, *Sociology and Scientism*, 132–134.

70. Jessie Bernard to Bruce Melvin, ca. April 1925, LLB.

71. Jessie to Luther Bernard, August 29, 1922, LLB.

72. Luther Bernard, "Journal of an Intimate Affair," January 26, 1923, LLB. On this occasion, Luther Bernard wrote to Heather on September 19, 1923: "Just the other day, Miss R, who for some reason always turns up as if by intuition when I am unhappy about you, came into my office. . . . But no one can satisfy me but you" (LLB).

73. Jessie to Luther Bernard, ca. April 1923, LLB.

74. Jessie Bernard, Diary, January 12, 1925, LLB.

75. Luther Bernard, Diary, January 12, 1925, LLB.

76. Ibid., January 12, June 8, 1925.

77. Frances to Luther Bernard, ca. 1925; Luther Bernard, "Statement of Motives," September 12, 1933; marriage contract, December 3, 1924, LLB.

78. The last two paragraphs are based on Luther Bernard, "Statement of Motives," September 12, 1933.

79. Clara Lambert to Jessie Bernard, February 16, 1926, LLB; David Ravitch to Jessie Bernard, February 7, 1926, LLB.

80. Luther to Jessie Bernard, March 26, 1938, LLB.

81. Luther Bernard to David Ravitch, February 6, 1926 [pencil draft], LLB.

82. Noah Lambert to Luther Bernard, July 2, 12, 1926, LLB.

83. Clara Lambert to Jessie Bernard, January 24, 1928, LLB.

84. Luther Bernard, Diary, February, 1926; F. Stuart Chapin to Luther Bernard, July 28, 1926, LLB.

85. Luther Bernard, Diary, July 1926, LLB.

86. Luther Bernard, "Statement of Motives," September 12, 1933, LLB.

87. Bernard, "Sins of the Mother," and "Joshua March's Revenge," MSS JB.

88. Bernard, "Little Sister," MS JB.

89. Jessie to Luther Bernard, ca. 1937, LLB.

90. Bernard, "Puritan's Mistress," MS JB.

91. Jessie to Luther Bernard, October 14, 1936, LLB.

92. Ehrenreich, *Hearts of Men*, chapter 4.

CHAPTER THREE: RESEARCH ASSISTANT

1. Odum to Steiner, June 24, 1927, HWO.

2. Odum to Luther Bernard, March 13, 1928, LLB.

3. For a full account of these developments see Bannister, *Sociology and Scientism*, chapters 13–15.

4. Bernard, "History and Prospects of Sociology."

5. Bernard, "Instrument for the Measurement of Neighborhood." For discussion of this and related studies of the 1930s see chapter 4.

6. These manuscripts are in JB. Since the frugal Bernards often wrote on the reverse side of old letters, exams, and other dated materials, it would appear that the original of most of the novels, including the semi-autobiographical "Sarah Gordon," were written about 1928. One exception is a short story, "The Runaway Wife," which was probably written in the mid-1930s.

7. Mathilde Weil to Jessie Bernard, February 2, 1931, LLB.

8. Of sixty chapters in *Origins of American Sociology*, Jessie wrote thirty-three. See Bernard, *Self-Portrait of a Family*, 341.

9. Luther to Jessie Bernard, May 4, 1936, LLB.

10. Jessie to Luther Bernard, June 19, 1928, JB.

11. Ibid. For an earlier example of a similar argument see Charlotte P. Gilman, *Women and Economics* (Boston: Small, Maynard, 1898).

12. Jessie to Luther Bernard, June 19, 1928, JB.

13. Luther to Jessie Bernard, September 20, 1930, LLB.

14. Ibid., September 20, 1930, June 19, 1931, January 7, 1932.

15. Ibid., January 21, 1932.

16. On Edger see Luther and Jessie Bernard, *Origins of American Sociology*, 163–172.

17. Luther to Jessie Bernard, October 11, December 15, 1935, LLB; Eda to Jessie Bernard, October 14, 1935, LLB.

18. Jessie to Luther Bernard, October 2, 1930, LLB.

19. Ibid., October 22, November 4, 26, December 10, 1935.

20. Ibid., October 19, and n.d., 1935.

21. Luther to Jessie Bernard, April 15, 1936, LLB; unsigned letters, June 1928–March 1929, LLB; "Me" to Luther Bernard, 1931, LLB; "Eda" to Luther Bernard, 1934–1935, LLB; Jessie to Luther Bernard, June 20, 1936, LLB; Luther to Jessie Bernard, May 9, 1936, LLB.

22. Jessie Bernard to Dr. Sidney Schwab, June 20, 1936, LLB.

23. Bernard, "Lucy Page," MS JB; Jesse to Luther Bernard, January 28, 1936, LLB.

24. Clara Lambert to Jessie Bernard, June 9, 1928, January 29, 1929, LLB; Jessie to Luther Bernard, December 29, 1931, LLB.

25. Jessie to Luther Bernard, 1924, LLB.

26. Jessie Bernard to Gwendolyn Safier, August 24, 1971, JB.

27. Luther Bernard, Diary, January 12, 1925, LLB.

28. Luther Bernard to David Ravitch, February 6, 1926, LLB.

29. Luther to Jessie Bernard, September 30, 1931, LLB.

30. Luther Bernard, Diary, June 12, 14, 1926, LLB.

31. Jessie to Luther Bernard, December 29, 1931, May 19, 1936, LLB.

32. Helen to Luther Bernard, April 23, 1932, "Monday A.M." [1932], LLB.

33. Luther to Jessie Bernard, October 18, 1935, LLB.

34. Ibid., October 19, 24, November 3, 1935.

35. Luther Bernard, Diary, August 18, 1936, LLB; Luther to Jessie Bernard, February 3, 1937, LLB.

36. Luther to Jessie Bernard, December 29, 1936, LLB; Luther Bernard, Diary, 1939, 15, LLB.

37. Luther to Jessie Bernard, April 13, July 23, 1938, LLB; Luther Bernard, Diary, September 9, 1939, LLB.

38. Jessie to Luther Bernard, ca. January 1924, LLB.

39. Jessie Bernard, Diary, ca. April 1926, LLB.

40. Jessie to Luther Bernard, December 22, 29, 1931, November 12, 1935, January 18, 1936, LLB.

41. Du Bois, *Souls of Black Folk,* 16–17.

42. Bernard, "Analysis of Jewish Culture," 448. This account "from the writer's files" was certainly autobiographical. It was omitted when the article was reprinted in *Jews in a Gentile World.*

43. Jessie to Luther Bernard, October 5, 1936, LLB.

44. Jessie to Luther Bernard, October 5, December 12, 25, 31, 1936, LLB; Jessie Bernard to T.V. Smith, January 1937, LLB. See also December 19, 1936, January 13, 1937, March 28, April 16, 1938, LLB.

45. Although not identified in the correspondence, the manuscript was probably the novel "Sarah Gordon" or a second autobiographical piece of which remnants remain in JB.

46. Jessie to Luther Bernard, February 26, 1937, LLB.

47. Ibid., December 19, 1936.

48. Bernard, "Analysis of Jewish Culture," 440, 430.

49. Ibid., 449–450.

50. Ibid., 439.

51. Jessie to Luther Bernard, March 3, April 16, 1938, LLB.

52. Luther to Jessie Bernard, October 1, 1938, LLB; Jessie to Luther Bernard, October 3, 1938, LLB.

53. For more detailed analysis see Bannister, *Sociology and Scientism,* chapter 9.

54. Bernard, "Analysis of Jewish Culture," 443.

55. Luther Bernard, Diary, September 6, 1939, LLB.

56. Ibid., January 25, 1948, LLB.

57. Bernard, "Analysis of Jewish Culture," 437.

CHAPTER FOUR: RUNAWAY WIFE

1. Bernard, Curriculum Vita, and "Coming of Age," ca. 1980s, MSS PPB; Jessie to Luther Bernard, May 24, 1938, LLB.

2. Jessie Bernard to George Lundberg, January 3, 1937, GAL.

3. Luther to Jessie Bernard, January 2, 13, March [n.d.], 1937, LLB.

4. Ibid., March 22, 1938, December 15, 1938.

5. Luther Bernard to Myking Mehus, June 4, 1939, LLB.

6. Luther to Jessie Bernard, November 8, 1936, LLB.

7. Jessie Bernard, Diary, April 18, 1940, LLB.

8. Luther to Jessie Bernard, June 11, 1936, LLB.

9. Ibid., March 2, 1938.

10. Luther Bernard, Diary, January 12, 1925, LLB. In 1959 the American Sociological Society (ASS) was renamed the American Sociological Association (ASA). Read Bain later credited the change to a desire to shed the earlier acronym, and specifically to the efforts of Earle E. Eubank of the University of Cincinnati ("damn his fat-headed and bottomed carcass"). Bain to Jessie Bernard, December 15, 1970, JB.

11. Jessie Bernard, Diary, January 10, 1925, LLB.

12. Bernard, "Coming of Age," 1, MS PPB.

13. Jessie to Luther Bernard, August 5, 1923, LLB.

14. Luther Bernard, "Attitudes and the Redirection of Behavior," 46–74. See also Bannister, *Sociology and Scientism*, 132–133.

15. Bernard, "Coming of Age," 3a, MS PPB.

16. Bernard, "Relative Rate of Change," 171. This article is a summary of the thesis.

17. Bernard, "Investigation into the Changes," 37.

18. Ibid., 38–39.

19. Bernard, "Questions: Sociology 230," MS JB.

20. Jessie Bernard to Guggenheim Foundation, September 6, 1926, LLB; Bernard, "History and Prospects of Sociology."

21. Bernard, "Culture as Environment."

22. Ibid.

23. Bernard, "Coming of Age," 3, MS PPB.

24. Jessie Bernard to Mildred Parton, January 5, 1930, LLB.

25. Bernard, "Sources and Methods of Social Psychology."

26. See Bernard, "Instrument for the Measurement of Success in Marriage"; "Distribution of Success in Marriage"; "Factors in the Distribution." A later study from a slightly different angle was "Differential Influence." Material in the next paragraph is also from these articles.

27. Bernard, "Instrument for the Measurement of Neighborhood"; "Neighborhood Behavior of School Children."

28. Bernard, "Coming of Age," 3a, MS PPB.

29. Jessie Bernard to Mildred Parton, January 5, 1930, LLB.

30. Luther Bernard to Susan Kingsbury, January 26, 1932, LLB.

31. Helen to Luther Bernard, December 3, 14, "Monday A.M." [1932], April 1, 22, 1946, LLB.

32. Bernard, "Experimental Comparison."

33. For a more detailed account see Bannister, *Sociology and Scientism*, 216–219.

34. Jessie to Luther Bernard, January 17, 1937, LLB.

35. See Jessie Bernard to Gwendolyn Safier, November 2, 1971, JB.

36. Jessie to Luther Bernard, February 13, 1937, LLB: "I want very much to sell something. Perhaps you are right that I am hungry for recognition."

37. Bernard, "Runaway Wife," 1, 2, 5–6, 12, MS JB.

38. Luther Bernard, not surprisingly, was sensitive to any charge that he was unbalanced. When word came to him that his colleagues at Washington University said he had a "paranoid personality," he was outraged. See Jessie Bernard to Luther Bernard, July 16, 1947, and Helen to Luther Bernard, July 27, 1947, LLB.

39. Luther to Jessie Bernard, April 7 [?], 1936, LLB. Since Bernard elsewhere said that Jessie filed for divorce on April 10, this letter—dated after the time—is probably misdated.

40. The "L" was almost certainly George Lundberg. See chapter five.

41. Luther to Jessie Bernard, April 31, 14, June 11, 9, 1936, LLB.

42. Luther Bernard, "Statement of Motives," September 12, 1933, LLB; Luther to Jessie Bernard, April 15, 1936, LLB.

43. Luther to Jessie Bernard, April 23, 30, 1936, LLB.

44. Ibid., April 23, 1936.

45. Ibid., April 25, 23, 15, 1936, LLB.

46. Virtually all of Luther's letters of April and May 1936, including some sent twice in duplicate, remained unopened in the Bernard Papers until the early 1980s, when the present author opened them with the permission and cooperation of the staff of the Pennsylvania State University Library.

47. Luther and Jessie Bernard, "Behavior, Individual and Social," *Social Force* 9 (1930): 127 (review of *The Adolescent, His Conflicts and Escapes*, by S. I. Schwab and B. S. Veeder [New York: Appleton, 1929]). See also Luther Bernard, "A Classification of Environments."

48. Sidney I. Schwab to Jessie Bernard, June 10, 22, 1936, LLB.

49. Jessie Bernard to Ellen Peck, January 9, 1973, JB.

50. Jessie Bernard to Sidney I. Schwab, June 20, 1936, LLB; Jessie to Luther Bernard, October 23, 1936, LLB.

51. Jessie to Luther Bernard, October 23, November 12, 10, December 5, 1936, LLB.

52. Ibid., March 30, 1938.

53. Jessie Bernard, Memorandum Book, January 18, March 29, 1940, LLB.

54. Jessie to Luther Bernard, March 20, 1938, LLB.

55. Ibid., July 17, 1940, JB.

56. Jessie to unborn child, ca. May 1941, quoted in *Self-Portrait of a Family*, xx–xxii.

57. Jessie to Luther Bernard, April 5, 1941, LLB.

58. Jessie Bernard to Clara Lambert, August 24, 1941, JB.
59. Jessie to Luther Bernard, July 26, 1941, LLB.
60. Quoted in Bernard, *Self-Portrait of a Family*, xxii.
61. Jessie Bernard to Clara Lambert, August 24, 1941, JB.
62. Bernard, *Female World*, 132.
63. Lasch discusses Ogburn's theory at some length; he also refers to *American Family Behavior* as "one of the standard family textbooks of the forties" (*Haven in a Heartless World*, 151).
64. Bernard, *American Family Behavior*, 256, 472, 474.
65. Ibid., 433, 538–539. For Bernard's later development of the "shock theory" see *Future of Marriage*, 41–42.
66. Kirkpatrick, review of *American Family Behavior*, 232.
67. Bernard, *American Family Behavior*, 35, 483.
68. [Name withheld], August 27, September 12, 1941, April 17, 1942, LLB.
69. Jessie to Luther Bernard, April 12, 1943, LLB.
70. In addition, see Bernard, *American Family Behavior* and *American Community Behavior*. See especially "Communication"; "Observation and Generalization"; and "Note on Sociological Research."

CHAPTER FIVE: LOSS OF FAITH

1. Luther Bernard to George Lundberg, January 12, 1946, GAL.
2. George E. Simpson to Drs. Bernard, January 21, 1947, JB; Bernard, "Academia 1947–1964," 1, 7, MS PPB. Safier quotes Bernard as saying that L.L.B. had come on her "shirttails" ("Jessie Bernard," 307).
3. Bernard, "Academia 1947–1964," 5, MS PPB.
4. Ibid.
5. Information from Pennsylvania State University catalogues; Lunday, *Sociology Dissertations;* and *Who's Who in America 1965–66* (Chicago: A. N. Marquis, 1966).
6. Bernard, "Academia 1947–1964," 4, MS PPB.
7. Jessie Bernard to George Lundberg, August 11, 1948, GAL. The article was Nancy Koplin Jack and Betty Schiffer, "The Limits of Fashion Control," *American Sociological Review* 13 (1948): 730–738. Bernard's reference was to an unspecified disagreement between Maurice Davie of Yale, the editor of the *ASR,* and Robert C. Angell of the University of Michigan, a member of the Executive Committee of the American Sociological Society.
8. Jessie Bernard to George Lundberg, August 11, 1948, GAL.
9. Lunday, *Sociology Dissertations,* lists a total of eighteen Ph.D.'s in sociology

granted at Penn State between 1947 and 1963. Of those listed in the annual graduation programs, Bernard directed only four: Charles H. Parmer, "The Relation between Scores on the McHugh Inventory and Self-Ratings of Marital Satisfaction" (1954); Eloise C. Snyder, "A Sociological Analysis of Supreme Court Opinions from 1921 to 1953" (1956); Salem Mohamed Abdus Ansari, "An Evaluation of the Quran and of Western Sociology as Guides for Implementing the Goals of the Pakistani Constitution, with Special Reference to Problems of Conflict" (1958); and Elliott H. Grosof, "Orientations of Senior Men toward Work Situations in a Bureaucratic Structure as Related to Social Class Background" (1959). Of these four, only the Snyder study was reflected in her published work. See Bernard, "Dimension and Axes."

10. Bernard, "Epiphany: Loss of Faith," 3, and "Twentieth Century Seen through the Life," ca. 1980s, MSS PPB.

11. William F. Ogburn, Diary, June 22, 1942, WFO; Read Bain to George Lundberg, December 1, 1938, RB. For a fuller discussion of this issue see Bannister, *Sociology and Scientism*, 225–226.

12. Luther to Jessie Bernard, October 1, 1938, LLB.

13. Luther Bernard to Earle Eubank, January 1, 1938, and to Maurice Parmelee, March 7, 1938, LLB; American Sociological Association, "Official Reports and Proceedings," 92. See also Clark, *Patrons and Prophets*, 228.

14. Luther Bernard, "Relations."

15. Jessie to Luther Bernard, October 5, 1936, LLB.

16. Ibid., September 26, 1938.

17. Ibid., October 8, 1938.

18. Ibid., November 23, 1938.

19. Bernard, "Analysis of Jewish Culture," 261, and "Biculturality," 291–293.

20. Isacque Graeber to Talcott Parsons, December 3, 1939, TP. Talcott Parsons wrote to Ben Halpern on June 26, 1942: "That article represents the worst experience with editorial interference with an author's work I have ever encountered" (TP). This collection also contains additional correspondence concerning Parsons's contribution.

21. Braunstein, "Social Problem," 16.

22. Jessie Bernard to George Lundberg, September 23, 1943, May 9, 1944, GAL. Although Graeber did not initially include Bernard among the contributors, her piece apparently pleased him. Apparently unknown to her, he offered at one point to send to Talcott Parsons a copy of her anonymous "Analysis of Jewish Culture" (Graeber to Parsons, "Tuesday," ca. November 1941, TP).

23. Bernard, *American Community Behavior*, 117, 208, 52, 603.

24. Ibid., 388–390. Except for adding some new materials for the 1962 edition

of *American Community Behavior,* none of which altered her position, she did not again return to the issue.

25. Jessie Bernard to George Lundberg, July 12, 1949, GAL.

26. Lundberg, *Can Science Save Us?,* 27.

27. Ibid., 31, 33–34, 46.

28. On Lundberg see De Grazia et al., *Behavioral Sciences;* Bierstedt, *American Sociological Theory,* chapter 8; and Lundberg, "Autobiography," LLB.

29. Larsen, "Lundberg's Encounters," 4.

30. Read Bain to George Lundberg, March 2, 1937, RB; Lundberg to Bain, March 22, 1937, RB.

31. George Lundberg to Read Bain, December 21, 1936, RB; Bain to Lundberg, March 2, 1937, RB; Lundberg to Bain, March 22, 1937, RB.

32. George Lundberg to Read Bain, February 7, 1941, RB.

33. Jessie Bernard to George Lundberg, September 25, 1940, LLB; Lundberg to Bernard, July 9, 1940, LLB.

34. Larsen, "Lundberg's Encounters," 21. For reaction see also Maurice Parmelee to Luther Bernard, May 25, 1944, LLB: "Have you read Lundberg's presidential address? . . . It has raised the question as to whether he is anti-semitic, although he protests against it."

35. Although Lundberg sometimes acknowledged his debt to Bernard, he believed that he owed a greater one to John M. Gillette, with whom he had studied at the University of North Dakota.

36. Larsen, "Lundberg's Encounters," 9. See Lundberg, "Case Work and Statistical Method," and *Social Research,* especially ix.

37. Jessie to Luther Bernard, July 7, 1923, LLB; Jessie Bernard to George Lundberg, June 5, 1934, GAL.

38. George Lundberg to Jessie Bernard, January 31, 1929, LLB.

39. Luther to Jessie Bernard, April 13, 1936, LLB. Because the number 3 on Bernard's typewriter was not working in this period, this letter is not in proper chronological order.

40. Jessie Bernard to George Lundberg, June 5, 1934, GAL. The Lundberg Papers (GAL) contain only this one letter between Bernard and Lundberg prior to 1935, although other evidence suggests that they corresponded during the early 1930s.

41. Jessie to Luther Bernard, December 13, 1936, LLB. Looking back years later, Bernard stated that she could easily have had Lundberg for a husband, but did not provide details (interview with author, August 1987).

42. Luther to Jessie Bernard, January 2, 1937, LLB.

43. Jessie Bernard to George Lundberg, ca. late autumn 1935, GAL.

44. Jessie to Luther Bernard, January 21, 1936, LLB.

45. Jessie Bernard to George Lundberg, September 15, 1937, GAL; Lundberg to Bernard, September 24, 1937, GAL; Bernard to Lundberg, October 25, 1937, GAL.

46. Jessie Bernard to George Lundberg, November 18, 1936, GAL; Jessie to Luther Bernard, November 26, 1938, LLB; Lundberg to Jessie Bernard, November 30, 1938, GAL.

47. Harold A. Phelps to Luther Bernard, January 4, 1938, LLB. Luther Bernard published the list of SRA members in the first number of his periodical *American Sociologist* (1938).

48. Jessie Bernard to George Lundberg, September 14, 1940, GAL.

49. George Lundberg to Jessie Bernard, September 22, 1940, GAL; Bernard to Lundberg, September 25, 1940, LLB. See also Bernard to Lundberg, February 2, 1940, GAL.

50. Luther Bernard to George Lundberg, January 20, March 1, 1941, GAL.

51. Jessie Bernard to George Lundberg, October 25, 1942, GAL; Lundberg to Bernard, November 9, 1942, GAL.

52. George Lundberg to Jessie Bernard, May 1, 1944, LLB.

53. Jessie Bernard to George Lundberg, September 23, 1943, GAL.

54. Jessie Bernard to George Lundberg, May 9, 1944, GAL; Lundberg to Bernard, July 18, 1955, LLB; Bernard to Lundberg, May 9, 1944, GAL.

55. Bernard, *American Family Behavior*, 203.

56. Winch, review of *American Family Behavior*.

57. Bernard, "Social Salvation through Science," 45–47, 55.

58. Bernard, "Power of Science," 580, 582; "Prescriptions for Peace," 256.

59. Ibid; Lundberg, "Some Comments," 796.

60. Alpert, "George Lundberg's Social Philosophy," 48–62.

61. Bernard, "Social Salvation through Science," 55.

62. Bernard, "Scientists and the Paradox of Power," 20.

63. Mills, *Sociological Imagination*, 24, 56–57.

64. Jessie to Luther Bernard, March 9, 1941, LLB.

65. Luther Bernard, Diary, January 20, 1948, LLB.

66. Jessie Bernard, "Twentieth Century Seen through the Life," 20, PPB.

67. Jessie Bernard to George Lundberg, December 24, 1954, GAL.

68. Ibid., November 22, 1950. GAL.

CHAPTER SIX: MARGINAL MAN

1. Hodgson, *America in Our Time*, chapter 4.

2. For example, Hartz, *Liberal Tradition in America,* and Hofstadter, *Age*

of Reform. For discussion of this group see Morton, *Terrors of Ideological Politics.*

3. Bernard, "Prescriptions for Peace," 246.

4. Lee and Lee, "Society for the Study of Social Problems," 5.

5. Bernard, "Twentieth Century Seen through the Life," 10, MS PPB; Jessie Bernard to Gwendolyn Safier, July 12, 1971, JB. To George Lundberg, August 26, 1954, GAL, she wrote of Parsons: "There ought to be a moratorium on discussions of that man. He has had brilliant students, better than he; otherwise no one would have paid any attention to him."

6. The interpretation in this and the preceding two paragraphs is reconstructed from various of Bernard's writings. See especially "Twentieth Century Seen through the Life," 10–11, MS PPB. Her source for the view that "career" is inherently "masculine" was Philip Slater, *The Pursuit of Loneliness* (Boston: Beacon, 1970), 72.

7. Hoyt B. Ballard and G. William Domhoff, eds., *C. Wright Mills and "The Power Elite"* (Boston: Beacon, 1968).

8. Although Bernard did not officially retire from Penn State until 1964, she commuted there from Washington several days a week during her remaining years on the faculty.

9. Jessie Bernard to George Lundberg, October 20, 1945, GAL.

10. See Bernard, "Where is the Modern Sociology of Conflict?"; "Conceptualizations of Inter-group Relations"; "Parties and Issues in Conflict"; "Autonomic and Decisive Forms of Competition"; "Some Current Conceptualizations"; and "Conflict as Research" [1966], MS, JB.

11. Warshay, "Current State of Sociological Theory," 31. In his book *Current State of Sociological Theory,* 28, Warshay nonetheless includes Bernard with the "classical" conflict theorists. Given Bernard's eclecticism, I skip the issue whether she was really a conflict theorist, a structural functionalist, or some combination thereof. For discussion of this point see Safier, "Jessie Bernard," 149–152.

12. Coser, *Functions of Social Conflict,* 165–166.

13. Bernard, "Conceptualizations of Inter-group Relations," 250.

14. Ibid, 251.

15. Jessie to Luther Bernard, January 20, 1937, LLB.

16. Bernard, "Biculturality," 290–291. See also *American Community Behavior,* 108. Bernard's anticommunist feelings may have been strengthened when the Soviets attacked the Bernards' *Origins of American Sociology* soon after its publication. See Baskin, "Campaign of American Sociology," 532–534, discussed in Safier, "Jessie Bernard," 62.

17. Lundberg, "Sociology versus Dialectical Immaterialism," 85.

18. Lundberg, "On Resolutions by the Society," *American Sociological Review* 15 (1950): 782, cited in Alpert, "George Lundberg's Social Philosophy," 59.

19. Lundberg, "Sociology versus Dialectical Immaterialism," 95; Lundberg, *Can Science Save Us?* 108–109.

20. Bernard, "Prescriptions for Peace," 251.

21. Bernard, "Where is the Modern Sociology of Conflict?" 11–12. Her source was *Stalin's Kampf: Joseph Stalin's Credo*, ed. M. R. Werner (New York: Howell, Soskin, 1940).

22. Bernard, *American Community Behavior*, 446; *Social Problems at Midcentury*, 166.

23. Dahlke, review of *Social Problems at Midcentury*.

24. See Bernard, "Theory of Games"; "Social Problems as Problems of Decision"; and "Counseling Techniques."

25. See Bernard, "Theory of Games."

26. Ibid., 415.

27. Ibid., 422.

28. Ibid., 424–425.

29. Bernard, "Counseling Techniques," 270.

30. Arthur G. Lindsay to Jessie Bernard, February 18, 1973, JB.

31. Bernard apparently recognized this problem since, by the mid-sixties she claimed that "scientific" thinking about conflict might itself "change values," as opposed to muckraking or moralistic reform, which simply inspired people to act on their values. But the point was not expanded. See Bernard, "Some Current Conceptualizations," 454.

32. Quoted in Safier, "Jessie Bernard," 72.

33. Bernard, "Some Current Conceptualizations," 443–444.

34. Jessie Bernard to Dorothy Fromm, November 4, 1962, JB. Bernard added: "I swept aside the policies and judgements of people who suspected the motives of, let us say, communists. But so often in the past they have been proved correct and I have been proved wrong that I hardly trust my own judgements."

35. Lee and Lee, "Society for the Study of Social Problems," 11; Bernard, "Social Problems as Problems of Decision." On the SSSP see also Lee, *Toward a Humanist Sociology*, 133–138; Skura, "Constraints on a Reform Movement"; Aurbach, "SSSP"; and Henslin and Roesti, "Trends and Topics."

36. Lee and Lee, "Society for the Study of Social Problems," 5, 7. T-O-R stood for Thomas-Ogburn-Rice.

37. Bernard, "My Four Revolutions," 774–775.

38. Skura, "Constraints on a Reform Movement," 16; Bernard, "My Four Revolutions," 774–775.

39. Horowitz, "Rise and Fall of Project Camelot," 4–5.

40. Nisbet, "Project Camelot," 313–338.

41. Ibid., 313–338. For statements of these criticisms see Horowitz, "Rise and Fall of Project Camelot," 5, 32. For the reaction of other social scientists see additional articles in the Horowitz volume, and comments in *Trans-action* 5 (January–February 1968): 10–12.

42. See Safier, "Jessie Bernard," 140–143; and Bernard, "Conflict as Research," 128–152.

43. Bernard, "Conflict as Research," 139, 143.

44. Ibid., 130, 132, 143, 146–149.

45. This criticism was recently expressed by an anonymous reader of this manuscript, with the conjecture that Bernard "must have been richly rewarded financially for this service." In an interview with the author October 3, 1989, Bernard specifically denied the latter charge, and continued to view her participation simply as the act of a loyal American (see also *Self-Portrait of a Family*, 335). In any case, her lifelong indifference to money matters argues that the size of the fee was not a consideration.

46. Bernard, "Social Science Fiction," 7.

47. Ibid.

48. Ibid.

49. Safier, "Jessie Bernard," 318

50. Bernard, "Social Science Fiction."

51. Bernard, *Female World*, 552–553.

CHAPTER SEVEN: ACADEMIC WOMAN

1. Bernard, "Academia 1947–1964," 1, 7, MS PPB; "Overview of American Society, 1968," lecture given at Georgetown University, August 5, 1968, 24, MS JB.

2. Jessie Bernard to George Lundberg, September 15, 1958, November 3, 1959, GAL. Although the possibility of a permanent position may have been in the offing, particularly given Princeton's relatively recent commitment to sociology, Bernard insisted to Lundberg that she could not and would not accept an offer even if extended. Professor Marvin Bressler (current Princeton chair) states that no records of Bernard's appointment exist (phone message to author, November 9, 1989).

3. The first of these issues is treated in Bernard, *Academic Women*, chapters 2–4; the second in chapters 5–7 and 14; and the third in chapters 8–13.

4. F. W. Shaper to Luther Bernard, May 10, 1939, JB.

5. Bernard to "Rufus-Gufus," March 25, 1940, JB. This correspondent is not otherwise identified, and Professor Bernard is unable to recall who it was.

6. Bernard, *Academic Women*, 99–105. This same person is probably the one referred to in ibid., 100, and note 14, 295.

7. Ibid., 11.

8. Henry Jones Ford, "The Pretensions of Sociology," *Nation* 88 (April 29, 1909): 433–435; reprinted *American Journal of Sociology* 15 (1909): 96–104. See also Ford, "The Claims of Sociology Examined," *American Journal of Sociology* 15 (1909): 244–259.

9. Lunday, *Sociology Dissertations*, lists one Ph.D. in sociology in 1939, a second in 1951, and a total of twenty-six between 1957 and 1966; Jessie Bernard to George Lundberg, November 5, 1959, GAL.

10. Jessie Bernard to colleagues, November 3 1959, GAL; Jessie Bernard to George Lundberg, November 5, 1959, GAL.

11. Jessie Bernard to George Lundberg, February 16, 1960, GAL; editorial comment in Bernard, "Breaking the Sex Barrier."

12. Bernard, "Breaking the Sex Barrier." The material in the following four paragraphs is also from this source.

13. Bernard, *Academic Women*, chapters 2, 3.

14. Ibid., 215, 222.

15. Bernard, "Academia 1947–1964," 6, MS PPB.

16. Ben Euwema, Foreword to *Academic Women*, xi; David Riesman, Introduction to ibid., xv–xxv.

17. Morse, review of *Academic Women;* Komarovsky, review of *Academic Women.*

18. Carter, "Academic Women Revisited." One factor, ironically, was probably the greater affluence of women's colleges in the postwar era.

19. Blitz, "Women in the Professions"; Graham, "Expansion and Exclusion"; Carter, "Academic Women Revisited"; Margaret Rossiter, "Money and Men at the Women's Colleges, 1945–1965," paper presented at the American Historical Association, December 1988, Cincinnati, Ohio.

20. Jessie to Luther Bernard, March 15, 1937, LLB.

21. Ibid., March 19, 1937.

22. On Sweet Briar see Jessie to Luther Bernard, July 1, 1938, LLB; on Stanford, Richard La Piere to Luther Bernard, April 6, 1938, LLB; on St. Louis colleges, Jessie to Luther Bernard, May 18, 1938, LLB; on the St. Louis schools, George R. Johnson to Jessie Bernard, May 7, 1938, LLB; on Bennington, Jessie Bernard to George Lundberg, September 15, 1937, Lundberg to Bernard, September 24, 1937, Bernard to Lundberg, October 25, 1937, GAL; on Reed, Jessie to Luther Bernard, July 21, 1938, LLB.

23. Luther to Jessie Bernard, June 22, 1938, LLB.

24. Ibid., December 16, 1938.

25. Jessie to Luther Bernard, January 27, 1938, LLB.

26. Ibid., July 21, 1938.

27. Ibid., October 28, 1938.

28. Ibid., August 28, November 14, 23, 1938; Luther to Jessie Bernard, December 15, 1938, LLB.

29. Jessie to Luther Bernard, July 7, 1947, LLB.

30. Friedan, *Feminine Mystique*, 118, 125; Bernard, review of *Women in the Modern World, American Sociological Review* 18 (1953): 709–710.

31. Bernard, *Academic Women*, 57–59, 47, 110–111.

32. Ibid., 92, 114.

33. Ibid., 66–67.

34. Graham, "Expansion and Exclusion," 760–761.

35. *Minnesota Daily*, January 17, 1924.

36. Bernard, *Women and the Public Interest*, 36–37, 113.

37. Bernard, *Self-Portrait of a Family*, 309.

38. Interestingly, Georg Simmel, a significant influence on Park, anticipated several ideas Bernard would later develop concerning "male" culture. Although the psychologist Karen Horney rediscovered these writings in the 1920s, Bernard apparently was unaware of them. See Coser, "Georg Simmel's Neglected Contributions."

39. Bernard, *American Community Behavior*, 510–516.

40. Bernard, *Social Problems at Midcentury*, chapters 15 and 16. Quotation is from 357–358.

41. Jessie Bernard to Gwendolyn Safier, July 12, 1971, JB.

42. D. Smith to Jessie Bernard, December 12, 1972, JB.

43. Jessie Bernard to Terry Clark, December 11, 1971, JB.

44. Jessie Bernard to Gwendolyn Safier, July 12, 1971, JB.

45. Bernard, "My Four Revolutions," 778–779. For explicit discussion of the implications of functional structuralism for feminism see Bernard, *Women and the Public Interest*, especially chapter 4. Examples are from 63, 158.

46. Works citing *Academic Women* in connection with further study of discrimination within academia include Astin, "Employment and Career Status"; Dinerman, "Sex Discrimination in Academia"; Divine, "Women in the Academy"; Fidell, "Empirical Verification"; and LaSorte, "Academic Women's Salaries." For a later version of Bernard's "supply side" argument, although one not citing her work, see Wolfe, De Fleur, and Slocum, "Sex Discrimination in Hiring."

47. Arlie Hochschild to Jessie Bernard, January 6, 1972, JB; Jessie Bernard to William S. Bier, January 3, 1974, JB. This collection contains other such letters.

48. Bernard, *Women and the Public Interest,* 36–37.
49. Jessie Bernard to Mr. Spectorsky, May 4, 1970, JB. See also Bernard, "Sexism and Discrimination."
50. See Tong, *Feminist Thought,* chapter 1.
51. M. Brewster Smith to Robert W. Wesner (Aldine Publishing), April 13, 1970, JB.

CHAPTER EIGHT: SINGLE PARENT

1. Bernard, "Academia 1947–1964," 9, MS PPB.
2. Ibid.
3. Bernard, *Self-Portrait of a Family,* 71, 90–126.
4. Ibid., 197, 268.
5. Fox, review of *Female World,* 260.
6. For these parallels see Freeman, "Origins of the Women's Liberation Movement."
7. Bernard quotes this statement to her son and describes this relationship in *Self-Portrait of a Family,* 3–8.
8. Ezra to Luther Bernard, March 21, 1947, JB; Bernard, *Self-Portrait of a Family,* 4–5.
9. Bernard, *Self-Portrait of a Family,* 6–7.
10. Ibid., 9–19, 328, 334.
11. Ibid., 7–8, 19.
12. Dorothy Lee to Jessie Bernard, ca. November 1963, quoted in ibid., 122–123; Jessie Bernard to Ezra, September 24, 1969, October 15, 1973, JB. In *Self-Portrait of a Family,* Bernard discusses a draft of the former letter (263). Aside from these brief communications, all other letters between the two have been withheld from the Jessie Bernard Papers.
13. Bernard, *Remarriage,* passim.
14. Nimkoff, review of *Remarriage;* Cuber, review of *Remarriage.*
15. See preface to 1971 edition of *Remarriage.*
16. Jessie to David Bernard, March 29, 1969, JB; Bernard, *Self-Portrait of a Family,* 339.
17. Jessie to Dorothy Lee Bernard, April 24, 1958, JB.
18. Jessie Bernard, Diary, January 18, 19, 1940, JB.
19. Jessie to Luther Bernard, October 14, 1936, March 25, 1938, LLB.
20. Helen to Luther Bernard, ca. 1947, March 22, 1948, LLB.
21. Luther Bernard, Diary, 1947, 54, 77, LLB.

22. Bernard, *Self-Portrait of a Family,* chapter 5.

23. Jeannette Alfrey to Jessie Bernard, January 1, 1943, JB.

24. Bernard, *Self-Portrait of a Family,* 274; Bernard, *Future of Marriage,* 47–52.

25. Will of L. L. Bernard, Statement of U.S. Savings Bonds as of January 23, 1951, JB; *Self-Portrait of a Family,* 329–330.

26. Jessie to Dorothy Lee Bernard, May 25, 1958, JB.

27. Bernard, undated memo ca. late 1960s, LLB; *Self-Portrait of a Family,* 9, 282, 337.

28. Bernard, *Self-Portrait of a Family,* 293. On the conference see Ruth B. Kundsin, ed., *Women and Success* (New York: Morrow, 1974).

29. Jessie to Dorothy Lee Bernard, February 23, 1968, JB.

30. Ibid., May 25, 1958; Bernard, memo, ca. 1967, JB; Jessie to David Bernard, March 29, 1969, JB.

31. Bernard, *Self-Portrait of a Family,* 292–293, 301, emphasized these evidences of her guilt.

32. Jessie to Dorothy Lee Bernard, May 25, 1958, JB.

33. Helen to Luther Bernard, July 9, 1945, LLB; Bernard, untitled manuscript fragment, probably for *Self-Portrait of a Family,* n.d., JB.

34. Bernard to Dr. Nardini, September 2, 1963, JB; Jessie to David Bernard, March 7, 1982, JB.

35. Bernard, *Self-Portrait of a Family,* 34–35; Jessie Bernard to Miss Willier, January 12, 1967, JB.

36. Katz, review of *Self-Portrait of a Family,* 58.

37. Jessie to Claude Bernard, November 10, 1963, JB. See also *Self-Portrait of a Family,* 21–28.

38. Jessie to Dorothy Lee Bernard, April 24, 1958, JB; *Self-Portrait of a Family,* 52, 91.

39. Jessie to Claude Bernard, April 20, 1960, November 10, 1963, JB.

40. Jessie to David Bernard, March 7, 1982, JB.

41. Bernard, *Self-Portrait of a Family,* 21.

42. Dorothy Lee quoted in Jessie to Dorothy Lee Bernard, ca. 1958, JB; *Self-Portrait of a Family,* 49, 51–52.

43. Jessie to Dorothy Lee Bernard, ca. fall 1962, quoted in *Self-Portrait of a Family,* 92; Jessie Bernard to Dr. Nardini, February 26, 1963, JB.

44. Jessie to Claude Bernard, July 28, August 17, 1963, JB. Also in *Self-Portrait of a Family,* 203–204.

45. Dorothy Lee to Jessie Bernard, ca. fall 1959, November 14, 1960, quoted in *Self-Portrait of a Family,* 54, 71.

46. Bernard, *Self-Portrait of a Family,* chapter 6.

47. Ibid., chapter 4.

48. Jessie Bernard to Dr. Nardini, July 3, 1963, JB; Jessie Bernard to Dr. Solomon, May 31, 1967, JB.

49. Jessie to Dorothy Lee Bernard, August [?], 1967, JB.

50. Bernard, "Points to Discuss with DLB," July 28, 1967, MS JB; Bernard, "To Whom it May Concern," August 4, 1967, JB.

51. Bernard, fragment, ca. 1967, JB.

52. For a detailed account of these later events see *Self-Portrait of a Family,* part 3.

53. Jessie to Dorothy Lee Bernard, February 23, 1968, JB.

54. Dorothy Lee to Jessie Bernard, ca. July 1963, quoted in *Self-Portrait of a Family,* 117; ibid., 126.

55. Bernard, *Sex Game,* 9–10, 73–94, 132.

56. Vance Packard to Jessie Bernard, June 5, 1968, JB.

57. Cisler, "Women: A Bibliography," 217–246, quoted in Safier, "Jessie Bernard," 268; ibid., 266.

58. Anon. marginalia in Bernard, *Sex Game* [1973 ed.], 307, secondhand copy purchased by author in Southhampton, New York, July 1988.

59. Bernard, *Marriage and Family among Negroes,* 68. Her source was Ashley Montagu, *The Natural Superiority of Women* (New York: Macmillan, 1953).

60. Bernard, *Future of Marriage,* 41, 58.

61. Ibid., 403, 113–115, 296–297. For criticism of the "shared-role" possibility see Ira L. Reiss to Jessie Bernard, September 12, 1973, JB.

62. Bernard, *Future of Marriage,* x–xvii, 326–327. See Robert Nisbet, "The Year 2000 and All That," *Commentary,* June 1968, 60–66.

63. Bernard, *Self-Portrait of a Family,* 57.

CHAPTER NINE: FEMINIST

1. Jessie Bernard, interview with author, October 3, 1989; *American Men and Women of Science* ed. Jacques Cattell Press, 130, 210, 734. 13th ed., New York: R. R. Bowker, 1978; Cantor, "Jessie Bernard—An Appreciation"; Lipman-Blumen, "Jessie Bernard—A 'Reasonable Rebel.' "

2. Jessie Bernard, in an interview with the author on October 3, 1989, identified both women as friends in the late 1960s. Quotations are from *Future of Marriage,* 239, 247; Jessie Bernard to Al, April, 20, 1970, JB. On Roxanne Dunbar see Morgen, *Sisterhood is Powerful,* 595.

3. On Charlotte Bunch and *Quest* see Wandersee, *On the Move,* 14, 53, 192. Quotation is from Karen Kollias, "Spiral of Change," *Quest* 1 (1974): 8, quoted ibid., 95. For a sample of the issues discussed see Charlotte Bunch and Nancy

Myron, eds., *Class and Feminism* (Baltimore: Diana Press, 1974), as quoted in Bernard, *Female World*, 329–330.

4. On Twin Oaks see Komar, *Living the Dream*. Quotation is from 62. Information supplied by Raphaela Best to author in phone interview, October 4, 1989, and in letter, December 17, 1989. B. F. Skinner, *Walden Two* (1948; reprint, New York: Macmillan, 1971), 7; Bernard, *Future of Motherhood*, 310, 325–330.

5. Jessie Bernard to Ms. Straub, October 22, 1973, JB; Bernard, *Female World*, 105–107. See also JB for correspondence between Bernard and the many women whose work she encouraged.

6. Arlie Hochschild to Jessie Bernard, January 6, 1972, JB; Kathryn Sklar to Jessie Bernard, October 3, 1973, JB; Jessie Bernard to [name withheld], ca. 1973, JB.

7. Unidentified letter fragment attached to Jessie Bernard to Gwendolyn Safier, September 12, 1971, JB.

8. Raphaela Best to author in phone interview, October 4, 1989.

9. [Name withheld at writer's request] to Jessie Bernard, September 25, 1974, JB.

10. Jessie Bernard to "Dear ————," December 9, 1976, JB.

11. Jessie Bernard to Mr. Spectorsky [editor of *Playboy*], May 4, 1970, JB; Jessie Bernard to Editor [not specified], August 25, 1971, JB; Jessie Bernard to Norman Lear, January 9, 1976, JB.

12. Jessie Bernard to Del Samson, December 12, 1976, JB.

13. In addition, Bernard later received honorary degrees at Syracuse (1983), George Washington University (1984), Lindenwood (1986), and Trinity (1987).

14. *Women's Caucus Newsletter* 1 (October 1970): 1.

15. Bernard, in "My Four Revolutions," wrote that she "was present . . . in Washington when the Women's Caucus began the process of transforming itself into Sociologists for Women in Society" (775). However, Alice Rossi, in a letter to me dated December 4, 1989, recalled that Bernard did not attend meetings of the group until February 1971 at Yale. Whether or not Bernard actually "listened," she was informed of the proceedings through the *Women's Caucus Newsletter* of October 1970.

16. Alice Rossi to author, December 4, 1989.

17. *Women's Caucus Newsletter* 1 (October 1970): 3; Bernard, "My Four Revolutions," 775.

18. Bernard, "Letters Department," 5–6.

19. Bernard, "My Four Revolutions,"

20. Alice Rossi, reply to Joy Held's letter, December 7, 1972, JB; Rossi, "A Biosocial Perspective on Parenting," *Daedalus* 106 (Spring 1977): 1–31; Rossi

to Jessie Bernard, June 20, 1977, JB. On responses to Rossi's article see Wandersee, *On the Move*, 200–201, and discussion in Epilogue.

21. Jessie to Luther Bernard, April 23, 1937, JB.

22. Howard, *Margaret Mead*, 367.

23. Jessie Bernard to [name withheld], ca. 1973, JB.

24. Bernard later stated that she was appointed "liaison" by Arlene Daniels, a sociologist then with the Scientific Analysis Corporation in San Francisco, later at Northwestern; Jessie Bernard to Pauline Bart, February 22, 1976, JB.

25. Pauline Bart to Jessie Bernard, February 3, 1976, JB; Bernard to Bart, February 22, 1976, JB.

26. Bernard, "Men Supporting Men: The Second National Conference on Men and Masculinity, July 30–August 1, 1976," MS JB; *Female World*, 356–358. On this issue at the Houston conference see L. Van Gelder, "Four Days That Changed the World," *MS.*, March 1978, and Rossi, *Feminists in Politics*, both cited in Ferree and Hess, *Controversy and Coalition*, 105.

27. Lipman-Blumen, "Jessie Bernard—A 'Reasonable Rebel,' " 273.

28. Bernard, *Marriage and Family among Negroes*, 69; Rodman review of *Marriage and Family among Negroes*, 413–414, quoted in Safier, "Jessie Bernard," 188. See also McIntyre, review of *Marriage and Family among Negroes*.

29. Bernard, *Marriage and Family among Negroes*, 88; Meier, "Negro Families in Caricature."

30. Bernard, *Female World*, chapter 2.

31. Ibid., 145, 230–256.

32. Ibid., chapters 12, 16–21.

33. Ibid., 88, 270, 551–552.

34. Epstein, review of *Female World;* Cavan, review of *Female World*.

35. Epstein, review of *Female World*.

36. Matthews, "Rethinking Sociology." The material in the following three paragraphs is based on comments by Jessie Bernard, Zillah Eisenstein, Alison Griffith, and Mary Jo Nitz published with this article.

37. Riesman, Introduction to *Academic Women*, xx–xxi; Bernard, *Academic Women*, 76, 96–113.

38. For example, Bernard, "Communication"; "Social Salvation through Science," 51.

39. Bernard, *American Community Behavior*, 319. For a similar example, see also "Biculturality," 265.

40. Bernard, *Social Problems at Midcentury*, 557–573; Jessie to Dorothy L. Bernard, October 30, 1964, JB.

41. Although Moynihan et al., *Negro Family*, was released in August 1965, some time before the publication of Bernard's book, she made no reference to

it. For discussion of this background see Rainwater and Yancey, *Moynihan Report.*

42. Bernard, *Marriage and Family among Negroes,* 28–32, vii.

43. Meier, "Negro Families in Caricature," 45–46. See also Podell, review of *Marriage and Family among Negroes;* and McIntyre, review of *Marriage and Family among Negroes.*

44. Jessie Bernard to Lee [possibly Lee Rainwater], July 28, 1967, JB.

45. Bernard, "Overview of American Society, 1968," 17–18.

46. Bernard, *Women and the Public Interest,* 128–130; J. B. Woods to Jessie Bernard, February 12, 1976, JB.

47. "For White Readers Only," n.d., n.p., MS JB. For an intermediate stage in Bernard's thinking about black power, see Bernard, *Sociology of Community* (1973), chapter 7. Since the focus here is Bernard's feminism, this analysis omits some of the complexities in her views on the race issue.

48. Bernard's major sources for this brief section were Wallace, "Black Macho," 4–5; and Hollie I. West, "Michelle Wallace."

49. Bernard, *Female World,* 339–342, 348–349.

50. Audrey West, "Class Roots," 109; Davis, review of *Female World,* 880; Deinhardt, "Vision of the Female World." Bernard returned to the issues of race, class, and ethnicity in *Female World from a Global Perspective* in the context of a worldwide feminist movement.

51. Jessie Bernard to Rae Carlson et al., January 1, 1973, JB. See also Bernard to Dr. Macoby, ca. 1970, JB: "I was reared in the research tradition established by male scientists and it is only relatively recently that its serious limitations have been clear to me."

52. Her examples were Rose's preface to *Human Behavior and Social Processes;* Jones, "Dynamics of Marriage and Motherhood"; and Mainardi, "Politics of Housework."

53. Bernard, "My Four Revolutions."

54. I here avoid the more complicated issue of whether this was a correct reading of Kuhn.

55. Kuhn, *Structure of Scientific Revolutions,* quoted in Bernard, *Sociology of Community,* 6.

56. Ibid., 6–7.

57. Ibid., 10; Fox, review of *Female World,* 260.

58. See Benston, "Political Economy of Women's Liberation; Gerda Lerner, *The Woman in American History* (Chicago: Addison-Wesley, 1971); and Carlson, "Sex Differences in Ego Functioning," and her "Understanding Women." For mention of Benston see Tong, *Feminist Thought,* 53.

59. Rae Carlson to Jessie Bernard, March 15, 1973, JB.

60. Schwendinger and Schwendinger, "Sociology's Founding Fathers."

61. In sociology these included Acker, "Women and Social Stratification"; Cook and Fonow "Knowledge and Women's Interests"; Epstein, "Different Angle of Vision"; Hochschild, "Review of Sex Role Research"; Kantor, "Skewed Sex Ratios"; Lofland, " 'Thereness' of Women"; Millman, "She Did It All for Love"; Millman and Kantor, *Another Voice;* Schneider and Hacker, "Sex Role Imagery"; Smith, "Women's Perspective"; Steinmetz, "Sexual Context of Social Research"; and Ward, "Feminist Critique." In anthropology, Fee, "Sexual Politics"; Golde, *Women in the Field;* Rosaldo, "Use and Abuse of Anthropology"; Scheper-Hughes, "Problem of Bias"; and Slocum, "Woman the Gatherer."

62. For example, Hall, "Biology, Sex Hormones, and Sexism"; Merchant, *Death of Nature;* and Ortner, "Is Female to Male." Works appearing after the *Female World* include Bleier, *Science and Gender;* Harding and Hintikka, *Discovering Reality;* Irigaray, "Is the Subject of Science Sexed?"; and Keller, *Reflections on Gender and Science.* For the jacket of the latter, Bernard commented: "A powerful book."

63. Bernard, *Female World*, 202–203.

64. Richardson, "Looking Forward," 497–499.

65. Mary Jo Deegan, "The Female Life World: Laminating the Feminist Sphere of Bernard and Taft," Unpublished MS, ca. 1981, provided to author by Professor Deegan.

66. Arthur G. Lindsay to Jessie Bernard, February 18, 1973, JB; Cavan, review of *Female World*, 261.

67. Bernard, "Have Patriarchs Had a Bad Press?"

68. See Bernard, *Female World*, 31.

69. On this point see Cott, *Grounding of Modern Feminism,* chapter 1; and Evans, *Born for Liberty,* chapter 9.

EPILOGUE

1. On the Houston meeting see Rossi, *Feminists in Politics.* On the post-Houston reaction see Wandersee, *On the Move,* chapter 9.

2. Alice Rossi to Jessie Bernard, June 20, 1977, JB; Bernard, "Considering," 698.

3. Pauline Bart, "Biological Determinism and Sexism," in *Biology as a Social Weapon,* ed. Ann Arbor Science for the People (Minneapolis: Burgess, 1977), quoted in Gross et al., "Considering," 697. See Rossi, "A Biosocial Perspective on Parenting," *Daedalus* 106 (Spring 1977): 1–31, the focus of the debate. For

examples of antifeminist writings, see Midge Decter, *The Liberated Woman and Other Americans* (New York: Coward, McCann and Geohegan, 1971), and *The New Chastity and Other Arguments against Women's Liberation* (New York: Coward, McCann and Geohegan, 1972). On the controversy over biology and feminism see Breines, Cerullo, and Stacy, "Social Biology, Family Studies, and Antifeminist Backlash."

4. Alice Rossi to Jessie Bernard, June 20, 1977, JB.

5. For this point I am indebted to Alice Rossi, whose letter of December 4, 1989, broached the subject.

6. Alice Rossi to Jessie Bernard, January 20, 1964, JB. Rossi commenting on Bernard's "Developmental Tasks."

7. Bernard, "Considering," 697–698; *Female World,* 166, 241, 243, 337, 361, 586.

8. For a treatment that links Rossi with Friedan and Elshstain see Wandersee, *On the Move,* 200–201. Also cf. the views of Friedan and Elshstain in Stacey, "New Conservative Feminism," and Tong, *Feminist Thought,* 22–28, 32–34.

9. Bernard, *Self-Portrait of a Family,* 210.

10. Bernard, *Future of Motherhood,* 275.

11. Bernard, *Female World,* 358, 498, 412.

12. Wandersee, *On the Move,* 197.

13. The most important of these are Mary Daly, *Gyn-ecology* (Boston: Beacon 1978); Dorothy Dinnerstein, *The Mermaid and the Minotaur* (New York: Harper and Row, 1976); Alison M. Jaggar and Paula R. Struhl, *Feminist Frameworks* (New York: McGraw-Hill, 1978); and Marge Piercy, *Woman on the Edge of Time* (New York: Fawcett Crest, 1976). For discussion of these titles and those in note 14 below, see Tong, *Feminist Thought.*

14. Examples of the former include Margaret E. Atwood, *The Handmaid's Tale* (Boston: Houghton-Mifflin, 1986); Gena Corea, *The Mother Machine* (New York: Harper and Row, 1985); Mary O'Brien, *The Politics of Reproduction* (Boston: Routledge and Kegan Paul, 1981) [radical]; Juliet Mitchell, *Psychoanalysis and Feminism* (New York: Vintage Books, 1974); and Nancy C. M. Hartsock, *Money, Sex, and Power: Toward a Feminist Historical Materialism* (New York: Longman, 1983) [socialist].

Examples of the latter include Luce Irigaray, *This Sex Which Is Not One* (Ithaca, N.Y.: Cornell University Press, 1985); Julia Kristeva, *Desire in Language* (New York: Columbia University Press, 1980), and Hélène Cixous, "Castration or Decapitation?" *Signs* 7 (1981): 41–55. On the implications of postmodernism for feminism see Alcoff, "Cultural Feminism"; Poovey, "Feminism and Deconstructionism"; Rabine, "Feminist Politics of Non-Identity"; Weedon,

Feminist Practice; Scott, "Deconstructing Equality-versus-Difference"; and Tong, *Feminist Thought,* chapter 8.

15. For example, Alcoff, "Cultural Feminism"; Poovey, "Feminism and Deconstructionism."

16. Jessie to Luther Bernard, March 28, 1938, LLB.

17. Bernard, *Female World,* 113.

18. For example, the Southern novelist Caroline Lee Hintz once wrote: "Book! Am I writing a book? No, indeed! This is only a record of my heart's life, written at random and carelessly thrown aside, sheet after sheet, sibylline leaves from the great book of fate" (quoted in Wood, " 'Scribbling Women' and Fanny Fern," 7).

19. Arthur G. Lindsay to Jessie Bernard, February 18, 1973, JB.

20. Bernard, "Twentieth Century Seen through the Life," MS PPB.

Selected Bibliography

WRITINGS BY JESSIE BERNARD

The following is a reasonably complete listing of the published writings of Jessie Bernard, with the exception of contributions to encyclopedias and introductions and afterwords to books. Coauthored works have been placed together at the end of this section.

Academic Women. University Park, Pa.: Pennsylvania State University Press, 1964. Reprint. New York: New American Library, 1974.

"The Adjustments of Married Mates." *Handbook of Marriage and the Family*, ed. Harold T. Christensen, 675–739. Chicago: Rand McNally, 1964.

"Adolescence and Socialization for Motherhood." In *Adolescence in the Life Cycle, Psychological Change, and Social Context*, ed. Sigmund E. Dragastin and Glen H. Elder, Jr. Washington, D.C.: Hemisphere, 1975.

"Age, Sexism, and Feminism." *Annals of the American Academy* 415 (1974): 120–137.

American Community Behavior. New York: Dryden, 1949; rev. ed., New York: Holt, Rinehart, Winston, 1962.

American Family Behavior. New York: Harper and Brothers, 1942. Reprint. New York: Russell and Russell, 1971.

"An Analysis of Jewish Culture." In *Jews in a Gentile World*, ed. Isacque Graeber and Steuart H. Britt, 43–63. New York: Macmillan, 1942.

"Areas for Research in Family Studies." *Sociology and Social Research* 42 (1958): 406–409.

"The Art of Science." *American Journal of Sociology* 55 (1949): 1–9.

"Autonomic and Decisive Forms of Competition." *Sociological Quarterly* 1 (1960): 25–38.

"Benchmark for the '80s." In *Handbook for Women Scholars*, ed. Monika Kehoe. San Francisco: Center for Women Scholars, 1983.

"Biculturality: A Study in Social Schizophrenia." In *Jews in a Gentile World*, ed.

Isacque Graeber and Steuart H. Britt, 264–293. New York: Macmillan, 1942.

"Breaking the Sex Barrier." *Princeton Alumni Weekly*, September 23, 1960.

"Can Science Transcend Culture?" *Scientific Monthly* 71 (1950): 268–273.

"Chance and Stability in Sex-Role Norms and Behavior." *Journal of Social Issues* 32 (1976): 207–224.

"Citizenship Bias in Scholarly and Scientific Work." *Sociological Inquiry* 30 (Spring 1960): 7–13.

"Class Organization in an Era of Abundance." *Transactions of the Third World Congress of Sociology* 3 (1956): 26–31.

"Comment" on "Rethinking Sociology from a Feminist Perspective," by Sarah Matthews. *American Sociologist* 17 (1982): 35–36.

"Comments on Current Legal Trends." *The Family Coordinator* 17 (1968): 62–64.

"A Communication." *American Sociological Review* 5 (1940): 415–417.

"The Conceptualizations of Inter-group Relations." *Social Forces* 29 (1951): 243–251.

"Conflict as Research and Research as Conflict." In *The Rise and Fall of Project Camelot,* ed. Irving L. Horowitz, 128–152. Cambridge, Mass: MIT Press, 1967.

"Considering 'A Biosocial Perspective on Parenting.' " *Signs* 4 (1979): 697–698.

" 'Contingency' or 'Career' Schedules for Women." In *Increasing Student Development Options in College,* ed. David E. Drew. San Francisco: Jossey-Bass, 1978.

"Counseling, Psychotherapy, and Social Problems in Value Contexts." In *Explorations in Sociology and Counseling,* ed. Donald A. Hansen, 378–414. Boston: Houghton Mifflin, 1969.

"Counseling Techniques for Arriving at Optimum Compromises: Game and Decision Theory." *Marriage and Family Living* 21 (1959): 264–274.

"Culture as Environment." *Sociology and Social Research* 15 (1930): 47–56.

"Developmental Tasks of the NCFR 1963–88." *Journal of Marriage and the Family* 26 (1964): 29–38.

"Dialogue with Catherine Chilman." *Journal of Home Economics* (1969).

"The Differential Influence of the Business Cycle on the Number of Marriages." *Social Forces* 18 (1940): 539–547.

"Dimension and Axes of Supreme Court Decisions." *Social Forces* 34 (1955): 19–27.

"The Distribution of Success in Marriage." *American Journal of Sociology* 39 (1933): 194–203.

"Divorce and Remarriage." In *Sex Ways in Fact and Faith,* ed. Evelyn Duvall and Sylvanus Duvall, 93–111. New York: Association Press, 1961.

"Education as a Demographic Variable." *International Population Conference* 3 (1969).

"The Eudaemonists." In *Why Men Take Chances,* ed. Samuel Z. Klausner, 6–47. Garden City, N.Y.: Doubleday, 1968.

"Expanding Academic Competence." *Society* 14 (May/June 1977): 8–9.

"An Experimental Comparison of Ranking and Paired Comparisons." *Proceedings of American Sociological Society* 37 (1933): 81–84.

"Facing the Future." *Society* 18 (1981): 53–59.

"Factors in the Distribution of Success in Marriage." *American Journal of Sociology* 40 (1934): 49–60.

"Facts and Facetiousness in Ethnic Opinionaires." *American Sociological Review* 5 (1950): 415–417.

"The Family and Stress." Symposium with Walter Mondale. *Journal of Home Economics* (Fall 1976).

"The Family: Does It Have a Future, and If So, How Will It Change?" *Radcliffe Quarterly* (June 1979).

The Female World. New York: Free Press, 1981.

"The Female World and Technology in 2020." *National Forum* 61 (1981): 8–10.

"The Female World from a Global Perspective." In *Women's Worlds,* ed. Marilyn Safir, Martha T. Mednick, Dafne Israeli, and Jessie Bernard, 3–14. New York: Praeger, 1985.

The Female World from a Global Perspective. Bloomington, Ind.: Indiana University Press, 1987.

"The Fourth Revolution." *Journal of Social Issues* 22 (1966): 76–87.

"Functions and Limitations in Counseling and Psychotherapy." In *Explorations in Sociology and Counseling,* ed. Donald A. Hansen, 348–377. Boston: Houghton Mifflin, 1969.

The Future of Marriage. New York: World, 1972.

The Future of Motherhood. New York: Dial Press, 1974. Reprint. New York: Penguin, 1975, and New Haven: Yale University Press, 1982.

"George Tucker: Liberal Southern Social Scientist." *Social Forces* 25 (1946): 131–145.

"The Good Provider Role: Its Rise and Fall." *American Psychologist* 36 (1981): 1–12.

"Ground Rules for Marriage." In *Challenge of Change,* ed. Metina Horner, Carol C. Nadelson, and Malkah T. Notman. New York: Plenum, 1983.

"Have Patriarchs Had a Bad Press?" *SWS Network* (May 1985).

"Historical and Structural Barriers to Occupational Desegregation." *Signs* 1 (1976): 87–94. Also in *Women and the Workplace*, ed. Martha Blaxall and Barbara Reagan, 87–94. Chicago: University of Chicago Press, 1976.

"The History and Prospects of Sociology in the United States." In *Trends in American Sociology*, ed. George A. Lundberg, Read Bain, and Nels Anderson, 1–71. New York: Harper and Bros., 1929.

"Homosociality and Female Depression." *Journal of Social Issues* 32 (1976): 213–235.

"The Housewife." In *Varieties of Work*, ed. Phyllis Stewart and Muriel Cantor, 73–93. Beverly Hills, Calif.: Sage, 1982.

"The Housewife: Between Two Worlds." In *Varieties of Work Experience* ed. Phyllis Stewart and Muriel Cantor. New York: Wiley, 1974.

"The Inferiority Curriculum." *Psychology of Women Quarterly* 12 (1988): 261–268.

"Infidelity: Some Moral and Social Issues." In *The Dynamics of Work and Marriage*, ed. Jules H. Masserman, 99–126. New York: Grune and Straton, 1970.

"An Instrument for the Measurement of Neighborhood." *Southwestern Social Science Quarterly* 18 (1937): 145–158.

"An Instrument for the Measurement of Success in Marriage." *Publications of the American Sociological Society* 27 (1933): 94–106.

"An Investigation into the Changes of Attitudes in Jews of the First and Second Generation under Influence of Social Environment." M.A. thesis, University of Minnesota, 1924. LLB.

"Jealousy and Marriage." In *Jealousy*, ed. Gordon Clanton and Lynn G. Smith, 141–150. Englewood Cliffs, N.J.: Prentice-Hall, 1977.

"Jealousy in Marriage." *Medical Aspects of Human Sexuality* 5 (April 1971): 200–215.

Letter to the Editor. *American Anthropologist* 51 (1949): 671–677.

Letter to the Editor. *American Sociologist* 1 (1960): 24–25.

"Letters Department," *Sociologists for Women in Society Newsletter* 1 (March 1971): 5–6.

"The Marital Bond vis-à-vis the Male Bond and the Female Bond." *American Family Therapy Newsletter* 1985.

"Marital Stability." *Journal of Marriage and the Family* 28 (1966): 421–439.

Marriage and Family among Negroes. Englewood Cliffs, N.J.: Prentice-Hall, 1966.

"Models for the Relationship between the World of Women and the World of Men." In *Research in Social Movements*, ed. Louis Kriesberg, 291–340. Greenwich, Conn.: JAI, 1978.

"My Four Revolutions." *American Journal of Sociology* 78 (1973): 773–791.

"The Neighborhood Behavior of School Children in Relation to Age and Socioeconomic Status." *American Sociological Review* 4 (1939): 152–162.

"New Issues: Some Solutions." *Women's Education* 7 (1968): 1.

"No-Fault—Whose Fault?" *Women's Review of Books* 3 (November 1985): 1–3.

"No News, but New Ideas." In *Divorce and After,* ed. Paul Bohannan, 3–25. Garden City, N.Y.: Doubleday, 1970.

"Normative Collective Behavior: A Classification of Societal Norms." *American Journal of Sociology* 47 (1941): 24–38.

"Note on Educational Homogamy in Negro-White and White-Negro Marriages, 1960." *Journal of Marrige and the Family* 28 (1966): 274–276.

"A Note on Sociological Research as a Factor in Social Change: The Reception of the Kinsey Report." *Social Forces* 28 (1949): 188–190.

"Observation and Generalization in Cultural Anthropology." *American Journal of Sociology* 50 (1945): 284–291.

"One Role, Two Roles, Shared Roles." *Issues in Industrial Society* 2 (1971): 21–28.

"On Resolutions by the Society." *American Sociological Review* 16 (1951): 103.

"One Alumna's Story." *University of Minnesota Alumni News,* October 1971.

"The Paradox of a Happy Marriage." In *Women in Sexist Society,* ed. Vivian Gornick and Barbara K. Moran, 89–119. New York: Basic, 1971.

"Parties and Issues in Conflict." *Journal of Conflict Resolution* 1 (1957): 111–121.

"Policy and Women's Time." In *Sex Roles and Social Policy,* ed. Jean Lipman-Blumen and Jessie Bernard, 303–333. Beverly Hills, Calif.: Sage, 1979.

"Political Leadership among North American Indians." *American Journal of Sociology* 34 (1928): 296–315.

"The Power of Science and the Science of Power." *American Sociological Review* 14 (1949): 575–585.

"Prescriptions for Peace." *Ethics* 59 (1949): 244–256.

"Present Demographic Trends and Structural Outcomes in Family Life Today." In *Marriage and Family Counseling,* ed. James A. Peterson, 44–109. New York: Association Press, 1968.

"The Present Situation in the Academic World of Women Trained in Engineering." In *Women in the Scientific Professions,* ed. Jacquelyn A. Mattfeld, 163–182. Cambridge, Mass: MIT Press, 1965.

"The Reconstituted Family." *Journal of Family Issues* 3 (1982).

"Reflections on Style, Structure, and Subject." In *Scholarly Writing and Publishing,* ed. Mary Frank Fox. Boulder, Colo.: Westview, 1985.

"Relative Rate of Change in Custom and Beliefs of Modern Jews." *Proceedings of the American Sociological Society* 19 (1925): 171–176.

Remarriage: A Study of Marriage. New York: Dryden, 1956. Reprint with new
    Introduction. New York: Russell and Russell, 1971.
"Reply to a Catholic Protest." *American Sociological Review* 15 (1950): 430–432.
"Reply to Lundberg's Comment." *American Sociological Review* 14 (1949):
    798–801.
"Scientists and the Paradox of Power." *Social Forces* 31 (1952): 14–20.
"The Second Sex and the Cichlid Effect." *Journal of the National Association of
    Women Deans* 31 (1967): 8–17.
Self-Portrait of a Family. Boston: Beacon, 1978.
"Sex as a Regenerative Force." In *The New Sexuality,* ed. Herbert A. Otto. Palo
    Alto, Calif.: Science and Behavior Books, 1971.
The Sex Game. Englewood Cliffs, N.J.: Prentice-Hall, 1968. Reprint. New York:
    Atheneum, 1972.
"Sex in Remarriage." *Medical Aspects of Human Sexuality* 2 (1968): 54–61.
"Sexism and Discrimination." *American Sociologist* 5 (1970): 374–375.
"Social Problems as Problems of Decision." *Social Problems* 6 (1958–1959):
    212–221.
Social Problems at Midcentury: Role, Status, and Stress in a Context of Abundance.
    New York: Dryden, 1957.
"Social-Psychological Aspects of Community Study: Some Areas Compara-
    tively Neglected by American Sociologists." *British Journal of Sociology*
    2 (1951): 12–30.
"Social Salvation through Science." *South Atlantic Quarterly* 46 (1947): 44–55.
"Social Science Fiction." *Trans-action* 5 (January–February 1968): 10–12.
"Social Theory of Samuel G. Howe." *Sociology and Social Research* 17 (1933):
    314–323.
"Social Work." In *Contemporary Social Science,* ed. Philip L. Harriman, 345–
    381. Harrisburg, Pa.: Stackpole, 1953.
"Societal Values and Parenting." *Counseling Psychologist* 9 (1981): 5–11.
"The Sociological Study of Conflict." In *The Nature of Conflict,* ed. Interna-
    tional Sociological Association, 33–117. Liege, Belgium: UNESCO,
    1957.
The Sociology of Community. Glenview, Ill.: Scott, Foresman, 1973.
"Some Biological Factors in Personality and Marriage." *Human Biology* 7
    (1935): 430–436.
"Some Current Conceptualizations in the Field of Conflict." *American Journal
    of Sociology* 70 (1965): 442–454.
"Some General Problems of Sociological Measurement." *Southwestern Social
    Science Quarterly* 12 (1932): 310–320.
"The Sources and Methods of Psychology." In *The Fields and Methods of Sociol-*

ogy, ed. Luther L. Bernard, 366–386. New York: R. Long and R. R. Smith, 1934.

"The Status of Women in Modern Patterns of Culture." *Annals of the American Academy* 375 (1968): 3–14.

"Subversive Sociology." *Women's Review of Books* 1 (Summer 1983): 3–4.

"Technology, Science, and Sex Attitudes." *Impact of Science on Society* 18 (1968): 213–228.

"Teen Age Culture." *Annals of the American Academy* 338 (1961): 1–12.

"The Theory of Games of Strategy as a Modern Sociology of Conflict." *American Journal of Sociology* 59 (1954): 411–424.

"The United States." In *The Institutions of Advanced Societies*, ed. Arnold M. Rose, 592–676. Minneapolis, Minn.: University of Minnesota Press, 1958.

"Update on Women." In *The Future American College*, ed. Arthur W. Chicering. Englewood Cliffs, N.J.: Prentice-Hall, 1980.

"Validation of Normative Social Theory." *Journal of Philosophy* 47 (1950): 481–493.

"What Do You Mean Participation!" *American Association of University Women Journal* 61 (1968): 147–150.

"Where Are We Now?" *Psychology of Women Quarterly* 1 (1976): 21–37.

"Where Is the Modern Sociology of Conflict? *American Journal of Sociology* 56 (1950): 11–16.

"Where the Action Is." *Probe* 1 (1971): 2–10.

"Who—What Makes a Family Today? *Lutheran Women* (November 1971): 5–7.

Women and the Public Interest. Chicago, Ill.: Aldine, 1971.

"Women, Marriage, and the Future." *Futurist* 4 (1970): 41–44. Reprinted in *Toward a Sociology of Women*, ed. Constantina Safilios-Rothschild, 367–371. Lexington, Mass.: Xerox College Pub., 1972.

Women, Wives, Mothers: Values and Options. Chicago: Aldine, 1975.

With Luther Bernard. *Origins of American Sociology.* New York: Thomas Y. Crowell, 1943. Reprint. New York: Russell and Russell, 1965.

With Luther Bernard. *Sociology and the Study of International Relations.* St. Louis, Mo.: Washington University Studies, 1934.

With C. B. Broderick, eds. *The Individual, Sex, and Society.* Baltimore: Johns Hopkins University Press, 1969.

With Deborah Jensen. *Sociology.* 4th ed. St. Louis, Mo.: C. V. Mosby, 1954.

With S.D.H. Kaplan and Faith Williams. *Family Income in the Southeast.* Washington, D.C.: U.S. Government Printing Office, 1939–1940.

With N. M. Lobsenz. "Why Husbands and Wives Remain Strangers." *Reader's Digest* 92 (February 1968): 63–66.

With Helen F. Buchanan Meahl and William M. Smith. *Dating, Mating, and Marriage.* Cleveland, Ohio: Howard Allen, 1958.
With Lida F. Thompson. *Sociology: Nurses and Their Patients in a Modern Society.* 8th ed. St. Louis, Mo.: C.V. Mosby, 1970.

SECONDARY SOURCES

Acker, Joan. "Women and Social Stratification." *American Journal of Sociology* 78 (1973): 936–945.
Alcoff, Linda. "Cultural Feminism versus Post-Structuralism." *Signs* 13 (1988): 405–436.
Alpert, Harry. "George Lundberg's Social Philosophy." In *The Behavioral Sciences: Essays in Honor of George A. Lundberg,* ed. Alfred De Grazia et al., 48–62. Great Barrington, Mass.: Behavioral Research Council, 1968.
American Sociological Association." Official Reports and Proceedings." *American Sociological Review* 3 (1938): 92.
Anderson, Karen. *Wartime Women: Sex Roles, Family Relations, and the Status of Women during World War II.* Westport, Conn.: Greenwood, 1981.
Astin, Helen. "Employment and Career Status of Women Psychologists." *American Psychologist* 27 (1972): 371–381.
Aurbach, Herbert A. "SSSP as the Organization of a Social Movement." *Social Problems* 24 (1976): 37–53.
Banner, Lois W. *Women in Modern America.* New York: Harcourt Brace Jovanovich, 1974.
Bannister, Robert C. *Sociology and Scientism: The American Quest for Objectivity.* Chaptel Hill, N.C.: University of North Carolina Press, 1987.
Baskin, M. "The Campaign of American Sociology against Reason." *Soviet Press* 3 (1948): 532–534.
Benston, Margaret. "The Political Economy of Women's Liberation." *Monthly Review* 21 (September 1969): 13–27.
Bernard, Luther L. "Attitudes and the Redirection of Behavior." In *Social Attitudes,* ed. Kimball Young, 46–73. New York: Henry Holt, 1931.
———. "A Classification of Environments." *American Journal of Sociology* 31 (1925): 318–332.
———. *Instinct: A Study in Social Psychology.* New York: Henry Holt, 1924.
———. "The Relations between the International Federation of Sociological Societies." *American Sociologist* 1 (1938): 3–4.
———. *The Transition to an Objective Standard of Social Control.* Chicago: Univer-

sity of Chicago Press, 1911. Also in *American Journal of Sociology* 16 (1910–1911): 171–212, 309–341, 517–537.

Bierstedt, Robert. *American Sociological Theory.* New York: Academic Press, 1982.

Bleier, Ruth. *Science and Gender: A Critique of Biology and Its Theories about Women.* New York: Pergamon, 1984.

Blitz, Rudolph C. "Women in the Professions, 1870–1970." *Monthly Labor Review,* May 1974, 34–39.

Braunstein, Baruch. "A Social Problem." *Saturday Review of Literature,* August 22, 1942, 16.

Breines, Wini, Margaret Cerullo, and Judith Stacy. "Social Biology, Family Studies, and Antifeminist Backlash." *Feminist Studies* 4 (1978): 43–76.

Brumberg, Joan, and Nancy Tomes. "Women in the Professions." *Reviews in American History* (1982): 275–296.

Cantor, Muriel G. "Jessie Bernard—An Appreciation." *Gender and Society* 3 (1988): 264–270.

Carlson, Rae. "Sex Differences in Ego Functioning: Exploratory Studies of Agency and Communion." *Journal of Consulting and Clinical Psychology* 37 (1971): 267–277.

———. "Understanding Women." *Journal of Social Issues* 28 (1972): 17–32.

Carter, Susan B. "Academic Women Revisited." *Journal of Social History* 14 (1981): 675–699.

Cavan, Ruth Shonle. "The Chicago School of Sociology, 1918–33." *Urban Life* 11 (1983): 407–419.

———. Review of *The Female World,* by Jessie Bernard. *American Journal of Sociology* 89 (1983): 260–261.

Cisler, Lucinda. "Women: A Bibliography." In *Voices of the New Feminism,* ed. M. L. Thompson, 217–246. Boston: Beacon, 1970.

Clark, Terry N. *Patrons and Prophets: The French Universities and the Emergence of the Social Sciences.* Cambridge, Mass.: Harvard University Press, 1973.

Cook, Judith A., and Mary Margaret Fonow. "Knowledge and Women's Interests." *Sociological Inquiry* 56 (1986): 2–29.

Coser, Lewis A. *The Functions of Social Conflict.* Glencoe, Ill.: Free Press, 1956.

———. "Georg Simmel's Neglected Contributions to the Sociology of Women." *Signs* 2 (1977): 869–876.

Cott, Nancy. *The Grounding of Modern Feminism.* New Haven: Yale University Press, 1987.

Cravens, Hamilton. *The Triumph of Evolution: American Scientists and the Heredity-Environment Controversy 1900–1941.* Philadelphia, Pa.: University of Pennsylvania Press, 1978.

Cuber, John F. Review of *Remarriage*, by Jessie Bernard. *American Sociological Review* 21 (1956): 652–653.

Dahlke, O. Otto. Review of *Social Problems at Midcentury*, by Jessie Bernard. *American Sociological Review* 22 (1957): 769–770.

Davis, Nancy J. Review of *The Female World*, by Jessie Bernard. *Social Forces* 63 (1985): 880.

De Grazia, Alfred, Rollo Handy, E. C. Harwood, and Paul Kurtz, eds. *The Behavioral Sciences: Essays in Honor of George A. Lundberg*. Great Barrington, Mass.: Behavioral Research Council, 1968.

Deinhardt, Carol L. "A Vision of the Female World." *Contemporary Psychology* 27 (1982): 207.

Dinerman, Beatrice. "Sex Discrimination in Academia." *Journal of Higher Education* 42 (1971): 253–264.

Divine, Thomas M. "Women in the Academy." *Journal of Law and Education* 5 (1976): 429–451.

Donovan, Josephine. *Feminist Theory: The Intellectual Traditions of American Feminism*. New York: Frederick Ungar, 1985.

Du Bois, William E. B. *The Souls of Black Folk*. New York: Mentor, 1961.

Ehrenreich, Barbara. *The Hearts of Men: American Dreams and the Flight from Commitment*. Garden City, N.Y.: Doubleday, 1983.

Ehrenreich, Barbara, and Deidre English. *For Her Own Good*. Garden City, N.Y.: Doubleday, 1979.

Elshtain, Jean B. *Public Man, Private Woman: Women in Social and Political Thought*. Princeton: Princeton University Press, 1981.

Epstein, Cynthia F. "A Different Angle of Vision: Notes on the Selective Eye of Sociology." *Social Science Quarterly* 55 (1974): 645–656.

———. Review of *The Female World*, by Jessie Bernard. *Sex Roles* 8 (1982): 935–937.

Evans, Sara M. *Born for Liberty: A History of Women in America*. New York: Free Press, 1989.

———. *Personal Politics: The Roots of Women's Liberation in the Civil Rights Movement and the New Left*. New York: Vintage, 1979.

Federal Writers' Project. *Minnesota: A State Guide*. St. Paul, Minn., 1938.

Fee, Elizabeth. "The Sexual Politics of Victorian Social Anthropology." In *Clio's Consciousness Raised*, ed. Mary S. Hartman and Lois Banner, 86–102. New York: Harper and Row, 1974.

Ferree, Myra Marx, and Beth B. Hess. *Controversy and Coalition: The New Feminist Movement*. Boston: Twayne, 1985.

Fidell, Linda. "Empirical Verification of Sex Discrimination in Hiring Practices in Psychology." *American Psychologist* 25 (1970): 1094–1098.

Fine, Gary A., and Janet S. Severance. "Great Men and Hard Times." *Sociological Quarterly* 26 (1985): 117–134.

Fox, Greer L. Review of *The Female World*, By Jessie Bernard. *American Journal of Sociology* 89 (1983): 260.

Freeman, Jo. "The Origins of the Women's Liberation Movement." *American Journal of Sociology* 78 (1973): 792–811.

Friedan, Betty. *The Feminine Mystique*. New York: Norton, 1963.

———. *The Second Stage*. New York: Summit Books, 1981.

Golde, Peggy, comp. *Women in the Field: Anthropological Experiences*. Chicago: Aldine, 1970.

Gordon, Albert I. *Jews in Transition*. Minneapolis: University of Minnesota Press, 1949.

Graham, Patricia A. "Expansion and Exclusion: A History of Women in American Higher Education." *Signs* 3 (1978): 760–761.

Gray, James. *The University of Minnesota*. Minneapolis: University of Minnesota Press, 1951.

Gross, Harriet Engel, et al. "Considering 'A Biosocial Perspective on Parenting.'" *Signs* 4 (1979): 695–717.

Hall, Diana Long. "Biology, Sex Hormones, and Sexism." *Philosophical Forum* 5 (1973–1974): 81–86.

Harding, Sandra. "The Instability of the Analytical Categories of Feminist Theory." *Signs* 11 (1986): 645–664.

Harding, Sandra, and Merill B. Hintikka, eds. *Discovering Reality: Feminist Perspectives on Epistemology, Metaphysics, Methodology in the Philosophy of Science*. Dortecht, Holland: D. Reidel, 1983.

Hartz, Louis. *The Liberal Tradition in America*. New York: Harcourt, Brace, 1955.

Henslin, James M., and Paul M. Roesti. "Trends and Topics in *Social Problems*, 1953–1975: A Content Analysis and a Critique." *Social Problems* 24 (1976): 54–68.

Hochschild, Arlie R. "A Review of Sex Role Research." *American Journal of Sociology* 78 (1973): 1011–1029.

Hodgson, Godfrey. *America in Our Time*. New York: Random House, 1976.

Hofstadter, Richard. *The Age of Reform*. New York: Alfred Knopf, 1955.

Honey, Maureen. *Creating Rosie the Riveter: Class, Gender, and Propaganda during World War II*. Amherst, Mass.: University of Massachusetts Press, 1984.

Horowitz, Irving L. "The Rise and Fall of Project Camelot." In *The Rise and Fall of Project Camelot*, ed. Irving I. Horowitz, 3–44. Cambridge, Mass.: MIT Press, 1967.

Howard, Jane. *Margaret Mead: A Life*. New York: Simon and Schuster, 1984.

Hughes, Helen M. "Maid of All Work or Departmental Sister-in-Law." *American Journal of Sociology* 78 (1973): 767–772.

――――. "Wasp/Woman/Sociologist." *Society* 14 (1977): 69–80.

Irigaray, Luce. "Is the Subject of Science Sexed?" *Cultural Critique* 1 (1985): 73–88.

Jaggar, Allison M. *Feminist Politics and Human Nature*. Sussex, Eng.: Harvester, 1983.

Jones, Beverly. "The Dynamics of Marriage and Motherhood." In *Sisterhood Is Powerful*, ed. Robin Morgan, 46–61. New York: Vintage, 1970.

Kantor, Rosabeth M. "Skewed Sex Ratios and Responses to Token Women." *American Journal of Sociology* 82 (1977): 965–990.

Katz, Molly. Review of *Self-Portrait of a Family*, by Jessie Bernard. *Change* (March 1977): 58.

Keller, Evelyn Fox. *Reflections on Gender and Science*. New Haven: Yale University Press, 1985.

Kirkpatrick, Clifford. Review of *American Family Behavior* by Jessie Bernard. *Annals of the American Academy* 221, (1942): 232.

Komar, Ingrid. *Living the Dream: A Documentary Study of the Twin Oaks Community*. Norwood, Pa.: Norwood, 1983.

Komarovsky, Mirra. Review of *Academic Women*, by Jessie Bernard. *Social Forces* 43 (1965): 605.

Kraditor, Aileen. *The Ideas of the Woman Suffrage Movement*. New York: Columbia University Press, 1965.

Kramer, Judith A., and Seymour Leventman. *Children of the Gilded Ghetto*. New Haven: Yale University Press, 1961.

Kuhn, Thomas. *The Structure of Scientific Revolutions*. Chicago: University of Chicago Press, 1962.

Larsen, Otto N. "Lundberg's Encounters with Sociology and Vice Versa." In *The Behavioral Sciences: Essays in Honor of George A. Lundberg*, ed. Alfred De Grazia et al., 1–22. Great Barrington, Mass.: Behavioral Research Council, 1968.

Lasch, Christopher. *Haven in a Heartless World*. New York: Basic, 1977.

LaSorte, Michael. "Academic Women's Salaries." *Journal of Higher Education* 42 (1971): 265–278.

Lee, Alfred M. *Toward a Humanist Sociology*. Englewood Cliffs, N.J.: Prentice-Hall, 1973.

Lee, Elizabth B., and Alfred M. Lee. "The Society for the Study of Social Problems: Parental Recollections and Hopes." *Social Problems* 24 (1976): 4–14.

Lemons, J. Stanley. *The Woman Citizen*. Urbana, Ill.: University of Illinois Press, 1973.

Lipman-Blumen, Jean. "Jessie Bernard—A 'Reasonable Rebel.' " *Gender and Society* 2 (1988): 271–273.

Lofland, Lyn H. "The 'Thereness' of Women: A Selective Review of Urban Sociology." *Sociological Inquiry* 45 (1975): 144–170.

Lunday, G. Albert. *Sociology Dissertations in American Universities, 1893–1966*. Commerce, Tex.: East Texas State University, 1969.

Lundberg, George A. *Can Science Save Us?* New York: Longmans, Green, 1947.

——. "Case Work and Statistical Method." *Social Forces* 5 (1926): 61–65.

——. *Social Research: A Study in Methods of Gathering Data*. New York: Longmans, Green, 1929.

——. "Sociology versus Dialectical Immaterialism." *American Journal of Sociology* 53 (1947): 85–96.

——. "Some Comments." *American Sociological Review* 14 (1949): 796.

McIntyre, Jennie. Review of *Marriage and Family among Negroes*, by Jessie Bernard. *Social Forces* 45 (1967): 456–457.

Mainardi, Pat. "The Politics of Housework." In *Sisterhood Is Powerful*, ed. Robin Morgan, 447–454. New York: Vintage, 1970.

Martindale, Don. *The Romance of a Profession*. St. Paul: Windflower, 1976.

Matthews, Sarah. "Rethinking Sociology from a Feminist Perspective." *American Sociologist* 17 (1982): 29–39.

Meier, August. "Negro Families in Caricature." *Transaction* 3 (July–August 1966): 45–46.

Merchant, Carolyn. *The Death of Nature: Women, Ecology, and the Scientific Revolution*. New York: Harper and Row, 1980.

Millman, Marcia. "She Did It All for Love: A Feminist View of the Sociology of Deviance." *Sociological Inquiry* 45 (1975): 251–279.

Millman, Marcia, and Rosabeth Kanter. *Another Voice*. Garden City, N.Y.: Doubleday, 1975.

Mills, C. Wright. *The Sociological Imagination*. New York: Oxford University Press, 1959.

Moore, Joan W. Review of *Academic Women*, by Jessie Bernard. *American Journal of Sociology* 72 (1966): 223–224.

Morgan, Robin, ed. *Sisterhood is Powerful*. New York: Vintage/Random House, 1970.

Morton, Marian J. *The Terrors of Ideological Politics: Liberal Historians in a Conservative Mood*. Cleveland: The Press of Case Western Reserve University, 1972.

Moynihan, Daniel P. et al. *The Negro Family: The Case for National Action.* Report prepared for the United States Department of Labor: Office of Planning and Research. Washington, D.C.: U.S. Government Printing Office, 1965.

Nimkoff, Meyer F. Review of *Remarriage,* by Jessie Bernard. *American Journal of Sociology* 62 (1956): 346–347.

Nisbet, Robert A. "Project Camelot and the Science of Man." In *The Rise and Fall of Project Camelot,* ed. Irving I. Horowitz, 3–15. Cambridge, Mass.: MIT Press, 1967.

Offen, Karen. "Defining Feminism: A Comparative Historical Approach." *Signs* 14 (1988): 119–157.

O'Neill, William. *Everyone Was Brave.* Chicago: Quadrangle Books, 1969.

Ortner, Sherry. "Is Female to Male as Nature Is to Culture?" *Women, Culture, and Society,* ed. Michele Z. Rosaldo and Louise Lamphere, 67–87. Stanford: Stanford University Press, 1974.

Plaut, W. Gunther. *The Jews in Minnesota: The First Seventy-Five Years.* New York, N.Y.: American Jewish Historical Society, 1959.

Podell, Lawrence. Review of *Marriage and Family among Negroes,* by Jessie Bernard. *American Journal of Sociology* 72 (1967): 688–689.

Poovey, Mary. "Feminism and Deconstructionism." *Feminist Studies* 14 (1988): 51–65.

Rabine, Leslie W. "A Feminist Politics of Non-Identity." *Feminist Studies* 14 (1988): 11–31.

Rainwater, Lee, and William L. Yancey. *The Moynihan Report and the Politics of Controversy.* Cambridge, Mass.: MIT Press, 1967.

Richardson, Laurel. "Looking Forward: Exploring the World of Women." *Contemporary Sociology* 11 (1982): 497–499.

Riesman, David. Introduction to *Academic Women,* by Jessie Bernard, xv–xxv. University Park, Pa.: Pennsylvania State University Press, 1964.

Rodman, Hyman. Review of *Marriage and Family among Negroes,* by Jessie Bernard. *Child Welfare* 46 (1967): 413–414.

Rosaldo, Michelle Z. "The Use and Abuse of Anthropology: Reflections of Feminism in Cross-Cultural Understanding." *Signs* 5 (1980): 389–417.

Rose, Arnold. Preface to *Human Behavior and Social Processes,* vii–xii. Boston: Houghton Mifflin, 1962.

Rossi, Alice. *Feminists in Politics: A Panel Analysis of the First National Woman's Conference.* New York: Academic Press, 1982.

Rupp, Leila J., and Verta Taylor. *Survival in the Doldrums: The American Women's Rights Movement, 1945 to the 1960s.* New York: Oxford University Press, 1987.

Safier, Gwendolyn. "Jessie Bernard: The Making of a Sociologist." Ph.D. diss., University of Kansas, 1972.

Salisbury, Harrison. "Victorian City in the Midwest." In *Growing Up in Minnesota*, ed. Chester G. Anderson, 49–75. Minneapolis: University of Minnesota Press, 1976.

Scheper-Hughes, N. "Problem of Bias in Androcentric and Feminist Anthropology." *Women's Studies* 10, no. 2 (1983): 109–116.

Schneider, Joseph W., and Sally L. Hacker. "Sex Role Imagery and the Use of Generic 'Man' in Introductory Texts." *American Sociologist* 8 (1973): 12–18.

Schwendinger, Herman, and Julia Schwendinger. "Sociology's Founding Fathers: Sexists to a Man." *Journal of Marriage and the Family* 33 (1971): 783–799.

Scott, Joan W. "Deconstructing Equality-versus-Difference: Or the Uses of Poststructuralist Theory for Feminism." *Feminist Studies* 14 (Spring 1988): 33–50.

———. "Gender: A Useful Category of Historical Analysis." *American Historical Review* 91 (1986): 1053–1075.

Sharf, L. *To Work and Wed: Female Employment, Feminism, and the Great Depression.* Westport, Conn.: Greenwood, 1980.

Skura, Barry. "Constraints on a Reform Movement: Relationships between the SSSP and the ASA, 1951–1970." *Social Problems* 24 (1976): 15–36.

Slocum, Sally. "Woman the Gatherer: Male Bias in Anthropology." In *Toward an Anthropology of Women*, ed. Rayna R. Reiter. New York: Monthly Review Press, 1975, 36–50.

Smith, Dorothy E. "Women's Perspective as a Radical Critique of Sociology." *Sociological Inquiry* 44 (1974): 7–13.

Stacey, Judith. "The New Conservative Feminism." *Feminist Studies* 3 (1983): 559–583.

Steinmetz, Suzanne K. "The Sexual Context of Social Research." *American Sociologist* 9 (1974): 111–116.

Tong, Rosemarie. *Feminist Thought: A Comprehensive Introduction.* Boulder, Colo.: Westview, 1989.

Voydanoff, Patrica. "Women, Work, and Family: Bernard's Perspective on the Past, Present, and Future." *Psychology of Women Quarterly* 12 (1988): 269–280.

Walker, Charles R. *American City: A Rank and File History.* New York: Farrar and Rinehard, 1937.

Wallace, Michelle. "Black Macho and the Myth of Superwoman." *Ms.*, January 1979, 4–5.

Wandersee, Winifred D. *On the Move: American Women in the 1970s*. Boston: Twayne, 1988.

Ward, K. B. "The Feminist Critique and a Decade of Published Research in Sociology Journals." *Sociological Quarterly* 26 (1985): 139–157.

Ware, Susan. *Beyond the New Deal*. Cambridge, Mass.: Harvard University Press, 1981.

Warshay, Leon. "The Current State of Sociological Theory." *Sociological Quarterly* 12 (1971): 31.

———. *The Current State of Sociological Theory*. New York: D. McKay, 1975.

Weedon, Chris. *Feminist Practice and Post-Structuralist Theory*. New York: Oxford University Press, 1987.

West, Audrey. "Class Roots of the 'Woman Question.' " *World Marxist Review* 24 (1984): 106–111.

West, Hollie I. "Michelle Wallace: Point, Counterpoint." *Washington Post*, February 7, 1979.

Winch, Robert F. Review of *American Family Behavior*, by Jessie Bernard. *Journal of Marriage and the Family* 4 (1942): 46–47.

Wolfe, Julie C. Melvin L. DeFleur, and Walter L. Slocum. "Sex Discrimination in Hiring Practices of Graduate Sociology Departments." *American Sociologist* 8 (1973): 159–168.

Wood, Ann D[ouglas]. "The 'Scribbling Women' and Fanny Fern: Why Women Wrote." *American Quarterly* 23 (1971): 3–24.

Young-Bruehl, Elisabeth. *Hannah Arendt: For Love of the World*. New Haven: Yale University Press, 1982.

Index

Bernard, Jessie (*continued*)
218–219; marriage to Luther Bernard, 5, 48–54, 59–74, 75–77, 88–95, 134, 152–154, 168–170, 219; and Marxism, 4, 128–129, 209, 220; and race, 195, 199–203, 217; on science and values, 101–102, 116–121, 131–134, 198–199, 203–208, 218, 220; and social class, 197–199, 203; and Society of Friends, 16, 72, 216; and sociology of conflict, 7, 122, 126–131, 217; and sociology of knowledge, 2–3, 119, 172. Teaching positions: Lindenwood College, 75, 76, 99, 143, 153, 169; Mills College, 190; Pennsylvania State University, 99–102, 142–144, 164–165; Princeton, 144–147; University of Delaware, 190; University of Southern California, 190. Works: *Academic Women,* 6, 7, 125, 142–143, 147–161, 162, 177, 194–195; 217; *American Community Behavior,* 105, 124, 127, 130, 133, 135, 158, 199; *American Family Behavior,* 7, 95–97, 116, 127, 163; "Analysis of Jewish Culture," 70–71, 74, 104; "Biculturality," 28, 36, 104, 129; "Conceptualizations of Inter-group Relations," 127–128; "Culture as Environment," 82; *Dating, Mating, and Marriage,* 124; "Distribution of Success in Marriage," 83–85; "Factors in the Distribution of Success in Marriage," 83–85; *Female World,* 2, 3, 5, 7, 23, 76, 95, 141, 185, 187, 190, 192, 194, 195–209, 212, 213, 214, 218; *Female World from a Global Perspective,* 2, 208; *Future of Marriage,* 2, 76, 163, 170, 181–184, 187, 188, 202; *Future of Motherhood,* 2, 187, 213; "History and Pros-

pects of Sociology," 57, 81, 111; "Instrument for the Measurement of Success in Marriage," 83–85; "Investigation into the Changes of Attitudes in Jews," 79–80, 85; "Joshua March," 53; "Little Sister," 53–54; "Lucy Page," 25, 75, 77; *Marriage and Family among Negroes,* 163, 195, 199–201, 217; "My Four Revolutions," 2, 191, 204, 207; *Origins of American Sociology,* 57, 116, 162; "Other People's Sins," 57, 58; "Power of Science," 117; "Puritan's Mistress," 54, 57, 59; "Purple Prose," 57; *Remarriage,* 124, 163, 166–168; "Runaway Wife," 88; "Sarah Gordon," 20, 23, 26; *Self-Portrait of a Family,* 14, 95, 97, 162–184, 188, 213; *Sex Game,* 2, 7, 163, 181–182; *Social Problems at Midcentury,* 124, 130–131, 133, 135, 158, 160, 199–200; "Social Salvation through Science," 117; "Theory of Games," 131–132; *Women and the Public Interest,* 2, 157, 160, 161, 163, 181

Bernard, Luther L.: analyzes Jessie, 31–32, 50–51, 76–77, 91–92; attitude toward women, 39–42, 50–51; background and career, 38–40, 49, 56–57; and behaviorism, 39, 41, 61, 79, 186; death of, 102, 121; edits *American Sociologist,* 114, 135; and fascism, 103, 120–121; and Judaism, 61, 65–69, 72–74, 89; and objectivism, 119; personality of, 38, 49, 50, 60–61, 72–73, 79, 215; politics of, 3, 66–67, 135; sexual affairs of, 40–42, 49, 61–63, 97; sociological influence on Jessie, 80, 137, 151, 163, 211, 215. Teaching positions: Cornell, 49, 56; Pennsylvania State University,